The More-Beef-For-Your-Money Cookbook

The More-Beef-For-Your-Money Cookbook

•••━━●◉●━━•••

by MARY DUNHAM

Peter H. Wyden/Publisher **W** New York

Photographs courtesy of Kent Van Slyke
Designed by Paula Wiener

Library of Congress Catalog Card Number: 74-76239
Manufactured in the United States of America
ISBN: 0-88326-054-9

DEDICATION

To homemakers everywhere, young and old,
to help them enjoy more tasty and nutritious meals
and to save them a few extra hours in the kitchen.

Acknowledgment

The author acknowledges the advice and counsel
of the National Live Stock and Meat Board in the
preparation of the beef information for this book.

Contents

Stretching the Beef Dollar

No matter how much or in which direction the price of beef may fluctuate, I suspect we will always be a nation of beef-eaters. We may consume less of it as prices rise, but only with great reluctance. And no wonder—beef tastes good in any way, shape, or form, and it's a particularly valuable food in terms of the vital nutrients it supplies.

Unfortunately, the days of cheap meat—indeed, the days of cheap *anything*—seem to have come and gone. (This may be a chronic complaint. Perhaps there never was a time when by common consent everything cost just about what it ought to. But that's beside the point. I for one remember serving certain tender, expensive cuts of beef frequently and as a matter of course, and those days are definitely in the past.)

So, in order to keep the beef we love so much on the family dinner table—and have cash left over for some of the other good things in life—it becomes important to find new, practical ways of getting better value for our money. That's what this book is all about.

I'm convinced that the best way to stretch one's beef dollar is to invest a greater proportion of it in the less tender, less familiar, less expensive cuts; to buy them at special prices whenever possible, and to cook and freeze them in quantity.

In order to take full advantage of these less tender, less familiar cuts, it's necessary to know at least a little bit about them—where they come from, how to identify them by name and appearance, and above all, what to do with them.

The guide-to-buying section (beginning on page 1) was put together with this in mind. In it, you will find a listing of *all* the basic retail cuts of beef, including information about their tenderness, the amount of fat and bone contained in each, and how to cook them. Here, as in all parts of this book, the various cuts are designated in accordance with the new standardized meat identification system established by the industrywide Cooperative Meat Identification Standards Committee. The committee was spearheaded by the National Live Stock and Meat Board. This innovation should be a great help to the consumer and go a long way toward eliminating confusion at the meat counter.

As you probably know, the less costly cuts are just as flavorful and nutritious as their more expensive counterparts. They're also—and this may come as a welcome surprise—every bit as *tender* when properly prepared. Technique makes the difference. Cooking the less tender cuts is almost always a matter of long, slow, moist-heat simmering—either *braising* or *cooking in liquid*. Once mastered, these techniques can be applied in an unlimited number of ways. All the recipes in this book call for one of the moist-heat methods of cooking and add up to a repertoire of meat dishes that are not only economical but relatively easy to prepare and as various as one could wish, ranging all the way from pot roasts with an international accent, such as Pot Roast Teriyaki and Pot Roast, Flemish Style (with beer), to outdoor specialties like Barbecue Beef with Savory Sauce.

These same techniques can be adapted to quantity cooking, whereby various less tender cuts of beef are turned into a number of different quick and easy meals. (My favorite plan is one in which an initial purchase of four beef chuck blade roasts yields *nine* different budget dishes!) I'm a staunch advocate of the concept of quantity buying and cooking, not only because it saves time and money, but, equally important, because by preparing two, three, four, or more meals at once it's possible to conserve significant amounts of fuel.

Buying in quantity at special prices is almost more economical than purchasing smaller amounts, and there is much to be said for the advantages of cooking and freezing ahead. But only with proper storage techniques can good nutritional value and flavor be maintained. For this reason, I've included a section (beginning on page 259) explaining the how-to of storing and freezing fresh and cooked meat (as well as many other foods). I hope it will be read with special care and attention.

All this is not by way of saying farewell forever to T-bone, Tenderloin, Porterhouse, and the like. On the contrary. Some of the money saved by investing in the budget cuts— good, wholesome food, remember, and appetizing in their own right—might very well be spent on the delectable fork-tender steaks and roasts whose very names have the power to activate our salivary glands. With good planning we can enjoy them all.

1

How to Know
What You're Buying—
and Buy What You Need

Tenderness is the single most important factor influencing the cost of a particular cut of beef. Some cuts are just naturally tender. They're the cuts we're least concerned with in this book—the glamour cuts from the rib and loin sections (the least exercised parts of the animal); the rib roast and steaks, the T-bone and Porterhouse and sirloin steaks; the tenderloin (filet mignon) roasts and steaks. In all, these tender cuts account for less than 28 percent of the beef carcass and they're in great demand. Consequently, we pay dearly for them.

The remaining 72 percent comes from the more heavily exercised parts of the animal where there is a great amount of connective tissue formed between the muscle fibers. Portions from these sections are often called—at times somewhat euphemistically—the "less tender" cuts.

Properly prepared, as I will show here, they're not "less tender" at all—in fact, they're every bit as tender and appetizing as the glamour cuts, and cheaper, too.

Getting more beef for your money begins with knowing more about beef—especially these less tender cuts—and how to buy it.

1

Fortunately, the new standardized identification system for labeling the various cuts of beef makes this a far easier undertaking than it would have been even a year or so ago.

Up until then, some confusion always arose from the ambiguous way in which meat was labeled. What could *properly* be labeled "beef rib eye steak," for example, might turn up in one store as "Delmonico steak," in another as "fillet steak," and in a third as "Spencer steak." Or what is now called "beef chuck blade roast" could be bought as "chuck blade roast" or "chuck roast." So, many consumers were never quite sure just what it was they were buying.

Under the new system there will be far less ambiguity in labeling. The purpose of the system is to banish fancy, regional names, which often tend to be misleading, and to aim instead for consistency: In all stores, in all parts of the country "beef rib eye steak" will be labeled as such.

Three categories of information will be included on the new labels: (1) the *kind* of meat (beef, pork, lamb, or veal); (2) the primal (or wholesale) cut; and (3) the retail cut.

Standardized labeling should go a long way toward eliminating confusion at the meat counter. I think that combined with a general knowledge of the various cuts themselves—their tenderness, their relative amounts of bone and the fat to lean ration, and most important, how to cook them—the new system will be a big help in getting more beef for your money.

I've used this new standard labeling in the following section, which describes the basic retail cuts of beef in some detail, as well as throughout this entire book.

Keep in mind, however, that this listing is not all-inclusive, but covers only the "basic" cuts. You may come across others, usually specialty cuts or regional variations, at your local meat counter. I think it would be a good idea to ask your butcher or supermarket meat-counter man for more information about any cuts that are not identified in this book.

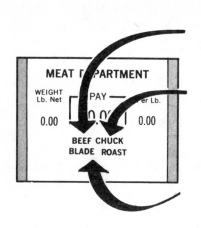

The kind of meat—BEEF, PORK, LAMB, or VEAL. It's listed first on every label.

The primal (wholesale) cut —CHUCK, RIB, LOIN, or ROUND —tells where the meat comes from on the animal.

The retail cut—BLADE ROAST, SPARERIBS, LOIN CHOPS, etc.—tells what part of the primal cut the meat comes from.

The Basic Beef Cuts—How to Recognize Them, What to Do with Them

As you will see from the illustration on pages 4-5, the *primal* or wholesale cuts of beef are:

CHUCK (or shoulder)
RIB
LOIN (subdivided into the short loin and sirloin)
ROUND
FLANK
SHORT PLATE
BRISKET
FORESHANK

(Incidentally, the various primal cuts of beef correspond closely to those of veal, lamb, and pork. Even the names are similar, except that the section called "chuck" in beef is "shoulder" in veal, lamb, and pork, while the section called "round" in beef is "leg" in veal and lamb and "ham" in pork.)

From these primal cuts we get the various specific portions offered at retail meat counters.

BEEF CHART

RETAIL CUTS OF BEEF — WHERE THEY COME FROM AND HOW TO COOK THEM

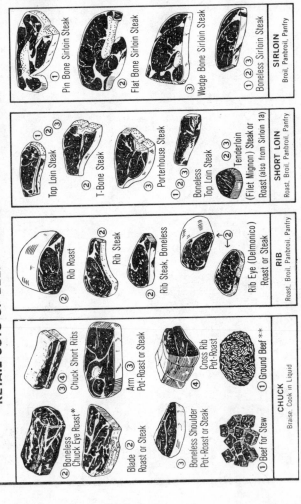

CHUCK
Braise. Cook in Liquid

② Boneless Chuck Eye Roast*
③④ Chuck Short Ribs
Blade ② Roast or Steak
Arm ③ Pot-Roast or Steak
Boneless Shoulder ③ Pot-Roast or Steak
Cross Rib ④ Pot-Roast
① Beef for Stew
① Ground Beef**

RIB
Roast. Broil. Panbroil. Panfry

② Rib Roast
② Rib Steak
Rib Steak, Boneless
Rib Eye (Delmonico) ②→ Roast or Steak

SHORT LOIN
Roast. Broil. Panbroil. Panfry

① ② ③ Top Loin Steak
② T-Bone Steak
③ Porterhouse Steak
① ② ③ Boneless Top Loin Steak
② ③ Tenderloin (Filet Mignon) Steak or Roast (also from Sirloin 1a)

SIRLOIN
Broil. Panbroil. Panfry

① Pin Bone Sirloin Steak
② Flat Bone Sirloin Steak
③ Wedge Bone Sirloin Steak
① ② ③ Boneless Sirloin Steak

ROUND
Braise. Cook in Liquid

④ Heel of Round
③ Round Steak
① Rolled Rump*
③ Top Round Steak*
③ Bottom Round Roast or Steak*
③ Cubed Steak*
③ Eye of Round*
Ground Beef**

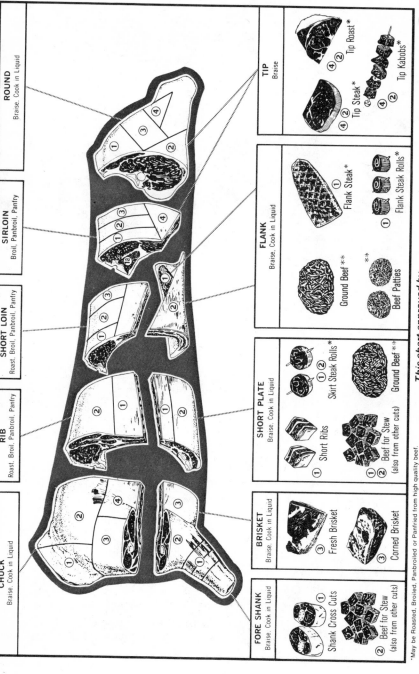

ROUND
Braise, Cook in Liquid

SIRLOIN
Broil, Panbroil, Panfry

SHORT LOIN
Roast, Broil, Panbroil, Panfry

RIB
Roast, Broil, Panbroil, Panfry

CHUCK
Braise, Cook in Liquid

TIP
Braise

④② Tip Roast *
④② Tip Steak *
④② Tip Kabobs *

FLANK
Braise, Cook in Liquid

① Flank Steak *
① Flank Steak Rolls *
Ground Beef **
Beef Patties **

SHORT PLATE
Braise, Cook in Liquid

①② Skirt Steak Rolls *
① Short Ribs
①② Beef for Stew (also from other cuts)
Ground Beef **

BRISKET
Braise, Cook in Liquid

① Fresh Brisket
③ Corned Brisket

FORE SHANK
Braise, Cook in Liquid

① Shank Cross Cuts
② Beef for Stew (also from other cuts)

*May be Roasted, Broiled, Panbroiled or Panfried from high quality beef.
**May be Roasted, (Baked), Broiled, Panbroiled or Panfried.

This chart approved by
National Live Stock and Meat Board

© National Live Stock and Meat Board

Meat Identification

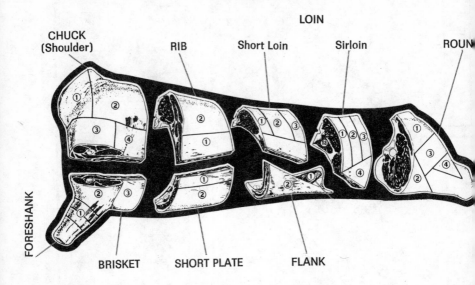

Beef Primal Cuts

Courtesy of National Live Stock and Meat Board.

Meat Grading

Meat is graded as an indication of its *quality*. This en- sures that the customer gets the quality meat he expects and pays for and is in fact a consumer service performed by the government, but paid for by meat packers. You can expect consistent eating qualities when you go to the retail store to buy beef, veal or lamb, depending on whether you buy U.S. Prime, Choice, Good, or Standard. Pork is not marketed by grades as it generally comes from youthful hogs which produce meat with fewer variations in eating quality and, therefore, has less reason to be graded.

Meat marketed under these labels therefore conforms with the following description:

U.S. Prime:	Top grade—meat containing a greater degree of marbling. (Marbling is the small flakes of fat that are interspersed with lean. It contributes to tenderness, juiciness, and flavor.) Considered a "gourmet" meat.
U.S. Choice:	The grade generally sold at retail stores. It's preferred by homemakers because it contains sufficient marbling but less than that found in U.S. Prime.
U.S. Good:	A less expensive grade of meat, with less marbling than U.S. Choice. It's good eating and as nutritious as the other grades.
U.S. Standard or U.S. Commercial:	U.S. Standard and U.S. Commercial are lower grades that are sometimes seen in meat cases. They're nutritious but often less tender. These grades are generally used in sausages.

The circle-shaped stamp you may see on the meat shows that the meat was processed under U.S.D.A. (or state/municipal) inspection. It indicates the meat is from healthy animals, processed under sanitary conditions.

Retail Cuts from the Chuck (Shoulder)

The shoulder is known as "chuck" in beef. It is a squarish section at the front end of the carcass, containing neck bones, blade bones, part of the arm bone, and the first through fifth ribs. Many of the retail cuts from the chuck take their name from the bone (or bones) running through them, i.e., beef chuck blade roast, or beef chuck arm steak.

The muscles in this section are much used and run in various directions. Because of this, the meat is a mixture of coarse-textured lean with a good deal of connective tissue and fat. Even so, it is juicy and very palatable.

BEEF CHUCK NECK POT ROAST

Formerly: Neck Boiling Beef
Neck Pot Roast
Neck Soup Meat
Yankee Pot Roast

Since there is little or no fat in this cut, a layer of fat is often added. The muscles here are heavily used, thus it is less tender and requires longer cooking than many of the other large cuts recommended for braising.

Cooking method for U.S. Prime, Choice, or Good: braise.

BEEF CHUCK NECK POT ROAST BONELESS

Formerly: Boneless Neck
Boneless Neck Pot Roast
Boneless Yankee Pot Roast

Same as above, but boneless.

BLADE CUTS

| (Cross Sections of Blade Bone) | Blade Bone (near neck) | Blade Bone (center cuts) | Blade Bone (near rib) |

Blade roasts are cut more or less straight down from the back bone to the upper part of the first through fifth ribs and contain part of the back bone, the blade bone, and part of the ribs. As you will note from the illustration, part of the blade bone resembles a reverse 7. The short 7 is near the neck and the long 7 is in the center, while the flat bone is adjacent to the sixth rib. Portions from the section near the rib are more tender than those near the neck, where the muscles are more heavily used.

BEEF CHUCK BLADE ROAST

Formerly: Blade Chuck Roast
Chuck Blade Roast
Chuck Roast Blade Cut
Chuck Roast First Cut

Cut from the blade section. Varies in thickness from 1½ to 3 inches.

Cooking method for U.S. Prime: roast or braise
for U.S. Choice or Good: roast if pretendered; otherwise, braise.

BEEF CHUCK BLADE STEAK

Formerly: Blade Steak
Chuck Blade Steak
Chuck Steak Blade Cut
Chuck Steak First Cut

Same as BEEF CHUCK BLADE ROAST, but cut to steak thickness.

Cooking method for U.S. Prime: broil, panbroil, panfry, braise
for U.S. Choice or Good: broil, panbroil, panfry if pretendered; otherwise, braise.

BEEF CHUCK EYE ROAST, BONELESS

Formerly: Boneless Chuck Roll
Boneless Chuck Fillet
Chuck Eye Roast
Inside Chuck Roll

Cut from blade section, boneless.

Cooking method for U.S. Prime: roast or braise
for U.S. Choice or Good: braise; roast if pretendered.

BEEF CHUCK EYE STEAK, BONELESS

Formerly: Boneless Chuck Fillet Steak
Boneless Steak Bottom Chuck
Chuck Boneless Slices
Chuck Eye Steak
Chuck Fillet Steak

Same as BEEF CHUCK EYE ROAST, BONELESS, but cut to steak thickness.
Cooking method for U.S. Prime: broil, panbroil, panfry, braise
for U.S. Choice or Good: braise; if pretendered, broil, panbroil, panfry.

Retail Cuts from the Arm Bone Section

Arm bone

Portions from this section of the chuck contain a cross section of the arm bone and occasionally a cross section of rib bones (though these are generally removed). The meat here is very lean and less tender than the blade cuts though both have the same well-developed flavor.

BEEF CHUCK ARM POT ROAST

Formerly: Arm Chuck Roast
Chuck Arm Roast
Chuck Round Bone Cut
Round Bone Pot Roast
Round Bone Roast

Cut across the rib bones; contains a section of the arm bone.
Cooking method for U.S. Prime, Choice or Good: braise.

BEEF CHUCK ARM POT ROAST, BONELESS

Formerly: Beef Chuck Arm Pot Roast

Same as BEEF CHUCK ARM POT ROAST, but boneless.
Cooking method for U.S. Prime, Choice or Good: braise.

BEEF CHUCK ARM STEAK

Formerly: Arm Chuck Steak
Arm Steak Beef Chuck
Arm Swiss Steak
Chuck Steak for Swissing
Round Bone Steak
Round Bone Swiss Steak

Same as BEEF CHUCK ARM POT ROAST, but cut to
steak thickness.
Cooking method for U.S. Prime, Choice or Good: braise.

BEEF CHUCK ARM STEAK BONELESS

Formerly: Boneless Arm Steak
Boneless Round Bone Steak
Boneless Swiss Steak

Same as BEEF CHUCK ARM STEAK, but boneless.
Cooking method for U.S. Prime, Choice, or Good: braise.

BEEF CHUCK SHOULDER POT ROAST, BONELESS

Formerly: Center Shoulder Roast
Chuck Roast, Boneless
Chuck Shoulder Roast
Clod Roast

Contains the largest muscle of the arm pot roast.
Cooking method for U.S. Prime, Choice, or Good: braise.

BEEF CHUCK SHOULDER STEAK BONELESS

Formerly: Chuck for Swissing
             Clod Steak, Boneless
             London Broil
             Shoulder Clod Steak, Boneless
             Shoulder Cutlet, Boneless
             Shoulder Steak

Same as BEEF CHUCK SHOULDER POT ROAST, BONELESS, but cut to steak thickness.
Cooking method for U.S. Prime, Choice, or Good: braise.

BEEF CHUCK CROSS RIB POT ROAST

Formerly: Boston Cut
             Bread and Butter Cut
             Cross Rib Roast
             English Cut Roast
             Thick Rib Roast

This is a squarish cut (often thicker at one end), with alternating layers of lean and fat; contains two or three rib bones.
Cooking method for U.S. Prime: roast or braise.
            for U.S. Choice or Good: braise; if pre-
            tendered, roast.

BEEF CHUCK CROSS RIB POT ROAST, BONELESS

Formerly: Boneless Boston Cut
             Boneless English Cut
             Cross Rib Roast, Boneless
             English Roll

Same as BEEF CHUCK CROSS RIB POT ROAST, but boneless.

Cooking method for U.S. Prime: roast or braise.
for U.S. Choice or Good: braise; if pretendered, roast.

BEEF CHUCK SHORT RIBS

Formerly: Barbecue Ribs
Braising Ribs
Brust Flanken
English Short Ribs, Extra Lean
Fancy Ribs
Short Ribs

Ribs cut from the beef chuck.
Cooking method for U.S. Prime, Choice, or Good: braise.

BEEF FOR STEW

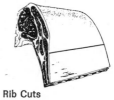

Formerly: Beef Cubed for Stew
Boneless Beef for Stew
Boneless Stew Beef
Stew Beef

One-inch to two-inch squares or cubes cut from the less
tender sections, often from the chuck, but also from the foreshank and short plate.
Cooking method for U.S. Prime, Choice, or Good: braise
or cook in liquid.

Retail Cuts from the Rib Section

Back Bone and Rib Bone   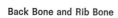   Rib Cuts

Rib roasts and steaks are cut from the rib section of the
carcass, located between the chuck (shoulder) and the short
loin.

A factor affecting the price of a rib roast is the length of the bone (measured from backbone to the tip end of the rib). The longer the rib, the greater the proportion of bone to meat and the lower the price per pound. A 10-inch roast contains a portion of the short ribs; a 7-inch roast is standard, though some retailers sell a 5-inch or 6-inch roast.

BEEF RIB ROAST, LARGE END

Formerly: Beef Rib Pot Roast, Short Cut (6-7)
Rib Roast, Oven Ready
Beef Rib Roast, Short Cut (6-7)
Standing Rib Roast (6-7)
Standing Rib Roast (6-8)
Standing Rib Roast (8-9)

Containing the sixth through ninth ribs, this cut is often referred to as "prime ribs," though this is a misnomer. Strictly speaking, the cut is prime only if it comes from prime-grade beef.

This cut has its own rack (the ribs), which allows heat to circulate during cooking. It is self-basting, because of the generous amount of exterior fat.

If a rib roast is to stand by itself, it must contain at least two or three ribs. For easier carving, ask the butcher to separate the backbone from the ribs so that it can be removed after roasting.

Cooking methods for U.S. Prime, Choice, or Good: roast.

BEEF RIB ROAST, SMALL END

Formerly: Rib Roast, Oven Ready
Standing Rib Roast
Sirloin Tip Roast

Same as BEEF RIB ROAST LARGE END, but containing the ninth through twelfth ribs.

Cooking method for U.S. Prime, Choice, or Good: roast.

BEEF RIB STEAK, LARGE END and
BEEF RIB STEAK, SMALL END

Both Formerly: Beef Rib Steak
              Beef Rib Steak, Bone-In

Rib steaks containing the eye of rib, rib bone, and sometimes a portion of the back bone.
    Cooking method for U.S. Prime, Choice, or Good: broil, panbroil, panfry.

BEEF RIB STEAK, SMALL END, BONELESS

Formerly: Beef Rib Steak, Boneless
            Beef Spencer Steak, Boneless

Same as BEEF RIB STEAK, SMALL END, but boneless.
Cooking method for U.S. Prime, Choice, or Good: broil, panbroil, panfry.

BEEF RIB, RIB EYE (DELMONICO) ROAST

Formerly: Delmonico Pot Roast
         Delmonico Roast
         Beef Rib Eye Pot Roast
         Regular Roll Roast

This tender, boneless roast is the large muscle of the BEEF RIB EYE ROAST. A thin layer of fat covers a portion of the lean.
    Cooking method for U.S. Prime, Choice, or Good: roast.

BEEF RIB, RIB EYE (DELMONICO) STEAK

Formerly: Delmonico Steak
         Boneless Rib Eye Steak
         Fillet Steak
         Spencer Steak
         Beauty Steak

Made by cutting across the grain of the BEEF RIB EYE ROAST. Thickness varies according to preference.

Cooking method for U.S. Prime, Choice, or Good: broil, panbroil, panfry.

BEEF RIB SHORT RIBS

Formerly: Beef Short Ribs

Cut from the ends of the ribs, these are sold either in long strips or cut into cubes. Layers of fat and lean alternate.

Cooking method for U.S. Prime, Choice, or Good: braise; broil if pretendered or precooked.

Retail Cuts from the Short Loin

Backbone (T-Shape) T-Bone Short Loin Cuts

The short loin is the "front" or "forward" part of the loin and is located between the rib and sirloin sections. Many retail cuts from the short loin contain parts of the T-shaped backbone. Top loin, T-bone, and Porterhouse steaks all come from the short loin.

Cut thin, these steaks tend to "curl" during cooking (although this is not a problem with thick steaks). To prevent curling, make incisions, at approximately 1-inch intervals in the fat that rims the meat.

BEEF LOIN TOP LOIN STEAK

Formerly: Shell Steak
　　　　　Strip Steak
　　　　　Club Steak
　　　　　Chip Club Steak
　　　　　Bone-In Club Sirloin Steak

Country Club Steak
Sirloin Strip Steak, Bone-In
Delmonico Steak

This steak differs from others cut from the short loin in that it contains none of the tenderloin muscle.
Cooking method for U.S. Prime, Choice, or Good: broil, panbroil, panfry.

BEEF LOIN TOP LOIN STEAK, BONELESS
also called BEEF LOIN STRIP STEAK

Formerly: Strip Steak
Kansas City Steak
New York Strip Steak
Sirloin Steak, Hotel Style
Beef Loin Ambassador Steak
Beef Loin Strip Steak, Hotel Cut
Boneless Club Sirloin Steak

Same as BEEF LOIN TOP LOIN STEAK, but boneless.
Cooking method for U.S. Prime, Choice, or Good: broil, panbroil, panfry.

BEEF LOIN T-BONE STEAK

Formerly: T-Bone Steak

So called because of the T-shaped bone; contains a small portion of the tenderloin muscle.
Cooking method for U.S. Prime, Choice, or Good: broil, panbroil, panfry.

BEEF LOIN PORTERHOUSE STEAK

Formerly: Porterhouse Steak

Similar to BEEF LOIN T-BONE STEAK, but contains a larger portion of the tenderloin muscle.
Cooking method for U.S. Prime, Choice, or Good: broil, panbroil, panfry.

BEEF LOIN TENDERLOIN ROAST

Formerly: Beef Tenderloin Tip Roast
Beef Tenderloin Filet Mignon Roast
Beef Tenderloin Chateubriand

Of all the cuts, this is the most tender, because it contains the tenderloin muscle (the least used of all the meat muscles). Beginning in the sirloin and ending at the rib end of the short loin, the roast is long and tapering, has very little fat and no bone. Weight varies from 3 pounds to 6 pounds. Also known as Filet Mignon.

Cooking method for U.S. Prime, Choice, or Good: roast.

BEEF LOIN TENDERLOIN STEAK

Formerly: Filet Mignon
Beef Fillet Steak
Beef Tenderloin, Filet DeBoeuf
Beef Tender Steak

Same as BEEF LOIN TENDERLOIN ROAST, but cut to steak thickness. Also known as Filet Mignon.

Cooking method for U.S. Prime, Choice, or Good: broil, panbroil, panfry.

Retail Cuts from the Sirloin

Sirloin Cuts

(Cross Sections
of Hip Bone) Pinbone
(near short loin)

 Flat Bone*
(center cuts)

 Wedge Bone†
(near round)

A portion of the hip bone is contained in every steak cut from the sirloin—except, of course, in the boneless steaks, from which it has been removed. Steaks from this section are named for the shape of the bone they contain.

BEEF LOIN SIRLOIN STEAK PIN BONE

Formerly: Beef Sirloin Steak Pin Bone
   Sirloin Steak

Pin bone sirloin steak contains the top (or front end) of the hip bone. It lies adjacent to the Porterhouse steaks (from the short loin) but has almost twice the amount of bone.
Cooking method for U.S. Prime, Choice, or Good: broil, panbroil, panfry.

BEEF LOIN SIRLOIN STEAK FLAT BONE

Formerly: Beef Sirloin Steak Flat Bone
   Sirloin Steak
   Flat Bone Sirloin Steak

The widest section of the hip bone is contained in this steak.
Cooking method for U.S. Prime, Choice, or Good: broil, panbroil, panfry.

* Formerly part of "double bone," but today the backbone is usually removed leaving only the "flat bone" (sometimes called "pinbone") in the sirloin steak.
† On one side of sirloin steak, this bone may be wedge-shaped, while on the other side the same bone may be round.

BEEF LOIN SIRLOIN STEAK WEDGE BONE

Formerly: Beef Sirloin Steak Wedge Bone
Beef Sirloin Steak, Short Cut
Sirloin Steak

Named for the wedge-shaped section of bone it contains, these steaks are located at the hindmost part of the sirloin, nearest the round.

Cooking method for U.S. Prime, Choice, or Good: broil, panbroil, panfry.

BEEF LOIN SIRLOIN STEAK, BONELESS

Formerly: Sirloin Steak, Boneless
Rump Steak

Any boneless steak from the sirloin.
Cooking method for U.S. Prime, Choice, or Good: broil, panbroil, panfry.

Retail Cuts from the Round

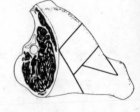

Round or
Leg Cuts

Leg or Round Bone

The muscles in this section are heavily used, thus retail cuts from the round are definitely among the least tender. There is a large amount of lean in proportion to fat and bone.

Many cuts from the round contain a portion of the leg bone.

BEEF ROUND TIP ROAST

Formerly: Beef Sirloin Tip Roast
Face Round Roast

Tip Sirloin Roast
Round Tip Roast
Crescent Roast

A boneless roast cut from the round but including a small portion from the lower sirloin.

Cooking method for U.S. Prime: roast or braise
for Choice or Good: braise; roast if pretendered.

BEEF ROUND TIP STEAK

Formerly: Beef Sirloin Tip Steak
Top Sirloin Steak

Same as BEEF ROUND TIP ROAST, but cut to steak thickness.

Cooking method for U.S. Prime, Choice or Good: panbroil, panfry; broil if pretendered.

BEEF CUBES FOR KABOBS

Formerly: Beef Sirloin Tip Kabob Cubes

Cubes or pieces often cut from the round but also from other parts of the carcass; usually served on skewers.

Cooking method for U.S. Prime, Choice, or Good: broil if cut from the sirloin; otherwise, braise, unless pretendered.

BEEF ROUND STEAK

Formerly: Beef Round Steak
Beef Round Steak, Center Cut
Beef Round Steak, Full Cut

The full-cut round steak (as illustrated) contains top round, bottom round, eye of round, plus part of the tip.

Cooking method for U.S. Prime: broil, panbroil, panfry,
braise
for U.S. Choice or Good: braise; if
pretendered, broil, panbroil, panfry.

BEEF ROUND STEAK, BONELESS

Formerly: Beef Round Steak
Beef Round Steak, Center Cut, Boneless
Beef Round, Full Cut, Boneless

Same as BEEF ROUND STEAK, but without the bone.
Cooking method for U.S. Prime: broil, panbroil, panfry,
braise
for U.S. Choice or Good: braise; if pretendered, broil, panbroil, panfry.

BEEF ROUND TOP ROUND STEAK

Formerly: Beef Top Round Steak
Beef Top Round Steak, Center Cut

Cut from the most tender muscle of the round.
Cooking method for U.S. Prime: broil, panbroil, panfry,
braise
for U.S. Choice or Good: braise; if pretendered, broil, panbroil, panfry.

BEEF ROUND BOTTOM ROUND ROAST

Formerly: Beef Bottom Round Pot Roast
Beef Bottom Round Oven Roast
Beef Bottom Round Steak Pot Roast

Varies in thickness and size and contains the bottom round
muscle.
Cooking method for U.S. Prime: roast or braise
for U.S. Choice or Good: braise.

BEEF ROUND BOTTOM ROUND STEAK

Formerly: Beef Bottom Round Steak
Bottom Round Steak

Same as BEEF ROUND BOTTOM ROUND ROAST, but cut to steak thickness. Less tender than the BEEF ROUND TOP ROUND STEAK, this cut requires longer cooking time. Cooking method for U.S. Prime, Choice, or Good: braise.

BEEF ROUND EYE ROUND ROAST

Formerly: Beef Eye Round Roast
Beef Round Eye Pot Roast
Eye Round Pot Roast
Beef Round Eye Roast

A round, compact, boneless cut, lean and fine grained.
Cooking method for U.S. Prime: roast
for U.S. Choice or Good: braise; roast if pretendered (when roasted, this cut is best cooked rare-to-medium and carved into very thin slices).

BEEF ROUND EYE ROUND STEAK

Formerly: Eye Round Steak
Beef Round Eye Steak

Same as BEEF ROUND EYE ROUND ROAST, but cut to steak thickness.
Cooking method for U.S. Prime, Choice, or Good: panbroil, panfry if sliced thin (about ⅜ inch) and cooked rare; otherwise, braise.

BEEF ROUND HEEL OF ROUND

Formerly: Beef Round Heel Pot Roast
Pike's Peak Roast

Diamond Roast
Denver Pot Roast
Horseshoe Roast

A boneless, wedge-shaped or triangular cut containing a large amount of connective tissue.
Cooking method for U.S. Prime, Choice, or Good: braise.

BEEF ROUND RUMP ROAST

Formerly: Beef Round Rump Roast, Bone-In
Beef Round Standing Rump

This cut has a large proportion of lean to fat.
Cooking method for U.S. Prime: roast or braise
for U.S. Choice or Good: braise; roast if pretendered.

BEEF ROUND RUMP ROAST, BONELESS

Formerly: Beef Round Boneless Rump
Beef Round Rump Roast, Rolled

Same as BEEF ROUND RUMP ROAST, but boneless.
Cooking method for U.S. Prime: roast or braise
for U.S. Choice or Good: braise; roast if pretendered.

BEEF CUBED STEAK

Formerly: Cubed Steak

Portions cut from the less tender parts of the round, made tender by a mechanical process that cuts through the connective tissue.
Cooking method for U.S. Prime, Choice, or Good: braise, panbroil, panfry.

Retail Cuts from the Foreshank

The foreshank contains considerable bone and connective tissue interspersed with varying amounts of lean. Cuts from this section are excellent for making soup.

BEEF SHANK CROSS CUTS

Formerly: Center Beef Shanks
Cross Shanks
Foreshank for Soup Meat, Bone-In

Easily identified by the round shank bone, these cuts vary in thickness from 1 to 2½ inches.
Cooking method for U.S. Prime, Choice, or Good: braise or cook in liquid.

Retail Cuts from the Brisket

The brisket is a rather small section of the carcass adjacent to the upper part of the foreshank. Cuts from this section tend to be rather "stringy" in texture.

BEEF BRISKET FLAT CUT, BONELESS

Formerly: Brisket Flat Cut

This requires long, slow cooking (simmering) to bring out the tenderness.
Cooking method for U.S. Prime, Choice, or Good: cook in liquid or braise.

BEEF BRISKET CORNED, BONELESS

Formerly: Corned Beef

Same as BEEF BRISKET, FLAT CUT, BONELESS, but cured in salt brine.

Cooking method for U.S. Prime, Choice, or Good: cook in
liquid unless pretendered.

Retail Cuts from the Short Plate

Located between the foreshank and the flank, the top section of the short plate contains the lower ends of the ribs.

BEEF PLATE SHORT RIBS

Formerly: Short Ribs

These cuts contain a cross section of the rib bones; layers of lean alternate with fat.

Cooking method for U.S. Prime, Choice, or Good: braise
or cook in liquid.

BEEF PLATE SKIRT STEAK ROLLS, BONELESS

Formerly: Beef London Broil
London Broil
Skirt Fillets
Skirt London Broil
London Grill Steak

For this cut the skirt steak, which is attached to the short plate, is rolled, fastened with wooden skewers, then sliced between the skewers.

Cooking method for U.S. Prime, Choice, or Good: braise;
broil if pretendered.

Retail Cuts from the Flank

The flank is a curved section of the carcass located between the short plate and the tip end of the sirloin.

BEEF FLANK

Formerly: Flank Steak Fillet
Plank Steak
London Broil
Jiffy Steak

This is a boneless cut, thin, flat, lean, and not very tender. Cooking method for U.S. Prime, Choice, or Good: broil if cooked rare and carved across the grain (should be sliced very thin); otherwise, braise.

BEEF FLANK STEAK ROLLS

Formerly: Beef London Broils
Cubed Flank Steak
Flank Steak Fillet
Flank Steak London Broils
London Broils

For this cut the flank steak is rolled, fastened with wooden skewers, then sliced between the skewers.
Cooking method for U.S. Prime, Choice, or Good: braise.

Ground Beef

A system to standardize the labeling of ground beef is being put into effect throughout the country, and will list the percentage of lean-to-fat in the meat. It should take some of the guesswork out of buying ground beef.

Lean-to-fat ratio of ground beef is important in relation to its use in recipes, as well as to its effect on the retail price. Normally, the less lean, the more fat, and the lower the price per pound.

Depending on the lean-to-fat ratio, sample labels and categorizing of ground beef is as follows:

GROUND BEEF
NOT LESS THAN 75% LEAN
70-75% Lean Ground Beef—Good for beefburgers, Sloppy Joes, chili, and spaghetti sauce.

GROUND BEEF
NOT LESS THAN 80% LEAN
75-80% Lean Ground Beef—Recommended for meat loaf, meat balls, Salisbury steak, tamale pie, beef and noodle and beef and rice casseroles.

GROUND BEEF
NOT LESS THAN 85% LEAN
80-85% Lean Ground Beef—Excellent for low-calorie entrees, including patties and loaves; also barbecued ground beef, stuffed cabbage.

Some meat retailers may label ground beef content in terms of percentage of fat. Whether it's stated in percentage of fat or percentage of lean, ground beef labeled as, say, 25 percent fat is the same as 75% lean.

Where ground beef is ground from a specific cut as the Chuck, Sirloin, or Round, the label will read:

GROUND BEEF CHUCK
NOT LESS THAN 75% LEAN

GROUND BEEF SIRLOIN
NOT LESS THAN 85% LEAN

GROUND BEEF ROUND
NOT LESS THAN 88% LEAN

The flavor and texture of ground beef depends more on the fat content than the actual cut of beef that is used. Therefore, there should not be much difference in flavor.

Cooking method: broil, panbroil, panfry, roast or bake (loaf), braise.

Variety Meats

Many organ, or variety, meats—which include liver, heart, kidneys, tongue, brains, sweetbreads, and tripe—are considered delicacies in other parts of the world.

Though in the past, we Americans have tended to pass them up in favor of the more familiar muscle meats, there does seem to be a recent trend toward greater consumption of these variety meats—a smart move, I think, since they are usually very good buys. They are excellent sources of many essential nutrients; for the adventurous cook, they're the means to more interesting and varied meals; and because many of them are still not in very great demand, their price per pound is often considerably less than that of the muscle meats.

Variety meats from beef, veal, pork, and lamb are often similar in flavor. In most cases, the size of the particular organ is consistent with the size of the animal from which it came—beef being the largest, lamb the smallest, with veal and pork somewhere between the two.

It's important to keep in mind that variety meats are more perishable than other meats and should be cooked and served (or frozen) on the day of purchase.

LIVER

Liver is probably the best known and most frequently served of all the variety meats. Beef, pork, lamb, and veal liver are all exceptionally rich sources of vital nutrients, particularly iron. (Pork liver is especially high in food value and is a good economy buy.)

HEART

Heart is very flavorful, though of all the variety meats it ranks as one of the least tender. Braising and cooking in liquid are the preferred cooking methods.

KIDNEY

Kidneys can be a great delicacy and they show up in a number of gourmet dishes. Veal and lamb kidneys are often left attached to chops and served as veal kidney chops or double lamb chops. (Both kinds, of course, are also sold separately.)

Beef kidney is less tender than other kidneys and should be cooked in liquid or braised. Veal, lamb, and pork kidneys are tender enough for broiling.

TONGUE

Tongue is a fairly popular variety meat and may be purchased fresh, corned, smoked, or canned. Because it's not very tender, it requires long, slow cooking in liquid.

SWEETBREADS

Sweetbreads—actually the two lobes of the thymus gland —gradually disappear as the animal matures. Thus, veal and young beef furnish nearly all the sweetbreads on the market.

Tender, with a delicate, piquant flavor, sweetbreads have long been regarded as party fare. They may be braised, broiled, or fried without precooking. Precooking is required when they are to be served in salads or with creamed ham or veal.

BRAINS

Brains are quite tender and delightfully mild in flavor, with a texture simliar to that of sweetbreads. A connoisseur ingredient in many breakfast, luncheon, and supper dishes, they may be broiled, fried, braised, or cooked in liquid.

TRIPE

Tripe has a pleasant, mild flavor and may be purchased fresh, pickled, and canned. It is one of the less tender variety meats and long, slow cooking in liquid is a must. (Fresh tripe is partially cooked before it is sold; even so, further cooking is preliminary to all ways of serving it.)

How to Buy What You Really Need

Knowing more about the various cuts of beef and what to do with them is important. So is knowing how to buy them in realistic amounts.

Though it may be next to impossible to calculate right down to the last mouthful the amount of meat (or poultry, or fish, for that matter) your family requires per meal, you should be able to figure closely enough to cut down on the kind of waste that results from having bought too much for one meal but not nearly enough for a second.

With items like chops or frankfurters, this is fairly easy to do. You probably already know that A will eat two, B will eat three, and C will eat one, so you buy accordingly. But estimating how much to buy of other items—especially those containing large amounts of bone or fat—is a bit trickier. You need to know the approximate number of servings per pound each cut can be expected to yield. The following table should be helpful:

LITTLE FAT AND NO BONE	Amount	Approximate number of servings
Rolled roasts, boneless roasts, tenderloin, flank steak, cube steaks, brisket, ground meat, veal cutlets, liver, heart, tongue, kidney, sausages, frankfurters, most canned meats	1 lb.	3 to 4

	Amount	Approximate number of servings

MEDIUM AMOUNT OF BONE AND SOME FAT

Beef chuck (shoulder)—blade and arm—roasts and steaks, rib roasts, loin roasts, rump roasts, chops, steaks, round steak, ham slices, leg of lamb — 1 lb. — 2 to 3

LARGE AMOUNT OF BONE AND FAT

Short ribs, spareribs, neck, breast, plate, shank, pork hocks — 1 lb. — 1 to 1½

The servings referred to in the following tables are "average"—in most cases ranging somewhere between 3½ and four ounces each of cooked lean meat. Nutritionally speaking, this "average" serving is adequate for a moderately active, medium-size adult. Obviously, an average serving of practically anything will be too much for a toddler, but nowhere near enough for a teen-age boy or very large, very active adult male. You'll have to make adjustments, then, in planning for your own family, perhaps allotting one-half the average serving for small children, and one to one and one-half (possibly two, or even three!) servings for the big eaters. (In theory, it might take only three average servings of meat to satisfy a family of four in which there are two sedentary adults and two very small children; while another family of four, with, say, two ever-famished teen-agers and two active adult members, might require eight!)

Cost for a Serving of Meat at Various Price Levels

APPROXIMATE COST PER SERVING

Cost Per Pound	1½ Servings per Pound	2 Servings per Pound	2½ Servings per Pound	3 Servings per Pound	3½ Servings per Pound	4 Servings per Pound	5 Servings per Pound	6 Servings per Pound
.59	.39	.30	.24	.20	.17	.15	.12	.10
.69	.46	.35	.28	.23	.20	.17	.14	.12
.79	.53	.40	.32	.26	.23	.20	.16	.13
.89	.59	.45	.36	.30	.25	.22	.18	.15
.99	.66	.50	.40	.33	.28	.25	.20	.17
1.09	.73	.55	.44	.36	.31	.27	.22	.18
1.19	.79	.60	.48	.40	.34	.30	.24	.20
1.29	.86	.65	.52	.43	.37	.32	.26	.22
1.39	.93	.70	.56	.46	.40	.35	.28	.23
1.49	.99	.75	.60	.50	.43	.37	.30	.25
1.59	1.06	.80	.64	.53	.45	.40	.32	.27
1.69	1.13	.85	.68	.56	.48	.42	.34	.28
1.79	1.19	.90	.72	.60	.51	.45	.36	.30
1.89	1.26	.95	.76	.63	.54	.47	.38	.32
1.99	1.33	1.00	.80	.66	.57	.50	.40	.33
2.09	1.39	1.05	.84	.70	.60	.52	.42	.35
2.19	1.46	1.10	.88	.73	.63	.55	.44	.37
2.29	1.53	1.15	.92	.76	.65	.57	.46	.38
2.39	1.59	1.20	.96	.80	.68	.60	.48	.40
2.49	1.66	1.25	1.00	.83	.71	.62	.50	.42
2.59	1.73	1.30	1.04	.86	.74	.65	.52	.43
2.69	1.79	1.35	1.08	.90	.77	.67	.54	.45

Servings per Pound to Expect from a Specific Cut of Meat

The servings per pound are only a guide to the average amount to buy to provide 3 to 3½ ounces of cooked lean meat. The cooking method and cooking temperature, the degree of doneness, the difference in the size of bone in the bone-in cuts and amount of fat trim are some of the factors that vary and will affect the yield of cooked lean meat.

BEEF

Steaks			
Chuck (Arm or Blade)	2	Chuck, Boneless	2½
"Cubed"	4	Cross Rib	2½
Filet Mignon	3		
Flank	3	*Other Cuts*	
Porterhouse	2	Brisket	3
Rib	2	Cubes, Beef	4
Rib Eye (Delmonico)	3	Loaf, Beef	4
Round	3	Patties, Beef	4
Sirloin	2½	Short Ribs	2
T-Bone	2		
Top Loin	3	*Variety Meats*	
		Brains	5
Roasts		Heart	5
Rib, Standing	2	Kidney	5
Rib Eye (Delmonico)	3	Liver	4
Rump, Boneless	3	Sweetbreads	5
Round Tip	3	Tongue	5
Pot Roasts			
Arm (Chuck)	2		
Blade (Chuck)	2		

34

A Few Words About Buying in Quantity

Unless one is a super planner, there will occasionally be times when the refrigerator and freezer take on the appearance of Old Mother Hubbard's cupboard. Unfortunately, this has a way of happening on the very days when dinner must be put together in a hurry and from scratch. What's needed is a small quantity (one meal's worth) of some quick-cooking item.

On the whole, though, it's far more economical to watch for specials and buy enough of a particular cut for two, three, or more meals. Much of this book is taken up with variations on the money-saving theme of buying and cooking in quantity.

Storage facilities, obviously, have a great bearing on the quantity of meat to purchase at any one time. With a freezer, one can take full advantage of meat specials—and *should*, in order to justify the expense of running it. But even with limited freezer space, it's possible to plan ahead and thus get better value for your meat dollar.

2
How to Cook the Thrift Cuts

Just as tenderness determines price, it also determines the way in which a particular cut of beef is cooked.

There are at least ten different ways to cook meat (the chart on page 38 gives a brief definition of each). But all are variations of only two basic methods: One utilizes *dry* heat—as in broiling in a pan or under a flame, or roasting in an oven or on a spit. The other utilizes *moist* heat, or steam—as in braising, where the meat is surrounded by a small amount of liquid and simmered in a tightly covered pan.

Most tender meat can be cooked successfully using one of the dry-heat methods, though I can think of a few exceptions: veal steaks and chops are one. They're often braised, because they have no fat to speak of and thus tend to dry out very quickly when cooked by other methods. Thick pork chops, too are sometimes braised, because the intense dry heat needed to assure a thoroughly done center may cause the outside to become overly dry.

As a general rule, the thrift cuts—the ones we're primarily concerned with in this book—should be *braised* or *cooked in liquid*. It's the long, slow, moist-heat simmering that makes them tender. (Alternatively, they may be pretendered—either with a commercial product or in homemade marinade.)

Basic Methods of Meat Cookery

Dry Heat	Moist Heat
Roasting	Braising
Broiling	Cooking in Liquid
Panbroiling	Pressure Cooking
Panfrying	
Deep-Fat Frying	
Barbecuing	

ROASTING—Meat is cooked by dry heat, uncovered, either in the oven or on a spit.

BROILING—Meat is cooked by direct heat, either in a broiler or on a grill.

PANBROILING—Meat is cooked by heat transmitted through the frying pan; fat is poured off as it accumulates.

PANFRYING—Meat is cooked in a small amount of fat.

DEEP-FAT FRYING—Meat is cooked by immersing in fat.

BARBECUING—Meat is roasted or broiled over an open fire.

BRAISING—Meat is simmered in a small amount of liquid.

COOKING IN LIQUID—Meat is simmered in enough liquid to cover it completely.

PRESSURE COOKING—Meat is cooked by means of superheated steam in a special appliance (pressure cooker).

Marinades and Tenderizers

Most often, moist-heat cooking is sufficient to "tenderize" even the (yes, let's say it) "toughest" budget cuts. However, there may be times when you will want to use a tenderizer or homemade marinade prior to cooking. Some recipes call for tenderizing or marinating; otherwise, I would say that their use is optional and purely a matter of choice.

There are many commercial tenderizers on the market. They're convenient and easy to use and they do the job they were made to do. Simply follow the manufacturers' instructions.

However, because of its potential for adding subtle new flavor, I'm partial to the homemade marinade as a tenderizing agent.

Marinades are a blend of three kinds of ingredients: (1) a fat—usually a salad oil or olive oil, though some recipes may call for peanut oil, butter, margarine, or lard; (2) a food acid, such as wine, vinegar, lemon juice, or fruit juice; and (3) seasonings.

In a marinade, it is the food acid that softens up the connective tissues and does the tenderizing. Meat to be marinated is covered and allowed to stand in the mixture for anywhere from 2 to 48 hours prior to cooking. As one might expect, the longer the marinating time, the more tender the meat. Often the marinade is reserved and used for basting or as part of the cooking liquid.

I've found that a plastic bag makes a fine container for marinating. (Pour a cup or so of water into the bag first to make sure there are no holes.) In any event, do avoid metal containers when wine is an ingredient in a marinade; choose glass or enamelware instead.

There are no hard and fast rules about the *seasonings* used in a marinade. Use your imagination, but do keep in mind that the idea is to enhance and complement—not mask—the flavor of the meat.

Here is a list of seasonings for guidance:
SPICES—Allspice, cayenne, cinnamon, cloves, ginger, mace, nutmeg, paprika, black pepper, white pepper, red pepper, saffron, turmeric.
HERBS—Basil, bay leaves, chervil, marjoram, mint, oregano, parsley, rosemary, sage, savory, tarragon, thyme.

AROMATIC SEEDS—Anise, caraway, cardamom, celery, coriander, cumin, dill, fennel, mustard, poppy.

OTHER SEASONINGS—Capers, catsup, chili powder, chili sauce, garlic, garlic salt, garlic powder, horseradish, liquid smoke, monosodium glutamate (MSG), onions, onion salt, poultry seasoning, soy sauce, tabasco, Worcestershire sauce.

How to Braise

In braising, sometimes called "pot-roasting," the meat is first browned in a small amount of hot fat; then liquid is added, and the meat is cooked slowly in a tightly covered pot, either on top of the range or in the oven.

Many of the recipes to follow call for braising. Though there are several steps involved, it's a rather simple technique and definitely a money-saver. Once mastered, it offers the means to an almost unlimited number of different ways to serve the thrifty, less tender cuts of beef.

Here is the complete procedure for braising:

1. Dry the meat with paper towels.

2. In a Dutch oven or other heavy pot with a tight-fitting lid, put two tablespoons of cooking fat. Place the pan over low-to-moderate heat. When the fat is hot, add the meat, turning it quickly so that all sides are immediately coated with fat. (This helps prevent the meat from sticking to the pot during browning.)

3. Brown the meat *slowly*, on all sides, using low-to-moderate heat. With slow browning, good flavor and color are developed and retained throughout the whole cooking process. (Too quick browning over high heat may impart a burnt taste.) As a general rule of thumb, I would suggest allowing between 20 and 25 minutes for browning; or, put an-

other way, approximately 5 minutes for each side. You needn't hover over the pot the whole time. You might, in fact, use a timer, setting it to call you back at 5-minute intervals.

4. Discard excess fat.

5. Season with salt and pepper. (Though seasonings are sometimes added to the fat in which the meat is browned, I find the meat retains more of its natural juices when seasoned *after* browning.)

6. Add a small amount of liquid. The liquid used might be water, soup stock, vegetable juice, tomato juice or sauce, canned or fresh tomatoes, or a marinade.

7. Cover the pan. A tight-fitting cover is important for holding in the steam needed to soften the connective tissues and make the meat tender.

8. Cook at a low temperature until meat is tender. *Simmer, don't boil.* In simmering, the temperature of the liquid reaches approximately 185°F.; bubbles form slowly and break below the surface. Oven-cooking at 325°F. makes it easier to retain even heat and moisture.

9. To assure uniform doneness, turn the meat once, about midway through the cooking time. (It helps to use tongs and a spatula, or two long-handled wooden spoons, for turning a big, unwieldy chunk of meat.)

10. Test for doneness by piercing with a sharp-tined fork. When the fork enters easily, the meat is done.

11. Make gravy or sauce from the liquid in the pan. A gravy or sauce is not only delicious when served as an accompaniment to the meat, but valuable, too, because the liquid from which it is made contains many soluble nutrients.

Unfortunately, *gravy* has a reputation for being tricky to make. It needn't be if you just follow these general rules:

To make 2 cups of gravy, pour liquid from pan into a 2-cup measure. Let stand for 1 minute to allow fat to rise to the top. Skim off all but 4 tablespoons (or less) of the fat. Then add enough water or other liquid to measure 1½ cups. Return mixture to pan.

In the same cup, measure ½ cup cold water, then blend in ¼ cup flour. Add slowly to the liquid in the pan. Bring to a boil, stirring constantly, and cook until thickened—about 3 minutes. If necessary, correct seasoning with salt and pepper.

This mixture will yield a medium-thick gravy. For a thicker gravy, use more flour; for a thinner gravy, use less flour.

To make a very thin sauce, simply skim off excess fat in the pan, then simmer the remaining liquid, uncovered, until it is slightly thickened.

The table on the following page shows how long some of the cuts require cooking for full flavor—and just how many people you can expect to serve from them.

How to Cook in Liquid

Another excellent way to prepare inexpensive cuts of beef is to cook in liquid. The technique is similar to braising, except, as one might expect, more liquid is used.

The rules for cooking in liquid are as follows:

1. Using low-to-moderate heat, brown the meat slowly on all sides. (For more complete instructions on browning, see step #3 in the *How to Braise* section, page 40). Browning develops flavor and encourages a nice, rich color. (Dredging the meat first in flour makes for an even richer, darker stew.) However, this step may be omitted entirely if one prefers a light stew. And, of course, corned beef and cured or smoked pork definitely should *not* be browned.

Large Beef Cuts to Braise

Cut	Approx. Weight	Approx. Servings	Approx. Total Cooking Time
Beef Chuck Blade Roast	4–5 pounds	8 to 10	3–3½ hours
Beef Chuck Blade Roast, Boneless	3–4 pounds	6 to 8	2½–3 hours
Beef Chuck Eye Roast, Boneless	4–5 pounds	8 to 10	3½–4 hours
Beef Chuck Arm Pot Roast	4–5 pounds	8 to 10	3–3½ hours
Beef Chuck Arm Pot Roast, Boneless	3–4 pounds	6 to 8	2½–3 hours
Beef Chuck Shoulder Pot Roast, Boneless	3½–4 pounds	7 to 8	2½–3½ hours
Beef Chuck Cross Rib Pot Roast	4–5 pounds	8 to 10	3–3½ hours
Beef Chuck Cross Rib Pot Roast, Boneless	3–4 pounds	6 to 8	2½–3 hours
Beef Round Bottom Round Roast	4–6 pounds	8 to 12	3½–4 hours
Beef Round Eye Round Roast	3–4 pounds	8 to 12	1½–2 hours
Beef Round Heel of Round	4–5 pounds	8 to 10	3–3½ hours
Beef Round Rump Roast, Boneless	4–6 pounds	8 to 12	3½–4 hours
Beef Round Tip Roast	3½–4 pounds	7 to 8	3–3½ hours

Note: Meat cuts in some of the pot roast recipes may be interchanged. Consult the above chart for approximate cooking time, weight, and servings.

2. Add enough liquid—either water, vegetable juice, soup stock, bouillon, or other liquid—to cover the meat. This assures uniform cooking without have to turn the meat. The liquid to be added may be either hot or cold. If it is hot, the meat will begin to cook at once.

3. Season with salt and pepper; add herbs and spices if desired. Imaginative use of seasonings adds much in the way of variety to the flavor of meats cooked in liquid. I hope you will experiment with at least some of the following: bay leaves, thyme, marjoram, parsley, green pepper,

celery, onion (and celery and onion tops), garlic, cloves, peppercorns, allspice.

4. Cover pan and simmer (do not boil) until done. (In simmering, bubbles form slowly and break just beneath the surface.)

5. Test for doneness by piercing the meat with a sharp-tined fork.

6. Add vegetables so that they and the meat will be done at the same time. Vegetables may be left whole, quartered, or cut in small, uniform pieces.

Large Beef Cuts to Cook in Liquid

Cut	Approx. Weight	Approx. Servings	Approx. Total Cooking Time
Beef Brisket Flat Cut, Boneless	4–5 pounds	8 to 10	3½–4½ hours
Beef Brisket Corned, Boneless	4–5 pounds	8 to 10	3½–4½ hours

How to Reduce Shrinkage

Meat always shrinks as it cooks. With heat, water and other volatile substances evaporate from the surface, while more water, fat, extractives, vitamins and other substances are released into the cooking liquid (in braising) or as pan drippings (in roasting), or else they are lost entirely. In any case, these losses should be kept to a minimum. Shrinkage not only reduces the meat by volume, but also affects its appearance and palatability.

Cooking at low-to-moderate temperatures can reduce shrinkage by as much as 15 to 20 percent. Much research has been done on the subject and it's been found that the lower the cooking temperature, the less shrinkage one can expect.

There are other advantages to low-temperature cooking: better flavor and tenderness are maintained; meat gets cooked more uniformly; and, though overall cooking time is increased, less fuel is used. In addition, meat cooked at low temperatures is easier to carve because the muscle fibers hold together better, and there is no hard crust to hack through. (I can think of one more advantage, not often mentioned in this context, but valid just the same: cleanup is easier, since racks, pans, etc., don't get so crusted over with burnt-on fat.)

Along these same lines, there is another point that is good to know about: The degree of doneness, as measured by the *internal* temperature to which the meat is cooked, may influence shrinkage just as much and sometimes more than the actual cooking temperature. In other words, the higher the internal temperature, the greater the degree of doneness and the more shrinkage one can expect.

Thus, if you want to have juicy, flavorful meat—neither dry and shrunken on the one hand, nor too rare on the other —it's important to be able to estimate when a particular cut has reached just the right degree of doneness.

A meat thermometer takes the guesswork out of roasting. When using a meat thermometer, it's a good idea to check its positioning within the cut when the desired degree of doneness is almost reached. (There is always the possibility that it may not have been placed exactly in the thickest part of the meat, or that it has shifted slightly during cooking.) If the temperature drops by a few degrees when the thermometer is pressed gently into the meat, more cooking is required.

Also keep in mind that meat continues to cook for a while even after it has been removed from the oven. For this reason, and because roasts and some other cuts need time to "rest" before carving, you may remove them from the oven when the thermometer registers about 5 degrees below the desired temperature.

Unfortunately, a meat thermometer doesn't work with all cuts and all methods of cooking. It's of no use when meat is braised or cooked in liquid. Neither can one depend entirely on the cooking time as stated in a recipe—it is meant only as a guide, and there are several variables that may make it necessary to increase, or reduce, the time required to reach just the right degree of doneness. Among them are:

1. *The size and shape of the cut.* In general, the larger the cut, the fewer minutes per pound required to cook it. However, a thick, chunky cut will require longer cooking than a flat, thin one of the same weight.

2. *The style of the cut.* Because it is less dense, a standing beef rib roast cooks in much less time than, say, the same cut rolled and boned.

3. *The amount of aging.* Cuts from aged beef require slightly less time to reach the desired degree of doneness than those from unaged beef.

4. *Tenderizing.* The use of a homemade or commercial tenderizer may reduce required cooking time by as much as 25 percent.

5. *Your particular oven.* Some ovens are a few degrees off in one direction or the other. You're probably aware of whether yours tends to be fast or slow, and if so, this should be taken into consideration. Even a slight variation in temperature affects the time required to cook meat to the proper degree of doneness.

So watch out for all these factors when you are about to assess the amount of time needed to cook your meat.

How to Add a Special Touch with Wine

The addition of wine as an ingredient makes even budget fare seem somehow special, more gracious.

Though there is a kind of mystique about wine in general, when one uses it in cooking it may be thought of as simply another ingredient. Actually, it is probably no more "difficult" to cook with wine than it is to cook with, say, garlic. In both cases, one proceeds with a bit of caution at first, keeping in mind that the goal is to bring out the special goodness of the food itself and not to supply the main flavoring.

When wine is used in cooking, the alcohol evaporates rather quickly (it boils at 172°F., while water boils at 212°F.) and only the flavor remains.

If you've never used wine, you might begin by trying a few recipes that call for it as an ingredient. Wine is marvelous in a marinade and is specified as an ingredient in some of the pot roast recipes in this book. But even where wine is not called for, it may be used as part of the cooking liquid —in which case, add about ¾ cup at the beginning of cooking and ¼ cup just before serving.

There's no need to buy the most expensive wines for cooking; the subtleties of a very fine wine may be lost when combined with the flavors of other ingredients in a recipe. (On the other hand, I certainly would not recommend cooking with any wine that you consider unfit to drink.)

All types of wine have a place in cooking. Though it was once felt that red wines belong with red meats only and white wines with fish and poultry, this generalization is usually regarded as being outmoded now. I know of some very good fish recipes calling for red wine, while a few recipes with red meat as the main ingredient are made with sweet dessert wines. With experience comes confidence and skill, and an adventuresome chef may find great pleasure in experimenting with different combinations of food and wine.

In cooking, wines of the same type are interchangeable. A recipe calling for burgundy, for example, certainly would not suffer if some other rather dry red wine were used instead. An adequate basic supply to have on hand for cooking might include a medium (dry) sherry (the most versatile wine, it can be used to advantage in almost anything), a burgundy or other red table wine, and a sauterne, or some sweetish white wine.

Again, though the mystique would have us believe otherwise, it is not difficult to care for and store wine. The only hard and fast rule is to keep it out of sunlight and in a cool, dry place or in the refrigerator if you prefer. Bottles with corks should rest on their sides so that the corks stay moist and tight. Screw-top bottles may be stored upright.

Though sherry keeps for a while after it's been opened, some other wines—table wines, such as burgundy, claret, sauterne, chablis, etc.—are perishable. Use them up within a very few days after opening the bottle. (A bottle of wine to be used for cooking only will keep longer if a bit of oil is dropped on the surface.)

3

Money-saving Ways
with Budget Beef

Pot Roasts International—
37 Hearty Meals Made with the Chunky Cuts

I've always liked the idea of the pot roast. There's something uniquely satisfying about starting with a good, chunky cut of inexpensive beef and—with a minimum of fuss—turning it into a meal that's not only hearty and nutritious, but marvelously good-tasting, too.

Unfortunately, so much of what we eat in the name of economy or convenience or both is apt to be rather complex, insubstantial stuff: either time-consuming or overly difficult to make, on the one hand, or nutritionally lacking on the other. Not so with the pot roast. It is good, honest, *real* food. And when prepared with reasonable care and skill, as flavorful and delicious as food can be. I for one will continue to serve and enjoy the pot roast no matter what happens to the price of beef.

Collected on the following pages is a group of thirty-seven different recipes for preparing pot roasts. Some are distinctively American; many others are adapted from the cuisines of other lands. All are good, thrifty eating. I'm sure you will enjoy them as much as I do.

Savory Pot Roast
(8 to 12 servings)

4- to 6-pound beef round rump roast, boneless
2   tablespoons cooking fat
Salt and pepper
½ cup chopped onion, fresh or frozen
1   can (10½ ounces) condensed bouillon, undiluted
½ cup catsup
¼ cup flour for gravy

1. In a Dutch oven, or large pan with a tight-fitting cover, brown meat in fat. Season with salt and pepper and remove from pan. Pour off fat drippings.
2. Cook onion in drippings remaining in pan until soft but not browned; stir often. Add bouillon and catsup; mix well.
3. Return meat to pan. Cover and simmer for 3½ to 4 hours, or until done. (Or cook in a 325°F. oven for same amount of time.)
4. Turn meat once to cook it evenly throughout. When done, remove meat and keep warm.
5. For 2 cups gravy, pour liquid from pan into a 2-cup measuring cup. Let stand for 1 minute to allow fat to come to top. Discard all but 4 tablespoons (or less) of fat. Add enough water (or other liquid) to measure 1½ cups of liquid. Return to pan.
6. In same cup, measure ½ cup cold water and blend in flour. Add mixture slowly to liquid in pan. Bring to a boil, stirring constantly, and cook until thickened, about 3 minutes. Taste gravy and correct seasoning, if necessary, with salt and pepper.
7. Slice meat; serve gravy separately, or spoon over meat.

Zesty Pot Roast
(6 to 8 servings)

3- to 4-pound beef chuck arm pot roast, boneless
2 tablespoons cooking fat
Salt and pepper
½ cup chopped onion, fresh or frozen
1 can (10¾ ounces) condensed tomato soup
1 soup can water
¼ cup vinegar
1 cup canned applesauce

1. In a Dutch oven, or large pan with a tight-fitting cover, brown meat in fat. Season with salt and pepper and remove from pan. Pour off fat drippings.
2. Cook onion in drippings remaining in pan until soft but not browned; stir often.
3. Add tomato soup, water, and vinegar; mix well.
4. Return meat to pan. Cover and simmer for 2½ to 3 hours, or until done. (Or cook in a 325°F. oven for same amount of time.)
5. Turn meat once to cook it evenly throughout. When done, remove meat and keep warm.
6. Skim off excess fat. Add applesauce and cook to desired consistency. Taste sauce and correct seasoning, if necessary, with salt and pepper.
7. Slice meat and serve with sauce.

Beef Pot Roast with Mushroom Soup–Wine Gravy
(7 to 8 servings)

3½- to 4-pound beef round tip roast
2 tablespoons cooking fat
Salt and pepper
1 medium-size onion, thinly sliced
1 can (10½ ounces) condensed cream of mushroom soup
¾ cup burgundy wine
2 tablespoons finely chopped parsley
⅛ teaspoon garlic powder
¼ cup flour for gravy

1. In a Dutch oven, or large pan with a tight-fitting cover, brown meat in fat. Season with salt and pepper and remove from pan. Pour off fat drippings.
2. Cook onion in drippings remaining in pan until soft but not browned; stir often.
3. Add mushroom soup, wine, parsley, and garlic powder; mix well.
4. Return meat to pan. Cover and simmer for 3 to 3½ hours, or until done. (Or cook in a 325°F. oven for same amount of time.)
5. Turn meat once to cook it evenly throughout. When done, remove meat and keep warm.
6. For 2 cups gravy, pour liquid from pan into a 2-cup measuring cup. Let stand for 1 minute to allow fat to come to top. Discard all but 4 tablespoons (or less) of fat. Add enough water (or other liquid) to measure 1½ cups of liquid. Return to pan.
7. In same cup, measure ½ cup cold water and blend in flour. Add mixture slowly to liquid in pan. Bring to a boil, stirring constantly, and cook until thickened, about 3 minutes. Taste gravy and correct seasoning, if necessary, with salt and pepper.
8. Slice meat; serve gravy separately, or spoon over meat.

Pot Roast with Tomatoes and Corn
(8 to 10 servings)

4- to 5-pound beef chuck blade roast
2 tablespoons cooking fat
Salt and pepper
1 medium-size onion, thinly sliced
2 cups canned tomatoes
1 teaspoon paprika
1 can (1 pound) whole-kernel corn, drained

1. In a Dutch oven, or large pan with a tight-fitting cover, brown meat in fat. Season with salt and pepper and remove from pan. Pour off fat drippings.
2. Cook onion in drippings remaining in pan until soft but not browned; stir often.
3. Add tomatoes and break up lumps, if desired, with a potato masher. (Or, tomatoes may be whirled in a blender for a few seconds.)
4. Add paprika. Return meat to pan. Cover and simmer 3 to 3½ hours, or until done. (Or cook in a 325°F. oven for same amount of time.)
5. Turn meat once to cook it evenly throughout. Add corn during the last 15 minutes of cooking. Skim off excess fat.
6. If sauce is too thin, remove meat to a serving platter and keep warm. Mix 2 tablespoons flour in ⅓ cup cold water. Add mixture slowly to sauce. Bring to a boil, stirring constantly, and cook until thickened, about 3 minutes. Taste sauce and correct seasoning, if necessary, with salt and pepper.
7. Serve sliced meat with vegetables and sauce.

Pot Roast, Italian Style
(7 to 8 servings)

3½- to 4-pound beef chuck shoulder pot roast, boneless
2 tablespoons cooking fat
Salt and pepper
½ cup chopped onion, fresh or frozen
½ cup chopped carrots
½ cup chopped celery
1 can (6 ounces) tomato paste
1 can (8 ounces) tomato sauce
½ cup dry red wine
2 beef bouillon cubes dissolved in 1½ cups hot water
1 teaspoon sugar
1 teaspoon basil
½ teaspoon oregano
1 pound spaghetti, or thin noodles
Grated Parmesan cheese

1. In a Dutch oven, or large pan with a tight-fitting cover, brown meat in fat. Season with salt and pepper and remove from pan. Pour off fat drippings.
2. Add onion, carrots, and celery; cook until vegetables are lightly browned, stirring often.
3. Add tomato paste, tomato sauce, wine, bouillon, sugar, basil and oregano; mix well.
4. Return meat to pan. Cover and simmer for 2½ to 3½ hours, or until done. (Or cook in a 325°F. oven for same amount of time.)
5. Turn meat once to cook it evenly throughout and stir sauce. When done, remove meat to a platter and keep warm. Skim excess fat.
6. If sauce is a little too thin, simmer, uncovered, until it is of desired thickness. Taste sauce and correct seasoning, if necessary, with salt and pepper.

7. Meanwhile cook spaghetti and drain. Serve sauce over spaghetti and sprinkle with Parmesan cheese.
8. Slice meat and spoon a little sauce over it.

Pot Roast in Barbecue Sauce
(8 to 10 servings)

4- to 5-pound beef chuck arm pot roast
2 tablespoons cooking fat
Salt and pepper
1½ cups catsup (or 1 cup catsup,
   ½ cup chili sauce)
1 cup water
¼ cup chopped onion, fresh or frozen
1 tablespoon Worcestershire sauce
¼ cup vinegar
1 teaspoon prepared mustard
1 tablespoon brown sugar

1. In a Dutch oven, or large pan with a tight-fitting cover, brown meat in fat. Season with salt and pepper and remove from pan. Pour off fat drippings.
2. Add remaining ingredients and mix well.
3. Return meat to pan. Cover and simmer 3 to 3½ hours, or until done. (Or bake in a 325°F. oven for same amount of time.)
4. Turn meat once to cook it evenly throughout and baste with sauce. Taste sauce and correct seasoning, if necessary, with salt and pepper.
5. When meat is done, remove and keep warm. Skim excess fat from sauce.
6. Slice meat, and serve sauce separately.

Hawaiian Pot Roast
(6 to 8 servings)

3- to 4-pound beef chuck cross rib pot roast, boneless
2   tablespoons cooking fat
Salt and pepper
¼ cup soy sauce
½ cup pineapple juice (drained from tidbits)
¼ teaspoon ginger
1   medium-size onion, thinly sliced
3   stalks celery, cut diagonally in 1-inch pieces
1   can (13¼ ounces) pineapple tidbits
1   can (4 ounces) mushroom slices
¼ cup water
1   tablespoon cornstarch

1. In a Dutch oven, or large pan with a tight-fitting cover, brown meat in fat. Season with salt and pepper and remove from pan. Pour off fat drippings.
2. Add soy sauce, pineapple juice, ginger, and onion; mix well.
3. Return meat to pan. Cover and simmer 2½ to 3 hours, or until done. (Or cook in a 325°F. oven for same amount of time.)
4. Turn meat once to cook it evenly throughout. During the last 20 minutes of cooking, add celery, pineapple tidbits, mushrooms, and juice. When meat is done, remove and keep warm. Skim fat from liquid.
5. Mix cornstarch in water. Add mixture slowly to liquid in pan. Bring to a boil, stirring constantly, and cook until thickened, about 3 minutes. Taste sauce and correct seasoning, if necessary, with salt and pepper.
6. Slice meat, and serve sauce separately.

Pot Roast with Dill Gravy
(6 to 8 servings)

3- **to 4-pound beef chuck arm pot roast, boneless**
2 **tablespoons cooking fat**
Salt and pepper
½ **cup water**
1 **tablespoon dill seed**
2 **medium-size onions, sliced thick**
¼ **cup flour for gravy**
½ **cup dairy sour cream**

1. In a Dutch oven, or large pan with a tight-fitting cover, brown meat in fat. Season with salt and pepper and remove from pan. Pour off fat drippings. Add water.
2. Return meat to pan and sprinkle with dill seed. Place onion slices on top.
3. Cover and simmer 2½ to 3 hours or until done. (Or cook in a 325°F. oven for same amount of time.)
4. When done, remove meat and onion to a platter and keep warm.
5. For 2 cups gravy, pour liquid from pan into a 2-cup measuring cup. Let stand for 1 minute to allow fat to come to top. Discard all but 4 tablespoons (or less) of fat. Add enough water (or other liquid) to measure 1½ cups of liquid. Return to pan.
6. In same cup, measure ½ cup cold water and blend in flour. Add mixture slowly to liquid in pan. Bring to a boil, stirring constantly, and cook until thickened, about 3 minutes.
7. Remove pan from heat. Add sour cream, a small amount at a time, and mix well. Taste gravy and correct seasoning, if necessary, with salt and pepper. If gravy is not hot enough when ready to serve, place pan over very low heat, but do not boil, or gravy may curdle. (Note:

The flavor of the gravy is not affected should curdling occur.)

8. Slice meat, and serve gravy separately.

Bavarian Pot Roast
(8 to 12 servings)

4- to 6-pound beef round bottom round roast
2   tablespoons cooking fat
Salt and pepper
1½ cups apple juice
1   can (8 ounces) tomato sauce
½   cup chopped onion, fresh or frozen
1   teaspoon ginger
1   teaspoon cinnamon
½   teaspoon salt
1   tablespoon vinegar
1   bay leaf
¼   cup flour for gravy

1. In a Dutch oven, or large pan with a tight-fitting cover, brown meat in fat. Season with salt and pepper and remove from pan. Pour off fat drippings.
2. Add the apple juice, tomato sauce, onion, ginger, cinnamon, salt, vinegar, and bay leaf; mix well.
3. Return meat to pan. Cover and simmer for 3½ to 4 hours, or until done. (Or cook in a 325° F. oven for the same amount of time.)
4. Turn meat once to cook it evenly throughout. When done, remove meat and keep warm. Discard bay leaf.
5. For 2 cups gravy, pour liquid from pan into a 2-cup measuring cup. Let stand for 1 minute to allow fat to come to top. Discard all but 4 tablespoons (or less) of fat. Add enough water (or other liquid) to measure 1½ cups of liquid. Return to pan.

6. In same cup, measure ½ cup cold water and blend in flour. Add mixture slowly to liquid in pan. Bring to a boil, stirring constantly, and cook until thickened, about 3 minutes. Taste gravy and correct seasoning, if necessary, with salt and pepper.
7. Slice meat, and serve gravy separately.

Beef Pot Roast, Oriental Style
   (8 to 10 servings)

4- to 5-pound beef chuck eye roast, boneless
2   tablespoons cooking fat
Salt and pepper
½ cup chopped onion, fresh or frozen
½ cup diced green pepper
¼ cup soy sauce
¼ cup dry sherry wine
1   teaspoon finely grated fresh ginger, or
    ¼ teaspoon ground ginger
½ cup water
1   can (4 ounces) sliced mushrooms, drained (save liquid)
2   tablespoons cornstarch
Hot cooked rice

1. In a Dutch oven, or large pan with a tight-fitting cover, brown meat in fat. Season with salt and pepper and remove from pan. Pour off fat drippings.
2. Add onion, green pepper, soy sauce, wine, ginger, water, and mushrooms; mix well.
3. Return meat to pan. Cover and simmer 3½ to 4 hours, or until done. (Or cook in a 325°F. oven for same amount of time.)
4. Turn meat once to cook it evenly throughout. When done, remove meat and keep warm.
5. For 2 cups sauce, pour liquid from pan into a 2-cup mea-

suring cup. Let stand for 1 minute to allow fat to come to top. Discard all but 4 tablespoons (or less) of fat. Add enough water to measure 1½ cups of liquid. Return to pan.

6. In same cup, add mushroom juice and enough water to measure ½ cup. Blend in cornstarch. Add mixture slowly to liquid in pan. Bring to a boil, stirring constantly, and cook until thickened, about 3 minutes. Taste sauce and correct seasoning, if necessary, with salt and pepper.

7. Slice meat and serve with sauce over hot rice.

Pot Roast Teriyaki
(7 to 8 servings)

3½- to 4-pound beef round tip roast
2   tablespoons flour
1   teaspoon salt
⅛ teaspoon black pepper
½ teaspoon curry powder
2   tablespoons cooking fat
¼ cup honey
¼ cup soy sauce
¼ cup water
¼ cup dry sherry wine
¼ teaspoon ground ginger
2   tablespoons cornstarch
Hot cooked rice

1. Combine flour, salt, pepper, and curry powder. Dredge meat in seasoned flour and brown in fat. Remove meat from pan and pour off fat drippings.

2. Add honey, soy sauce, water, wine, and ginger; mix well.

3. Return meat to pan. Cover and simmer 3 to 3½ hours, or until done. (Or cook in a 325°F. oven for same amount of time.)

4. Turn meat once to cook it evenly throughout. When done, remove meat and keep warm.

5. For 2 cups of sauce, pour liquid from pan into a 2-cup measuring cup. Let stand for 1 minute to allow fat to come to top. Discard fat. Add enough water to measure 1½ cups of liquid. Return to pan.

6. In same cup, measure ½ cup cold water and blend in cornstarch. Add mixture slowly to liquid in pan. Bring to a boil, stirring constantly, and cook until thickened, about 3 minutes. Taste sauce and correct seasoning, if necessary, with salt and pepper.

7. Slice meat and serve with sauce and hot rice.

Pot Roast, Mexican Style
(8 to 10 servings)

4- to 5-pound beef chuck cross rib pot roast
2 tablespoons flour
1 teaspoon salt
⅛ teaspoon pepper
1 teaspoon paprika
2 tablespoons cooking fat
1 large onion, thinly sliced
1 can (8 ounces) tomato sauce, plus 1 can water
½ cup catsup
1 tablespoon brown sugar
1 tablespoon (or to taste) chili powder
2 tablespoons vinegar
1 tablespoon Worcestershire sauce
1 can (1 pound) baby lima beans, or kernel corn, drained

1. Combine flour, salt, pepper, and paprika; rub into meat. In a Dutch oven, or large pan with a tight-fitting cover, brown meat in fat. Remove from pan and pour off fat drippings.

2. Cook onion in drippings remaining in pan until soft but not browned; stir often.
3. Add tomato sauce, water, catsup, brown sugar, chili powder, vinegar, and Worcestershire sauce; mix well.
4. Return meat to pan. Cover and simmer for 3 to 3½ hours, or until done. (Or cook in a 325°F. oven for same amount of time.)
5. Turn meat once to cook it evenly throughout. Add lima beans, during the last 15 minutes of cooking. When meat is done, remove and keep warm.
6. Skim off any excess fat. Taste sauce and correct seasoning, if necessary, with salt and pepper.
7. Slice meat and serve with sauce and vegetables.

Sloppy Joe Pot Roast
(7 to 8 servings)

3½- to 4-pound beef round tip roast
2   tablespoons cooking fat
Salt and pepper
1   can (8 ounces) tomato sauce
1½ cups water
1   package Sloppy Joe seasoning mix
2   medium-size potatoes, pared and quartered
1   cup sliced carrots, cut ½ inch thick
1   cup sliced zucchini, cut ½ inch thick

1. In a Dutch oven, or large pan with a tight-fitting cover, brown meat in fat. Season with salt and pepper and remove from pan. Pour off fat drippings.
2. Add tomato sauce, water, and seasoning mix.
3. Return meat to pan. Cover and simmer for 3 to 3½ hours, or until done. (Or cook in a 325°F. oven for same amount of time.)
4. Turn meat once to cook it evenly throughout. Add po-

tatoes and carrots during the last 35 minutes of cooking, zucchini the last 15 minutes.

5. Remove meat and keep warm. Skim off any excess fat. Taste sauce and correct seasoning, if necessary, with salt and pepper.
6. Serve sliced meat with vegetables and sauce.

Pot Roast with Onion Soup Mix and Vegetables
(8 to 10 servings)

4- to 5-pound beef round heel of round
2 tablespoons cooking fat
Salt and pepper
1 cup water
1 package onion soup mix
8 or more medium-size carrots, cut in 2-inch pieces
4 stalks celery, cut in 3-inch pieces

1. In a Dutch oven, or large pan with a tight-fitting cover, brown meat in fat. Season with salt and pepper and remove from pan. Pour off fat drippings.
2. Add water and soup mix.
3. Return meat to pan. Cover and simmer for 3 to 3½ hours, or until done. (Or cook in a 325°F. oven for same amount of time.)
4. Turn meat once to cook it evenly throughout. Add carrots and celery during the last 35 minutes of cooking.
5. Skim off any excess fat. Taste gravy and correct seasoning, if necessary, with salt and pepper.
6. If gravy is too thin, remove meat and vegetables to a platter and keep warm. Mix 2 tablespoons flour in ⅓ cup cold water. Add mixture slowly to liquid in pan. Bring to a boil, stirring constantly, and cook until thickened, about 3 minutes.
7. Serve sliced meat with vegetables and gravy.

Pot Roast with Beef Stew Seasoning Mix
(6 to 8 servings)

3- to 4-pound beef chuck blade roast, boneless
2 tablespoons cooking fat
Salt and pepper
1 large onion, thinly sliced
1 can (15 ounces) tomato sauce
2 tablespoons dry sherry wine
1 package beef stew seasoning mix

1. In a Dutch oven, or large pan with a tight-fitting cover, brown meat in fat. Season with salt and pepper and remove from pan. Pour off fat drippings.
2. Cook onion in drippings remaining in pan until soft but not browned; stir often.
3. Add tomato sauce, wine, and seasoning mix.
4. Return meat to pan. Cover and simmer for 2½ to 3 hours, or until done. (Or cook in a 325°F. oven for same amount of time.)
5. Turn meat once to cook it evenly throughout. When done, remove meat to a platter and keep warm. Skim off any excess fat.
6. If sauce is too thin, mix 2 tablespoons flour in ⅓ cup cold water. Add mixture slowly to liquid in pan. Bring to a boil, stirring constantly, and cook until thickened, about 3 minutes. Taste sauce and correct seasoning, if necessary, with salt and pepper.
7. If sauce needs only a little thickening, remove meat, skim off excess fat, and simmer, uncovered, for a few minutes.
8. Slice meat and serve with sauce.

Individual Pot Roasts with Bouillon Noodles
(6 to 8 servings)

3- to 4-pound beef chuck arm pot roast, boneless
⅓ cup flour seasoned with 1 teaspoon salt, ⅛ teaspoon pepper
2 tablespoons cooking fat
1 large onion, thinly sliced
2 cups tomato juice
2 teaspoons Worcestershire sauce
4 ounces (or more) noodles
1 can (10½ ounces) condensed beef bouillon
1 can water

1. Cut meat into 6 or 8 portions. Rub meat with seasoned flour. Save any leftover flour to thicken gravy.
2. In a Dutch oven, or large pan with a tight-fitting cover, brown meat in fat. Remove meat from pan and pour off fat drippings.
3. Cook onion in drippings remaining in pan until onion is soft but not browned; stir often.
4. Add tomato juice and Worcestershire sauce.
5. Return meat to pan. Cover and simmer for 2½ to 3 hours, or until done. (Or cook in a 325°F. oven for same amount of time.)
6. Turn meat once to cook it evenly throughout. When done, remove meat to a platter and keep warm. Skim off any excess fat.
7. If sauce is too thin, mix 2 tablespoons seasoned flour in ⅓ cup cold water. Add mixture slowly to liquid in pan. Bring to a boil, stirring constantly, and cook until thickened, about 3 minutes. Taste sauce and correct seasoning, if necessary, with salt and pepper.
8. Cook noodles in bouillon and water; drain.
9. Spoon gravy over noodles and serve with pot roasts.

Pot Roast with Tomato-Red Wine Sauce
(7 to 8 servings)

3½- to 4-pound beef chuck shoulder pot roast, boneless
2   tablespoons cooking fat
Salt and pepper
½ cup chopped onion, fresh or frozen
1   can (8 ounces) tomato sauce
¾ cup dry red wine
1   bay leaf, crushed
⅛ teaspoon garlic powder

1. In a Dutch oven, or large pan with a tight-fitting cover, brown meat in fat. Season with salt and pepper and remove from pan. Pour off fat drippings.
2. Cook onion in drippings remaining in pan until soft but not browned; stir often.
3. Add tomato sauce, wine, bay leaf, and garlic powder; mix well.
4. Return meat to pan. Cover and simmer for 2½ to 3½ hours, or until done. (Or cook in a 325°F. oven for same amount of time.) Turn meat once to cook it evenly throughout. Skim off excess fat.
5. If sauce is too thin, remove meat to a serving platter and keep warm. Mix 2 tablespoons flour in ⅓ cup cold water. Add mixture slowly to sauce. Bring to a boil, stirring constantly, and cook until thickened, about 3 minutes. Taste sauce and correct seasoning, if necessary, with salt and pepper.
6. If sauce needs only a little thickening, skim off excess fat and simmer, uncovered, for a few minutes.
7. Slice meat and serve with sauce.

Beef Pot Roast, Danish Style
(8 to 10 servings)

4- to 5-pound beef chuck eye roast, boneless

Marinade:
½ **cup chopped onion**
½ **cup water**
½ **cup red wine vinegar**
1 **teaspoon salt**
¼ **teaspoon black pepper**
½ **teaspoon ginger**
4 **whole cloves**
1 **bay leaf**

2 **tablespoons cooking fat**
2 **beef bouillon cubes**
¼ **cup flour**
2 **tablespoons brown sugar**
½ **cup dairy sour cream**
Salt and pepper

1. Prepare marinade by combining in a bowl the onion, water, vinegar, salt, pepper, ginger, cloves, and bay leaf. Pour half into a shallow dish large enough to hold the meat.
2. Place meat in dish and pour rest of marinade on top of meat. Cover and refrigerate 2 to 3 hours, turning once.
3. Drain meat in a colander, saving marinade; discard cloves. Pat meat dry with paper towels.
4. In a Dutch oven, or large pan with a tight-fitting cover, brown meat in fat. Remove meat from pan and pour off fat drippings.
5. Add marinade and bouillon cubes. Simmer until brown particles are dissolved. Return meat to pan.

6. Cover and simmer for 3½ to 4 hours, or until done. (Or cook in a 325°F. oven for same amount of time.) Turn meat once to cook it evenly throughout. When done, remove meat and keep warm. Discard bay leaf.

7. For 2 cups gravy, pour liquid from pan into a 2-cup measuring cup. Let stand for 1 minute to allow fat to come to top. Discard all but 4 tablespoons (or less) of fat. Add enough water (or other liquid) to measure 1½ cups of liquid. Return to pan.

8. In same cup, measure ½ cup cold water and blend in flour and brown sugar. Add mixture slowly to liquid in pan. Bring to a boil, stirring constantly, and cook until thickened, about 3 minutes. Taste gravy and correct seasoning, if necessary, with salt and pepper.

9. Remove pan from heat. Add sour cream, a small amount at a time, and mix well. If gravy is not hot enough when ready to serve, place pan over very low heat, but do not boil, or gravy will curdle. (Note: The flavor of the gravy is not affected should it curdle.)

10. Slice meat and serve with gravy.

Pot Roast Stroganoff
(7 to 8 servings)

3½- to 4-pound beef chuck shoulder pot roast, boneless
2 tablespoons cooking fat
Salt and pepper
½ cup chopped onion, fresh or frozen
½ cup water
1 beef bouillon cube
¼ cup catsup
¼ cup dry sherry wine
1 tablespoon Worcestershire sauce
1 teaspoon caraway seeds (optional)
1 can (4 ounces) sliced mushrooms, drained (save liquid)

¼ cup flour for gravy

½ to 1 cup dairy sour cream, depending on desired
 thickness of gravy

Hot cooked noodles

1. In a Dutch oven, or large pan with a tight-fitting cover, brown meat in fat. Season with salt and pepper and remove from pan. Pour off fat drippings.
2. Cook onion in drippings remaining in pan until soft but not browned; stir often.
3. Add water; bring to a boil and dissolve bouillon cube. Reduce heat and add catsup, wine, Worcestershire sauce, and caraway seeds.
4. Return meat to pan. Cover and simmer for 2½ to 3 hours, or until done. (Or cook in a 325°F. oven for same amount of time.)
5. Turn meat once to cook it evenly throughout. When done, remove meat and keep warm.
6. For 2 cups gravy, pour liquid from pan into a 2-cup measuring cup. Let stand for 1 minute to allow fat to come to top. Discard all but 4 tablespoons (or less) of fat. Add enough water (or other liquid) to measure 1½ cups of liquid. Return to pan.
7. In same cup, add mushroom juice and enough water to measure ½ cup, and blend in flour. Add mixture slowly to liquid in pan. Bring to a boil, stirring constantly, and cook until thickened, about 3 minutes.
8. Remove pan from heat. Add sour cream, a small amount at a time and mix well. Taste gravy and correct seasoning, if necessary, with salt and pepper. If gravy is not hot enough when ready to serve, place pan over very low heat, but do not boil, or gravy will curdle. (Note: The flavor of the gravy is not affected should curdling occur.)
9. Slice meat and serve with gravy and noodles.

Hungarian Pot Roast with Noodles
(8 to 12 servings)

4- to 6-pound beef round rump roast, boneless
2 tablespoons cooking fat
Salt and pepper
1 cup chopped onion, fresh or frozen
1 tablespoon paprika
1 cup tomato juice
1 teaspoon caraway seeds
½ cup water
¼ cup flour
½ cup dairy sour cream
Hot cooked noodles

1. In a Dutch oven, or large pan with a tight-fitting cover, brown meat in fat. Season with salt and pepper and remove from pan. Pour off fat drippings.
2. Cook onion in drippings remaining in pan until soft but not browned; stir often.
3. Add paprika and mix well. Add tomato juice and caraway seeds.
4. Return meat to pan. Cover and simmer for 3½ to 4 hours, or until done. (Or cook in a 325°F. oven for same amount of time.) Turn meat once and cook it evenly throughout. When done, remove meat and keep warm.
5. For 2 cups gravy, pour liquid from pan into a 2-cup measuring cup. Let stand for 1 minute to allow fat to come to top. Discard all but 4 tablespoons (or less) of fat. Add enough water (or other liquid) to measure 1½ cups of liquid. Return to pan.
6. In same cup, add ½ cup water and blend in ¼ cup flour. Add mixture slowly to liquid in pan. Bring to a boil, stirring constantly, and cook until thickened, about 3 minutes.

7. Remove pan from heat. Add sour cream, a small amount at a time, and mix well. Taste gravy and correct seasoning, if necessary, with salt and pepper. If gravy is not hot enough when ready to serve, place pan over very low heat, but do not boil, or gravy may curdle. (Note: The flavor of the gravy is not affected should curdling occur.)

8. Slice meat and serve with gravy and noodles.

Pot Roast with Enchilada Sauce Mix
(6 to 8 servings)

3- to 4-pound beef chuck cross rib pot roast, boneless
2 tablespoons cooking fat
Salt and pepper
1 large onion, thinly sliced
1 medium-size green pepper, chopped
1 can (8 ounces) tomato sauce
1 package enchilada sauce mix*
¾ cup water

1. In a Dutch oven, or large pan with a tight-fitting cover, brown meat in fat. Season with salt and pepper and remove from pan. Pour off fat drippings.

2. Cook onion and green pepper in drippings remaining in pan until onion is soft but not browned; stir often.

3. Add tomato sauce, enchilada sauce mix, and water.

4. Return meat to pan. Cover and simmer for 2½ to 3 hours, or until done. (Or cook in a 325°F. oven for same amount of time.) Turn meat once to cook it evenly throughout.

5. Taste sauce and correct seasoning, if necessary, with salt and pepper.

6. Remove meat to a platter and slice. Skim fat from sauce; serve sauce with meat.

* Or use taco seasoning mix.

Beef Pot Roast, French Style
(8 to 12 servings)

4- to 6-pound beef round rump roast, boneless
2 tablespoons cooking fat
Salt and pepper
½ cup chopped onion, fresh or frozen
1 can (8 ounces) tomato sauce
¼ cup dry red wine
⅛ teaspoon garlic powder
1 small bay leaf
1 teaspoon bouquet garni, or mixed herbs

1. In a Dutch oven, or large pan with a tight-fitting cover, brown meat in fat. Season with salt and pepper and remove from pan. Pour off fat drippings.
2. Cook onion in drippings remaining in pan until soft but not browned; stir often.
3. Add remaining ingredients; mix well.
4. Return meat to pan. Cover and simmer for 3½ to 4 hours, or until done. (Or cook in a 325°F. oven for same amount of time.)
5. Turn meat once to cook it evenly throughout. When done, remove bay leaf and discard. Taste sauce and correct seasoning, if necessary, with salt and pepper.
6. Skim any excess fat from sauce, and serve sauce with sliced meat.

Note: Frozen peas may be added during the last 10 minutes of cooking; canned peas, drained, during the last 5 minutes.

Fruited Pot Roast
(6 to 8 servings)

3- to 4-pound beef chuck blade roast, boneless
2   tablespoons cooking fat
Salt and pepper
½ cup chopped onion, fresh or frozen
½ cup finely chopped carrots
½ cup finely chopped celery
⅛ teaspoon garlic powder
½ cup dry red wine
½ cup water
1   package (12 ounces) mixed dried fruit
1½ cups hot water
¼ cup flour for gravy

1. In a Dutch oven, or large pan with a tight-fitting cover, brown meat in fat. Season with salt and pepper and remove from pan.
2. Cook onion in drippings remaining in pan until soft but not browned; stir often. Add carrots, celery, garlic powder, wine, and water. Return meat to pan.
3. Cover and simmer for 2 hours on top of range or in a 325°F. oven. Turn meat once to cook it evenly throughout.
4. Meanwhile, pour hot water over fruit; let stand at least 1 hour. Drain fruit, reserving liquid. Place fruit on meat (after it has cooked for 2 hours). Cover and continue cooking 45 minutes to 1 hour, or until meat is done. Remove meat and fruit to a platter and keep warm.
5. For 2 cups of gravy, pour liquid from pan into a 2-cup measuring cup. Let stand for 1 minute to allow fat to come to top. Discard all but about 4 tablespoons (or less) of fat. Add enough liquid from fruit to measure 1½ cups. Return liquid to pan.

6. In same cup, measure ½ cup cold water and blend in flour. Add mixture slowly to liquid in pan. Bring to a boil, stirring constantly, and cook until thickened, about 3 minutes. Taste gravy and correct seasoning, if necessary, with salt and pepper.
7. Slice meat and serve with fruit and gravy.

Pot Roast in Savory Cheese Sauce
(8 to 10 servings)

4- to 5-pound beef chuck arm pot roast*
2 tablespoons cooking fat
Salt and pepper
1 medium-size onion, sliced
1 can (10¾ ounces) condensed Cheddar cheese soup
1 can (8 ounces) tomato sauce
1 can (4 ounces) sliced mushrooms, drained
¼ teaspoon oregano
¼ teaspoon basil

1. In a Dutch oven, or large pan with a tight-fitting cover, brown meat in fat. Season with salt and pepper and remove from pan. Pour off fat drippings.
2. Cook onion in drippings remaining in pan until soft but not browned; stir often.
3. Add soup, tomato sauce, mushrooms, oregano, and basil; mix well.
4. Return meat to pan. Cover and simmer 3 to 3½ hours, or until done. (Or cook in a 325°F. oven for same amount of time.) Turn meat once to cook it evenly throughout. Skim off excess fat.

* Frozen beef chuck arm pot roasts and beef chuck blade roasts may be browned under the broiler. Place meat on broiler pan rack, then place pan in center of oven. Brown to one side, about 10 minutes. Turn meat and brown other side, about 8 to 10 minutes. Meat should be completely thawed after browning.

5. If sauce is too thin, remove meat to a platter and keep warm. Mix 2 tablespoons flour in ⅓ cup cold water. Add mixture slowly to sauce. Bring to a boil, stirring constantly, and cook until thickened, about 3 minutes. Taste sauce and correct seasoning, if necessary, with salt and pepper.
6. If sauce needs only a little thickening, remove meat, skim off excess fat, and simmer, uncovered, for a few minutes.
7. Slice meat and serve with sauce.

Barbecued Chili Pot Roast
(8 to 10 servings)

4- to 5-pound beef round heel of round
2 tablespoons cooking fat
Salt and pepper
1 cup chopped onion, fresh or frozen
1 can (15 ounces) tomato sauce
1 small green pepper, chopped
½ teaspoon paprika
2 tablespoons brown sugar
1 tablespoon (or to taste) chili powder
1 tablespoon prepared mustard
2 tablespoons vinegar
1 tablespoon Worcestershire sauce

1. In a Dutch oven, or large pan with a tight-fitting cover, brown meat in fat. Season with salt and pepper and remove from pan. Pour off fat drippings.
2. Cook onions in drippings remaining in pan until soft but not browned; stir often.
3. Add remaining ingredients; mix well.
4. Return meat to pan. Cover and simmer for 3 to 3½ hours, or until done. (Or cook in a 325°F. oven for same amount of time.) Turn meat once to cook it evenly throughout.
5. Remove meat to a platter and keep warm. Skim off excess

fat. If sauce needs only a little thickening, simmer, uncovered, for a few minutes.
6. Taste sauce and correct seasoning, if necessary, with salt and pepper.
7. Slice meat and serve with sauce.

Chili Bean Pot Roast
(8 to 12 servings)

4- to 6-pound beef round bottom round roast
2 tablespoons cooking fat
Salt and pepper
½ cup chopped onion, fresh or frozen
1 can (15 ounces) tomato sauce
1 tablespoon (or to taste) chili powder
1 can (15½ ounces) red kidney beans

1. In a Dutch oven, or large pan with a tight-fitting cover, brown meat in fat. Season with salt and pepper and remove from pan. Pour off fat drippings.
2. Cook onions in drippings remaining in pan until soft but not browned; stir often.
3. Add tomato sauce and chili powder; mix well.
4. Return meat to pan. Cover and simmer for 3½ to 4 hours, or until done. (Or cook in a 325°F. oven for same amount of time.) Turn meat once to cook it evenly throughout.
5. Add undrained kidney beans during the last 15 minutes of cooking. Taste sauce and correct seasoning, if necessary, with salt and pepper.
6. If sauce is too thin, remove meat to a platter and keep warm. Mix 2 tablespoons flour in ⅓ cup cold water. Add mixture slowly to sauce. Bring to a boil, stirring constantly, and cook until thickened, about 3 minutes.
7. If sauce needs only a little thickening, remove meat from pan, skim off excess fat, and simmer, uncovered, for a few minutes.
8. Slice meat and serve with kidney bean sauce.

Pot Roast in Savory Wine Gravy
(6 to 8 servings)

3- to 4-pound beef chuck arm pot roast, boneless
1   package onion soup mix
2   medium-size potatoes, pared and cut in sixths
6   or more medium-size carrots, scraped
½ cup dry red wine
½ teaspoon thyme
¼ teaspoon pepper
1   bay leaf, crushed
¼ cup flour for gravy

1. Preheat oven to 350°F.
2. Place an 18-by-30-inch piece of heavy-duty foil in the center of a shallow baking pan.
3. Sprinkle a little of the soup mix in center of foil. Place meat over mix. Arrange carrots and potatoes around meat. Pour wine over meat; sprinkle balance of soup mix and seasonings over meat and vegetables.
4. Bring the two edges of foil together above the meat and fold down in 1-inch locked folds, but do not draw the foil too tightly. Fold ends over and over to make an *airtight seal.*
5. Cook for 2½ hours, or until done. Remove roast from oven and fold foil back. Transfer to a serving platter, arrange vegetables around roast, and keep warm.
6. For 2 cups gravy, pour liquid into a 2-cup measuring cup. Let stand for 1 minute to allow fat to come to top. Discard all but 4 tablespoons (or less) of fat. Add enough water (or other liquid) to measure 1½ cups of liquid. Pour into a medium-size saucepan.
7. In same cup, measure ½ cup cold water and blend in flour. Add mixture slowly to liquid in pan. Bring to a boil, stirring constantly, and cook until thickened, about

3 minutes. Taste gravy and correct seasoning, if necessary, with salt and pepper.
8. Slice meat and serve with vegetables. Serve gravy separately.

Pot Roast with Horseradish Sauce
(6 to 8 servings)

3- to 4-pound beef chuck cross rib pot roast, boneless
2   tablespoons cooking fat
Salt and pepper
½   cup chopped onion, fresh or frozen
2¼ cups tomato juice (No. 2 can)
¼   cup prepared horseradish
2   tablespoons dry sherry wine

1. In a Dutch oven, or large pan with a tight-fitting cover, brown meat in fat. Season with salt and pepper and remove from pan. Pour off fat drippings.
2. Cook onion in drippings remaining in pan until soft but not browned; stir often. Add tomato juice, horseradish, and wine; mix well. Return meat to pan.
3. Cover and simmer for 2½ to 3 hours, or until done. (Or cook in a 325°F. oven for same amount of time.) Turn meat once to cook it evenly throughout and baste with sauce. Skim off excess fat.
4. If sauce is too thin, remove meat to a platter and keep warm. Mix 2 tablespoons flour in ⅓ cup cold water. Add mixture slowly to sauce. Bring to a boil, stirring constantly, and cook until thickened, about 3 minutes. Taste sauce and correct seasoning, if necessary, with salt and pepper.
5. If sauce needs only a little thickening, remove meat, skim off excess fat, and simmer, uncovered, for a few minutes.
6. Slice meat and serve with sauce.

Pot Roast, Spanish Style

(8 to 12 servings)

4- to 6-pound beef round rump roast, boneless
2   tablespoons olive or salad oil
½ teaspoon salt, few dashes pepper
¼ teaspoon marjoram leaves, crushed
½ teaspoon cinnamon
⅛ teaspoon ground cloves
1   tablespoon minced parsley
⅛ teaspoon garlic powder
2   tablespoons cooking fat
1   medium-size onion, thinly sliced
1   medium-size green pepper, chopped
1   can (15 ounces) tomato sauce with tomato bits
¾ cup dry red wine
½ cup orange juice
1   cup pimiento-stuffed olives (optional)
1   tablespoon cornstarch
¼ cup water

1. In a small bowl, mix 2 tablespoons oil with salt, pepper, marjoram, cinnamon, cloves, parsley, and garlic powder. Spread mixture on meat with a small spoon and allow to stand in room temperature not more than 1 hour.
2. In a Dutch oven, or large pan with a tight-fitting cover, brown meat in fat. Remove from pan and pour off fat drippings.
3. Cook onion in drippings remaining in pan until soft but not browned; stir often. Add green pepper, tomato sauce with bits, wine, and orange juice; mix well. Return meat to pan.
4. Cover and simmer 3½ to 4 hours, or until done. (Or cook in a 325°F. oven for same amount of time.) Turn meat once to cook it evenly throughout. Remove meat and keep warm. Skim off any excess fat.

5. Add olives. Mix cornstarch with water. Add mixture slowly to liquid in pan. Bring to a boil, stirring constantly, and cook until thickened, about 3 minutes. Taste sauce and correct seasoning, if necessary, with salt and pepper.
6. Spoon sauce over sliced meat, or serve sauce separately.

Supreme Pot Roast
(7 to 8 servings)

3½- to 4-pound beef round tip roast
2   tablespoons cooking fat
Salt and pepper
½ cup chopped onion, fresh or frozen
1   can (10½ ounces) condensed golden mushroom soup
¼ cup water
2   tablespoons dry sherry wine
8   small carrots, scraped
2   medium-size potatoes, pared and quartered

1. In a Dutch oven, or large pan with a tight-fitting cover, brown meat in fat. Season with salt and pepper and remove from pan. Pour off fat drippings.
2. Cook onion in drippings remaining in pan until soft but not browned; stir often.
3. Add soup, water, and wine; mix well. Return meat to pan.
4. Cover and simmer 3 to 3½ hours, or until done. (Or cook in a 325°F. oven for same amount of time.) Turn meat once to cook it evenly throughout.
5. Add carrots and potatoes during the last 35 minutes of cooking.
6. Skim off any excess fat. Taste sauce and, if necessary, correct seasoning with salt and pepper.
7. Serve sliced meat with vegetables and sauce.

Oven Pot Roast, Bag Style
(6 to 8 servings)

3- to 4-pound beef chuck arm pot roast, boneless
10-by-16-inch roasting bag, with twist tie
1 can (15 ounces) tomato sauce
½ cup chopped onion, fresh or frozen
1 medium-size green pepper, chopped
1 package taco seasoning mix
Salt and pepper

1. Preheat oven to 350°F.
2. In a small bowl, mix together tomato sauce, onion, green pepper, and taco seasoning mix.
3. Place empty bag in a roasting pan at least 2 inches in depth and larger than the bag.
4. Place meat in bag and spoon tomato sauce mixture over meat. Twist end of bag and secure with twist tie. Puncture three small holes in top of bag.
5. Cook for 2 hours, or until meat is done.
6. When done, carefully remove pan from oven and allow juices to stop bubbling.
7. Slit top of bag and remove meat. Taste sauce and correct seasoning, if necessary, with salt and pepper.
8. Slice meat and serve with sauce.

My Favorite Pot Roast
(7 to 8 servings)

3½- to 4-pound beef chuck shoulder pot roast, boneless
2   tablespoons cooking fat
Salt and pepper
1   can (10¾ ounces) condensed tomato soup
½ cup chili sauce
¼ cup dry sherry wine
1   package onion soup mix
2   medium-size potatoes, pared and quartered
4   large carrots, scraped and cut in half lengthwise

1. In a Dutch oven, or large pan with a tight-fitting cover, brown meat in fat. Season with salt and pepper and remove from pan. Pour off fat drippings.
2. Add tomato soup, chili sauce, sherry, and onion soup mix. Return meat to pan.
3. Cover and simmer 2½ to 3½ hours, or until done. (Or cook in a 325°F. oven for same amount of time.) Turn meat once to cook it evenly throughout.
4. Add potatoes and carrots during the last 35 minutes of cooking.
5. If sauce is too thin, remove meat and vegetables to a platter and keep warm. Skim off any excess fat.
6. Mix 2 tablespoons flour in ⅓ cup cold water. Add mixture slowly to sauce. Bring to a boil, stirring constantly, and cook until thickened, about 3 minutes. Taste sauce and correct seasoning, if necessary, with salt and pepper.
7. Slice meat and serve with vegetables and sauce.

Pot Roast with Beef Mushroom Mix

(8 to 12 servings)

4- to 6-pound beef round rump roast, boneless
2   tablespoons cooking fat
Salt and pepper
½ cup chopped onion, fresh or frozen
1   can (10¾ ounces) condensed tomato soup
¾ cup water
1   package beef flavor mushroom mix
¼ cup sherry wine
⅛ teaspoon garlic powder
¼ teaspoon oregano

1. In a Dutch oven, or large pan with a tight-fitting cover, brown meat in fat. Season with salt and pepper and remove from pan. Pour off fat drippings.
2. Cook onion in drippings remaining in pan until soft but not browned; stir often.
3. Add tomato soup, water, mushroom mix, sherry, garlic powder, and oregano; mix well. Return meat to pan.
4. Cover and simmer for 3½ to 4 hours, or until done. (Or cook in a 325°F. oven for same amount of time.)
5. Turn meat once to cook it evenly throughout. When done, remove meat to a platter and keep warm.
6. Skim off any excess fat. Taste sauce and correct seasoning, if necessary, with salt and pepper.
7. Slice meat and serve with sauce.

Pot Roast in Wine Marinade Sauce
(7 to 8 servings)

3½- to 4-pound beef round tip roast

Marinade:

2 cups dry red wine

¼ cup red wine vinegar

½ teaspoon garlic powder

1 large onion, thinly sliced

1 cup thinly sliced carrots

¼ cup salad oil

1 teaspoon salt

**Herb bouquet: 2 small bay leaves, 6 peppercorns, 4 cloves,
    ½ teaspoon thyme, all tied in cheesecloth**

2 tablespoons cooking fat

3 strips bacon, diced

1 large fresh tomato, unpeeled and chopped

2 beef bouillon cubes dissolved in 1 cup hot water

Salt and pepper

1. Place meat in a plastic bag. (Pour a small amount of water in bag first to check for any holes.)
2. Combine marinade ingredients in a bowl and pour into bag. Twist top of bag and fasten with a closure.
3. Place bag in a flat baking dish and refrigerate for 24 hours, turning occasionally.
4. Remove meat from bag, drain (save marinade), and pat dry with paper towels.
5. In a Dutch oven, or large pan with a tight-fitting cover, brown meat in fat. Remove meat and pour off fat drippings.
6. Cook bacon until slightly crisp. Add marinade (liquid, vegetables, and herb bouquet), tomatoes, and bouillon.
7. Return meat to pan. Cover and simmer 3 to 3½ hours, or until done. (Or cook in a 325°F. oven for same

amount of time.) Turn meat once to cook it evenly throughout.

8. When meat is done, remove and keep warm. Discard herb bouquet. Skim off any excess fat.

9. *Optional*: Strain sauce into a pan, pressing vegetables through a strainer, or leave sauce as it is.

10. Taste sauce and correct seasoning, if necessary, with salt and pepper.

11. If sauce is too thin, mix 2 tablespoons flour in ⅓ cup cold water. Add mixture slowly to sauce. Bring to a boil, stirring constantly, and cook until thickened, about 3 minutes.

12. If sauce needs only a little thickening, simmer, un-covered, for a few minutes.

13. To serve, slice meat and spoon some sauce over it. Serve balance of sauce in a bowl.

Spicy Pot Roast
(6 to 8 servings)

3- to 4-pound beef chuck cross rib pot roast, boneless
2   tablespoons cooking fat
Salt and pepper
1   medium-size onion, thinly sliced
1½ cups tomato juice
⅛   teaspoon garlic powder
¼   teaspoon each ground cloves, mace, allspice
2   tablespoons lemon juice
1   tablespoon vinegar
2   small bay leaves

1. In a Dutch oven, or large pan with a tight-fitting cover, brown meat in fat. Season with salt and pepper and remove from pan. Pour off fat drippings.

2. Cook onion in drippings remaining in pan until soft but not browned; stir often.

3. Add remaining ingredients; mix well.

4. Return meat to pan. Cover and simmer for 2½ to 3 hours, or until done. (Or cook in a 325°F. oven for same amount of time.)

5. Turn meat once to cook it evenly throughout. When meat is done, remove to a platter and keep warm. Discard bay leaves.

6. Skim off any excess fat. Taste sauce and correct seasoning, if necessary, with salt and pepper.

7. If sauce is too thin, mix 2 tablespoons flour in ⅓ cup cold water. Add mixture slowly to sauce. Bring to a boil, stirring constantly, and cook until thickened, about 3 minutes.

8. If sauce needs only a little thickening, simmer, uncovered, for a few minutes.

9. Slice meat and serve with sauce.

Pot Roast, Flemish Style
(6 to 8 servings)

3- to 4-pound beef chuck blade roast, boneless
2 tablespoons cooking fat
Salt and pepper
1 large onion, thinly sliced
2 cloves garlic, minced (or ¼ teaspoon garlic powder)
2 beef bouillon cubes dissolved in ½ cup hot water
2 tablespoons red wine vinegar
1 cup beer
1 teaspoon dark brown sugar
1 bay leaf
¼ teaspoon dried thyme leaves
2 medium-size potatoes, pared and quartered
6 carrots, scraped and sliced diagonally in 1-inch pieces

1. In a Dutch oven, or large pan with a tight-fitting cover, brown meat in fat. Season with salt and pepper and remove from pan. Pour off fat drippings.

2. Cook onion and garlic in drippings remaining in pan until soft but not browned; stir often.
3. Add bouillon, wine vinegar, beer, sugar, bay leaf, and thyme.
4. Return meat to pan. Cover and simmer for 2½ to 3 hours, or until done. (Or cook in a 325°F. oven for same amount of time.) Turn meat once to cook it evenly throughout.
5. Add potatoes and carrots during the last 35 minutes of cooking.
6. Remove meat and vegetables to a platter and keep warm. Discard bay leaf.
7. If sauce is too thin, mix 2 tablespoons flour in ⅓ cup cold water. Add mixture slowly to sauce. Bring to a boil, stirring constantly, and cook until thickened, about 3 minutes. Taste sauce and correct seasoning, if necessary, with salt and pepper.
8. If sauce needs only a little thickening, simmer, uncovered, for a few minutes.
9. Slice meat and serve with vegetables and sauce.

Pot Roast with Spicy Wine Sauce
(8 to 10 servings)

4- to 5-pound beef round heel of round
2 tablespoons cooking fat
Salt and pepper
½ cup chopped onion, fresh or frozen
1 package brown gravy mix
1 cup water for gravy mix
½ cup light cream
¼ cup catsup
½ cup dry red wine
2 teaspoons Dijon-style mustard
1 teaspoon Worcestershire sauce
⅛ teaspoon garlic powder
Hot cooked noodles

1. In a Dutch oven, or large pan with a tight-fitting cover, brown meat in fat. Season with salt and pepper ·and remove from pan. Pour off fat drippings.
2. Cook onion in drippings remaining in pan until soft but not browned; stir often.
3. Add remaining ingredients except noodles; mix well.
4. Return meat to pan. Cover and simmer for 3 to 3½ hours, or until done. (Or cook in a 325°F. oven for same amount of time.) Turn meat once to cook it evenly throughout.
5. When meat is done, remove to a platter and keep warm.
6. Skim off any excess fat. Taste sauce and correct seasoning, if necessary, with salt and pepper.
7. If sauce is too thin, mix 2 tablespoons flour in ⅓ cup cold water. Add mixture slowly to sauce. Bring to a boil, stirring constantly, and cook until thickened, about 3 minutes.
8. If sauce needs only a little thickening, simmer, uncovered, for a few minutes.
9. Slice meat and serve with sauce and hot noodles.

Leftovers—What to Do with Them

Though I personally prefer the concept of "planned-overs" —where one *purposely* buys enough beef for two meals (or three, or more, as the case may be), leftovers remain a fact of life in any family. And these few suggestions and recipes can help transform the lowly leftover into something quite special indeed.

Pot roast leftovers, of course, make fine sandwiches, either to be eaten within a day or so or frozen for future use (in which case, see page 270 for *How to Prepare Sandwiches for Freezing*). Two deliciously out-of-the-ordinary sandwiches are the French Dip Sandwiches, page 89; and Pot Roast Barbecued Sandwiches, page 89.

Bits and pieces of leftover meat can be used to good advantage—again, either within a day or so, or frozen for future use—in any of these recipes: Pot Roast Pizza, page 128; Pot Roast Fried Rice, page 130; Pot Roast Luncheon Salad, page 131; Pot Roast Sloppy Joes, Creole Style, page 132; Hot Pot Roast Barbecued Sandwiches, page 133; Pot Roast Skillet Hash, page 134.

French Dip Sandwiches
(makes 6 sandwiches)

Thinly sliced pot roast meat for 6 sandwiches
1 package of au jus mix
Long loaf of French bread
Softened butter or margarine (optional)

1. If frozen, place slices of meat on a cookie tray in a 325°F. oven just long enough to thaw and heat through. It is not necessary to preheat oven.
2. While meat is heating, prepare au jus mix according to manufacturer's directions. Keep hot until ready to serve.
3. Cut bread lengthwise in half and then in sandwich size, about 4 inches long.
4. Butter bread (optional) and make up sandwiches. Serve au jus mix in individual bowls for dunking sandwiches. Allow ½ cup, or more, for each sandwich.

Pot Roast Barbecued Sandwiches
(makes 2 sandwiches)

1 cup leftover pot roast meat, cut into shreds
⅓ cup barbecue sauce, homemade or commercial
   (see page 33 for recipe)
4 slices bread, or 2 buns
Softened butter or margarine

1. In a small pan combine meat and barbecue sauce.
2. Heat mixture to a simmer and cook over very low heat for 5 minutes, stirring frequently.
3. Transfer mixture to a small bowl, cover, allow to cool.
4. Butter bread or buns to edges. Spread the mixture on two slices of bread, or bottom half of buns. Add tops, and cut sandwiches in half.
5. For freezing instructions, refer to chapter on *How to Prepare Sandwiches for Freezing*, page 270.

4

More Money-saving Ways with Budget Beef

19 Tasty Recipes Calling for Thrift Steaks
and Other Nonchunky Cuts

The following recipes call for various odd-size, nonchunky cuts, such as short ribs, round steaks, flank steaks, brisket, and stew beef. They're not truly pot roasts, though they too require long, slow simmering for tenderness and to marry the flavors of their different ingredients. But they definitely belong here. My feeling about them is much the same as for the pot roasts: They make good, hearty eating, and I would not forsake them altogether for sirloin even if, by some strange twist of events, their places relative to each other on the price scale were reversed.

Many of the recipes in this section are particularly well-suited to simple quantity cooking. For two meals, double the ingredients; freeze one meal-size portion and serve the other immediately. (Refer to instructions on *How to Prepare Cooked Food for the Freezer*, page 266, and *How to Reheat Frozen Cooked Food*, page 269).

Braised Short Ribs and Gravy
(4 servings)

3- to 4-pounds beef rib short ribs
2   tablespoons cooking fat
Salt and pepper
½ cup chopped onion, fresh or frozen
1   cup water
¼ cup dry sherry wine
¼ cup flour for gravy
Hot buttered noodles

1. In a Dutch oven, or large pan with a tight-fitting cover, brown meat on all sides in fat. Season with salt and pepper and remove from pan. Pour off fat drippings.
2. Cook onion in drippings remaining in pan until soft but not browned; stir often.
3. Add water and sherry.
4. Return meat to pan. Cover tightly and simmer for 1½ to 2 hours, or until done. (Or cook in a 325°F. oven for same amount of time.) Turn meat once to cook it evenly throughout. When done, remove meat and keep warm. Skim off any excess fat.
5. For 2 cups gravy, pour liquid from pan into a 2-cup measuring cup. Let stand for 1 minute to allow fat to come to top. Discard all but 4 tablespoons (or less) of fat. Add enough water to measure 1½ cups of liquid. Return to pan.
6. In same cup, measure ½ cup cold water and blend in flour. Add mixture slowly to liquid in pan. Bring to a boil, stirring constantly, and cook until thickened, about 3 minutes. Taste gravy and correct seasoning, if necessary, with salt and pepper.
7. Spoon gravy over meat and noodles.

Short Ribs with Garbanzos
(4 servings)

3- to 4-pounds beef rib short ribs
2 tablespoons cooking fat
Salt and pepper
½ cup chopped onion, fresh or frozen
1 small green pepper, chopped
½ cup thinly sliced celery
1 can (10¾ ounces) condensed tomato soup
½ soup can water
1 teaspoon sugar
1 teaspoon Worcestershire sauce
1 teaspoon prepared mustard
½ teaspoon paprika
1 can (15 ounces) garbanzos, drained

1. In a Dutch oven, or large pan with a tight-fitting cover, brown meat on all sides in fat. Season with salt and pepper and remove from pan. Pour off fat drippings.
2. Cook onion in drippings remaining in pan until soft but not browned; stir often.
3. Add green pepper, celery, tomato soup, water, sugar, Worcestershire sauce, mustard, and paprika; mix well.
4. Return meat to pan. Cover tightly and simmer for 1½ to 2 hours, or until done. (Or cook in a 325°F. oven for same amount of time.) Turn meat once to cook it evenly throughout.
5. Add garbanzos during the last 5 minutes of cooking. Taste sauce and correct seasoning, if necessary, with salt and pepper.
6. Skim off any excess fat before serving.

Short Ribs with Stewed Tomatoes
   (4 servings)

3- to 4-pounds beef rib short ribs
2   tablespoons cooking fat
Salt and pepper
½ cup chopped onion, fresh or frozen
¼ cup chopped green pepper
2   cans (1 pound each) stewed tomatoes
1   teaspoon chili powder, or to taste
Hot fluffy rice, or cooked noodles

1. In a Dutch oven, or large pan with a tight-fitting cover, brown meat on all sides in fat. Season with salt and pepper and remove from pan. Pour off fat drippings.
2. Cook onion in drippings remaining in pan until soft but not browned; stir often.
3. Add green pepper, tomatoes, and chili powder. If desired, break up large tomato chunks with a potato masher or fork.
4. Return meat to pan. Cover tightly and simmer for 1½ to 2 hours, or until done. (Or cook in a 325°F. oven for same amount of time.) Turn meat once to cook it evenly throughout.
5. Taste sauce and correct seasoning, if necessary, with salt and pepper.
6. Skim any excess fat from sauce.
7. Serve meat and sauce over rice or noodles.

Barbecued Short Ribs
(4 servings)

3- to 4-pounds beef rib short ribs
2 tablespoons cooking fat
Salt and pepper
½ cup chopped onion, fresh or frozen
1 can (8 ounces) tomato sauce
1 cup hot water
1 beef bouillon cube
¼ cup brown sugar, lightly packed
¼ cup vinegar
1 tablespoon Worcestershire sauce

1. In a Dutch oven, or large pan with a tight-fitting cover, brown meat on all sides in fat. Season with salt and pepper and remove from pan. Pour off fat drippings.
2. Cook onion in drippings remaining in pan until soft but not browned; stir often.
3. Add tomato sauce, water, bouillon cube, brown sugar, vinegar, and Worcestershire sauce.
4. Return meat to pan. Cover tightly and simmer for 1½ to 2 hours, or until done. (Or cook in a 325°F. oven for same amount of time.) Turn meat once to cook it evenly throughout. Skim off any excess fat.
5. If sauce is too thin, remove meat and keep warm. Mix 2 tablespoons flour in ⅓ cup cold water. Add mixture slowly to sauce. Bring to a boil, stirring constantly, and cook until thickened, about 3 minutes.
6. If sauce needs only a little thickening, remove meat, skim off excess fat, and simmer, uncovered, for a few minutes.

Swiss Steak with Brown Gravy

(Ingredients based on two meals with 4 servings each meal; gravy for one meal only)

3 pounds beef round steak boneless, cut ½ inch thick
2 to 3 tablespoons flour
3 to 4 tablespoons cooking fat
Salt and pepper
½　cup chopped onion, fresh or frozen
1½ cups water
½　teaspoon liquid gravy seasoning (optional)
¼　cup flour for gravy

1. Cut meat for 8 servings.
2. Place meat on a cutting board and sprinkle with flour. With a meat mallet, or edge of heavy saucer, pound flour into meat. Repeat on other side.
3. In a large skillet, or Dutch oven, brown meat on both sides in fat, a few pieces at a time. Season with salt and pepper. Remove meat from pan and pour off fat drippings.
4. Cook onion in drippings remaining in pan until soft but not browned; stir often. Add water and gravy seasoning.
5. Return meat to pan. Cover tightly and simmer for 1 to 1½ hours, or until done. (If using beef round bottom round steak, more cooking time may be necessary.) Turn meat once to cook it evenly throughout. When done, remove portions to be served for immediate meal and keep warm while making gravy.
6. For second meal, refer to instructions on *How to Prepare Cooked Food for the Freezer*, page 266, and recipes calling for frozen cooked Swiss steak, beginning on page 232.
7. For 2 cups gravy, pour liquid from pan into a 2-cup measuring cup. Let stand for 1 minute to allow fat to come to top. Discard all but 4 tablespoons (or less) of fat. Add enough water (or other liquid) to measure 1½ cups of liquid. Return to pan.

8. In same cup, measure ½ cup cold water and blend in flour. Add mixture slowly to liquid in pan. Bring to a boil, stirring constantly, and cook until thickened, about 3 minutes. Taste gravy and correct seasoning, if necessary, with salt and pepper.
9. To serve, spoon gravy over meat, or serve separately.

Barbecued Beef Round Steak
(4 servings)

1½ **pounds beef round top round steak, cut ½ inch thick**
2 **tablespoons cooking fat**
Salt and pepper
½ **cup chopped onion, fresh or frozen**
1 **can (8 ounces) tomato sauce**
1 **cup hot water**
1 **beef bouillon cube**
¼ **cup brown sugar, lightly packed**
2 **tablespoons vinegar**
1 **tablespoon Worcestershire sauce**

1. Cut meat for 4 servings.
2. In a large skillet, brown meat on both sides in fat. Season with salt and pepper. Remove meat from pan and pour off fat drippings.
3. Cook onion in drippings remaining in skillet until soft but not browned; stir often.
4. Add tomato sauce, water, bouillon cube, brown sugar, vinegar, and Worcestershire sauce. Return meat to skillet.
5. Bring to a boil; reduce heat. Cover tightly and simmer for 1 hour, or until done. Turn meat once to cook it evenly throughout. Taste sauce and correct seasoning, if necessary, with salt and pepper.
6. If sauce is a little thin, remove cover last few minutes of cooking.

Round Steak in Chili Wine Sauce
(4 servings)

1½ pounds beef round bottom round steak, cut ½ inch thick
2 tablespoons cooking fat
Salt and pepper
½ cup chopped onion, fresh or frozen
1 medium-size green pepper, chopped
1 can (15 ounces) tomato sauce with tomato bits
¼ cup dry red wine
1 tablespoon (or to taste) chili powder

1. Cut meat for 4 servings.
2. In a large skillet, brown meat on both sides in fat. Season with salt and pepper. Remove meat from pan and pour off fat drippings.
3. Cook onion and green pepper in drippings remaining in skillet until onion is soft but not browned; stir often.
4. Add tomato sauce with tomato bits, wine, and chili powder; mix well. Return meat to skillet.
5. Bring to a boil; reduce heat. Cover tightly and simmer for 1½ hours, or until done. Turn meat once to cook it evenly throughout. Taste sauce and correct seasoning, if necessary, with salt and pepper.
6. If sauce is a little too thick, add hot water, a small amount at a time, to desired consistency.

Round Steak in Creole Sauce
(4 servings)

1½ pounds beef round bottom round steak, cut ½ inch thick
2 tablespoons cooking fat
Salt and pepper
1 cup chopped onion, fresh or frozen
1 can (10¾ ounces) condensed tomato soup

2   **teaspoons Worcestershire sauce**
⅛ **teaspoon garlic powder**
2   **medium-size green peppers, chopped**
1   **cup thinly sliced celery**

1. Slice meat into thin strips about ½ inch wide by 2 inches or 3 inches long.
2. In a large skillet, brown meat in fat, stirring frequently. Season with salt and pepper. Remove meat from pan and pour off fat drippings.
3. Cook onions in drippings remaining in pan until soft but not browned; stir often.
4. Add soup, Worcestershire sauce, and garlic powder. Return meat to skillet.
5. Bring to a boil; reduce heat. Cover tightly and simmer for 1 hour, stirring occasionally.
6. Add green pepper and celery. Continue cooking for 15 minutes, or until meat and vegetables are done. If sauce thickens, add a small amount of hot water.
7. Taste sauce and correct seasoning, if necessary, with salt and pepper.

Braised Individual Round Steaks
(4 servings)

1½ **pounds beef round top round steak, cut ½ inch thick**
Salt and pepper
2   **medium-size carrots, scraped and cut lengthwise**
    into 8 pieces
1   **small green pepper, cut into 8 strips**
2   **tablespoons cooking fat**
1   **medium-size onion, thinly sliced**
1½ **cups water**
1   **beef bouillon cube**
¼   **cup flour for gravy**

1. Cut meat into 4 equal servings. Pound meat with a mallet, or edge of a heavy saucer, on both sides to flatten and tenderize meat. Season with salt and pepper.
2. Place two carrot strips and two green pepper strips in center of each piece of meat. Roll meat lengthwise and fasten with wooden picks, skewers, or tie with string.
3. In a Dutch oven, or large pan with a tight-fitting cover, brown meat in fat. Remove from pan and pour off fat drippings.
4. Cook onion in drippings remaining in pan until soft but not browned; stir often. Add water and bouillon cube.
5. Return meat to pan. Bring to a boil; reduce heat. Cover and simmer for 1½ to 2 hours, or until done. Turn meat once to cook it evenly throughout. When done, remove meat and keep warm.
6. For 2 cups gravy, pour liquid from pan into a 2-cup measuring cup. Let stand for 1 minute to allow fat to come to top. Discard all but 4 tablespoons (or less) of fat. Add enough water, or other liquid, to measure 1½ cups liquid. Return to pan.
7. In same cup, measure ½ cup cold water and blend in flour. Add mixture slowly to liquid in pan. Bring to a boil, stirring constantly, and cook until thickened, about 3 minutes. Taste gravy and correct seasoning, if necessary, with salt and pepper.
8. Remove wooden picks from meat. Serve gravy separately, or spoon over meat.

Brisket of Beef, Pot Roast Style
(8 to 10 servings)

4- to 5-pound beef brisket flat cut, boneless
2   tablespoons flour
1½ teaspoons paprika
1   teaspoon salt

¼   **teaspoon pepper**
2   **tablespoons cooking fat**
1   **large onion, thinly sliced**
1   **cup water**
2   **medium-size potatoes, pared and quartered**
8   **medium-size carrots, scraped and cut lengthwise**

1. Blend flour, paprika, salt, and pepper.
2. Cut meat in half for faster cooking and easier handling. Dust meat with seasoned flour. (Save any leftover mixture to thicken gravy.) In a Dutch oven, or large pan with a tight-fitting cover, brown meat in fat. Remove meat and pour off fat drippings.
3. Cook onion in drippings remaining in pan until soft but not browned; stir often. Add water and return meat to pan.
4. Cover tightly and cook in a 325°F. oven for 3 hours, or until very tender. Turn meat once to cook it evenly throughout.
5. Arrange potatoes and carrots around meat and spoon cooking liquid over vegetables. Season with salt and pepper. Cover and cook for 30 minutes, or until vegetables and meat are done.
6. Turn off oven. Remove meat and vegetables to a heatproof platter and keep warm in oven while making gravy.
7. Place Dutch oven on range burner to make gravy. Mix 1 tablespoon of seasoned flour in ⅓ cup of cold water. Add to liquid in pan. Bring to a boil, stirring constantly, and cook until thickened, about 3 minutes. Taste gravy and correct seasoning, if necessary, with salt and pepper.
8. Slice meat; serve gravy with meat and vegetables.

Brisket-of-Beef Stew
(4 servings)

A fresh brisket—beef brisket flat cut boneless—weighing 4 to 5 pounds, may be too large for one meal for many families. The meat can be utilized for two meals: Brisket of Beef, Pot-Roast Style, and Brisket-of-Beef Stew. Uncooked meat for second meal can be cubed and frozen for stew for future use. Or, stew can be cooked within a few days of purchase of meat. Here is the recipe for a delicious, unusual, tasty stew.

1 to 1½ pounds beef brisket, flat cut, boneless,
   cut in 1-inch cubes
2 tablespoons cooking fat
Salt and pepper
½ cup chopped onion, fresh or frozen
4 cups water
1 package beef stew seasoning mix
2 medium-size potatoes, pared and cut in 1-inch cubes
4 medium-size carrots, scraped and sliced ¼ inch thick
1 package (10 ounces) frozen peas

1. In a Dutch oven, or large pan with a tight-fitting cover, brown meat in fat. Season with salt and pepper and remove from pan. Pour off fat drippings.
2. Cook onion in drippings remaining in pan until soft but not browned; stir often.
3. Add water and beef stew seasoning mix.
4. Return meat to pan. Cover tightly and simmer for 1½ hours, or until meat and vegetables are done. Stir occasionally.
5. Add vegetables during the last 15 minutes of cooking. Taste sauce and correct seasoning, if necessary, with salt and pepper.

6. If a thicker sauce is desired, mix 2 tablespoons flour in
   ⅓ cup water. Add to stew, stirring constantly, and cook
   until thickened, about 3 minutes.

Corned-Beef Dinner
(8 to 10 servings)

4- to 5-pound beef brisket corned, boneless
Water
1 medium-size onion, sliced
6 peppercorns
1 bay leaf
2 or more medium-size potatoes, pared and quartered
8 or more carrots, scraped
1 medium-size cabbage, cut in 6 wedges

1. In a Dutch oven, or large pan with a tight-fitting cover,
   cover meat with cold water. Add onion, peppercorns,
   and bay leaf. Bring to boiling point; reduce heat. Cover
   pan tightly and simmer about 1 hour per pound of meat,
   or until fork tender. (Note: The meat must be covered
   with water during the cooking time. Add boiling water
   to replace that which cooks away.)
2. One-half hour before end of cooking time, spoon off
   any scum and add the potatoes and carrots.
3. Add cabbage 20 minutes before end of cooking time.
4. To serve, slice meat and put on platter. Remove vegetables with a slotted spoon and place around meat, or
   serve separately. Pass Hot Mustard Sauce* for meat.

* Hot Mustard Sauce: In a small saucepan, slightly beat 1 egg, add ½ cup
vinegar, 1 tablespoon butter or margarine, 1 tablespoon sugar, 2 tablespoons
prepared mustard, and 1 teaspoon paprika. Cook over low heat until
thickened, stirring constantly, for 3 minutes. Makes ¾ cup.

Marinated Flank Steak

(4 to 5 servings)

1½- to 1¾-pounds beef flank steak

Marinade:

½ cup salad oil

3 tablespoons honey

¼ cup soy sauce

¼ cup dry sherry wine

½ teaspoon garlic powder

1 teaspoon ground ginger

1 green onion and tops, chopped fine

1. Put salad oil in a small bowl or 2-cup measuring cup. Dip measuring tablespoon in oil to facilitate measuring honey (this prevents a tendency to put in more honey).
2. Add remaining ingredients and mix well.
3. Cut flank steak in half for easier handling.
4. Pour half of marinade in a flat glass container. Place meat on top of marinade. Pour remaining marinade over meat.
5. Cover with foil and marinate in refrigerator for 24 hours, turning occasionally.
6. Drain meat. Broil about 5 to 6 minutes on each side, basting with marinade.
7. To serve, carve thin diagonal slices across the grain.

Braised Stuffed Flank Steak
(4 to 5 servings)

1½- to 1¾ pounds beef flank steak

Stuffing:

2 tablespoons cooking fat
⅓ cup chopped onion, fresh or frozen
4 cups dry bread cubes
¼ teaspoon salt
Dash pepper
¼ teaspoon poultry seasoning

2 tablespoons cooking fat
Salt and pepper
½ cup chopped onion, fresh or frozen
1 can (15 ounces) tomato sauce
½ cup chopped green pepper
½ cup thinly sliced celery
1 can (4 ounces) sliced mushrooms and liquid

1. Pound flank steak evenly to about 9-by-12 inches, and ¼ inch thick.
2. *To make stuffing*: In a skillet, cook onion in fat until soft but not browned; add bread cubes and seasonings. Cook until bread is lightly toasted, stirring often.
3. Spread stuffing over one end of meat, and roll meat up lengthwise. Fasten with metal skewers or tie with string. Close ends with skewers or tie one piece of string around the length of the roll.
4. In a Dutch oven, or large pan with a tight-fitting cover, brown meat on all sides in 2 tablespoons fat. Season with salt and pepper. Remove meat from pan and pour off fat drippings. Add onion and cook until soft but not browned; stir often. Add tomato sauce and return meat to pan.

5. Cover tightly and simmer for 1½ hours or until meat is done. A fork will pierce it easily when it's done.
6. Add green pepper, celery, and mushrooms and liquid 15 minutes before meat is done.
7. Remove meat roll to a serving platter. Remove skewers or string, and slice meat with a sharp knife.
8. Taste sauce and correct seasoning, if necessary, with salt and pepper.
9. Serve sliced meat with sauce.

Flank Steak in Wine Sauce
(4 to 5 servings)

1½- to 1¾-pounds beef flank steak
2 tablespoons cooking fat
Salt and pepper
1   medium-size onion, thinly sliced
1   can (15 ounces) tomato sauce
1   cup dry red wine
⅛ teaspoon garlic powder
¼ cup chopped parsley
¼ teaspoon oregano
¼ teaspoon basil
1   can (4 ounces) sliced mushrooms, drained (save liquid)
Cooked, buttered noodles

1. Cut steak in half lengthwise. Cut each piece into diagonal slices crosswise, about ¼ inch thick.
2. In a large skillet, brown slices a few at a time in fat. Season with salt and pepper and remove from pan. Continue until all slices are browned. Remove last batch of meat and pour off fat drippings.
3. Cook onion in drippings remaining in skillet until soft but not browned; stir often.
4. Add tomato sauce, wine, garlic powder, parsley, oregano, and basil. Return meat to pan.

5. Bring to a boil; reduce heat. Cover tightly and simmer for 1 hour, or until meat is done, stirring occasionally.
6. Add mushrooms and continue to simmer for 5 minutes. If sauce is too thick, add juice from mushrooms.
7. Taste sauce and correct seasoning, if necessary, with salt and pepper.
8. Serve meat and sauce over hot buttered noodles.

Flank Steak with Savory Sauce
(4 to 5 servings)

1½- to 1¾-pounds beef flank steak
Unseasoned meat tenderizer
2 tablespoons fat
⅓ cup commercial French dressing (not the creamy type)
¼ cup water
⅓ cup bleu cheese, crumbled
2 tablespoons cream
Few drops Worcestershire sauce
4 teaspoons flour
Salt and pepper

1. Remove meat from refrigerator and let stand not more than one hour at room temperature before tenderizing. Cover meat to prevent drying out. Cut meat in two pieces for easier handling.
2. Follow manufacturer's directions for tenderizing meat. DO NOT SALT MEAT, rather correct seasoning toward end of cooking.
3. Brown meat slowly on both sides in fat. Place in a shallow baking dish.
4. Combine French dressing and water and pour over meat. Make a lid of heavy-duty foil. Cook in a 325°F. oven for 1 hour, turning meat once.
5. Combine bleu cheese, cream, and Worcestershire sauce. Spread over top of meat. Cover and cook 30 minutes

more, or until meat is done. Baste meat once. Remove meat to a platter and keep warm.

6. For 1 cup of sauce, pour liquid into a 1-cup measuring cup. Let stand for 1 minute to allow fat to come to top. Discard all but 2 tablespoons of fat. Add enough water to measure 1 cup of liquid. Pour into a small saucepan.

7. In same cup, measure ¼ cup cold water and blend in 4 teaspoons flour. Add mixture slowly to liquid in pan. Bring to a boil, stirring constantly, and cook until thickened, about 3 minutes. Taste sauce and correct seasonings, if necessary, with salt and pepper. Makes an unusual, tasty sauce.

8. To serve, carve thin diagonal slices across the grain.

Marinated Beef Stew
(4 to 5 servings)

1½-pounds beef for stew

Marinade:
1   **cup burgundy wine, or dry red wine**
1   **medium-size onion, thinly sliced**
1   **carrot, thinly sliced**
2   **tablespoons salad oil**
½ **teaspoon thyme**
⅛ **teaspoon garlic powder**
2   **tablespoons chopped parsley**
1   **bay leaf**
½ **teaspoon salt**
⅛ **teaspoon black pepper**

2   **tablespoons cooking fat**
1   **can (4 ounces) sliced mushrooms**
1   **beef bouillon cube dissolved in 1½ cups hot water**
2   **medium-size potatoes, pared and cut in 1 inch cubes**
Salt and pepper

1. Place meat in a plastic bag. (Pour a small amount of water in bag first to check for any holes.)

2. Combine marinade ingredients in a bowl and pour into bag. Twist top of bag and fasten with a closure.
3. Move contents of bag around to blend. Place bag in a flat container and marinate meat in refrigerator for 24 hours, turning occasionally.
4. Remove meat from bag, drain, and pat dry with paper towels.
5. In a Dutch oven, or large pan with a tight-fitting cover, brown meat on all sides in fat.
6. Add marinade, sliced mushrooms and liquid, bouillon; mix well.
7. Cover and simmer for 1½ to 2 hours, or until meat is done. (Or cook in a 325°F. oven for same amount of time.)
8. Stir several times during cooking. Add potatoes (and a small amount of water, if necessary) 12 to 15 minutes before meat is done. Discard bay leaf.
9. Taste sauce and correct seasoning, if necessary, with salt and pepper.

Easy Pot Roast Casserole
(4 to 6 servings)

1½-pounds beef for stew
1   medium-size onion, sliced
1   can (10½ ounces) condensed consommé, undiluted
½ cup burgundy, claret, or other dry red wine
½ teaspoon salt
⅛ teaspoon pepper
⅛ teaspoon marjoram
⅛ teaspoon thyme
⅛ teaspoon garlic powder
4   or more carrots, scraped and cut in 1 inch pieces
1   medium-size potato, pared and cut in 1 inch cubes
¼ cup fine, dry bread crumbs
¼ cup flour

1. In a buttered 2½-quart casserole, combine beef, onion, consommé, wine, and seasonings; mix well.
2. Add carrots and potato.
3. Mix bread crumbs with flour and stir into mixture.
4. Cover and cook in a slow oven (300°F.) for 3 hours, or until meat is done.
5. Stir mixture twice during cooking.

Beef Shanks in Tomato Sauce
(4 servings)

3- to 4-pounds beef shank cross cuts
2   tablespoons flour combined with ½ teaspoon salt,
    ⅛ teaspoon pepper
2   tablespoons cooking fat
½ cup chopped onion, fresh or frozen
2   cups tomato juice
2   tablespoons dry sherry wine
½ teaspoon basil
2   medium-size potatoes, pared and quartered
Salt and pepper

1. Rub meat with seasoned flour. Save any leftover flour to thicken sauce.
2. In a Dutch oven, or large pan with a tight-fitting cover, brown meat in fat. Remove meat from pan and pour off fat drippings.
3. Cook onion in drippings remaining in pan until onion is soft but not browned; stir often.
4. Add tomato juice, wine, and basil; mix well.
5. Return meat to pan. Cover and simmer for 1½ hours, turning meat once to cook it evenly throughout.
6. Add potatoes and simmer for 30 minutes more, or until meat is tender and potatoes are done.

7. If sauce is too thin, remove meat and potatoes to a platter and keep warm. Mix 2 tablespoons flour in ⅓ cup cold water. Add mixture slowly to sauce. Bring to a boil, stirring constantly, and cook until thickened, about 3 minutes. Taste sauce and correct seasoning, if necessary, with salt and pepper.
8. Serve meat with sauce and potatoes.

5

Quantity Cooking

How to Get 9 Different Meals from
16 Pounds of Budget Beef

I know of no better time- and money-saving technique
than that of buying—at special prices—and cooking in
quantity.

At its simplest, quantity cooking involves very little
more than doubling or tripling a recipe, then freezing the
portions to be used for future meals. No great amount of
freezer storage space is required for this—no more, actually,
than for equivalent servings of TV dinners—so almost anyone can reap the benefits of simple quantity cooking.

There's another, slightly more elaborate technique that
allows for even greater savings of time and money. It also
enables you to prepare the makings of a wide variety of
meals all at once. With the culinary slight of hand described
in this section and a few hours of preparation, sixteen pounds
of relatively inexpensive beef yields *nine different meals*.

It's a tremendously practical technique. Not only does it
pretty much do away with the day-to-day bother of menu
planning, shopping, and cooking from scratch—for a while,
at any rate—but the cash savings, figured on a cost-per-
serving basis, are cause for real glee. (And if you're thrifty
by nature and abhor waste, as I do, it's also gratifying to

know that with this plan *everything* gets used—even bones, which may ultimately keep the dog happy, and fat trimmings.)

The plan calls for 16 pounds of beef chuck blade roast. I buy it on special, of course, and from it I get:

—one dinner of four individual pot roasts
—a filling and delicious beef-vegetable soup
—enough pot roast pieces (about 6 pounds) to form the basis of 6 more quick-and-easy 30-minute meals, and
—a bonus meal prepared from bits and shreds of meat from the soup bones.

The average beef chuck blade roast is about 2 inches thick and weighs around 4 pounds. It seems most practical and economical to work with four of these (total weight, approximately 16 pounds), and the plan is based on this amount. However, there's no reason why you shouldn't modify the quantity and work instead with 12, or perhaps 8, pounds of beef chuck blade roast. IF YOU DO DECIDE TO WORK WITH ONLY 8 POUNDS OF MEAT, I SUGGEST YOU OMIT THE PREPARATION OF INDIVIDUAL POT ROASTS.

The breakdown is something like this:

4 individual pot roasts	1 lb.	12 oz.
Meat cubes	6 lbs.	
Soup meat	1 lb.	8 oz.
Bones and cartilage	3 lbs.	8 oz.
Fat	3 lbs.	
Total:	15 lbs.	12 oz.

It's a good idea to arrange to do this kind of quantity cooking on a day that is relatively free for you. Though it's by no means a sun-up to sun-down affair, you will need to stay fairly close to the kitchen for a fair amount of time.

How to Prepare 16 Pounds of Beef Chuck Blade Roast for a Variety of Meals: a Step-by-Step Guide

Very briefly, the sequence is as follows. You will:
  I. DIVIDE THE MEAT
 II. PREPARE SOUP STOCK
III. REFRIGERATE, OR (III-A) FREEZE THE STOCK
 IV. FREEZE BITS AND SHREDS OF MEAT REMOVED FROM SOUP BONES
  V. PREPARE BITE-SIZE POT ROAST PIECES
 VI. FREEZE BITE-SIZE POT ROAST PIECES, OR (VI-A) IN MEAL-SIZE AMOUNTS

Before you begin, do make sure that you understand the procedure by reading through the step-by-step guide one or more times.

I. DIVIDE THE MEAT

For the Soup Stock:

1. Place meat on a cutting board and with a sharp knife remove all the bones, leaving enough meat on them— a layer of between ½ inch and ¾ inch—for the soup. Trim excess fat.

2. In a large skillet, heat enough of the fat trimmings to make about 2 tablespoons liquid fat (or use 2 tablespoons cooking fat). Add bones to the skillet and brown slowly over low heat.

For Individual Pot Roast Portions (This step may be omitted when working with less than 12 pounds of meat.):

1. While the bones brown, cut pieces of solid meat from each blade roast measuring approximately 4 inches long by 2 inches wide by 1½ inches thick. These are the individual pot roast portions.

2. If you plan to serve the individual pot roasts as the im- mediate meal, place the meat in a bowl, cover and re-

Individual pot roasts; and in two trays, 1″ meat cubes.

frigerate until about 3 hours before serving time. (It takes about 2 hours for the pot roasts to cook; for recipe see p. 124.) However, if you prefer to serve them at some other time, by all means store the meat in the freezer now. (See page 260 for how to freeze fresh meat.)
For Bite-size Pot Roast Pieces:
1. Trim any fat from the balance of the meat, then cut into 1-inch cubes.
2. Place meat in a bowl, cover, and refrigerate until ready to brown.

The soup bones should be browned by now. The next step is making stock for soup. However, if it's more convenient to proceed with the soup at some other time, the bones may be frozen. Simply cool the browned bones, wrap in freezer paper, seal with tape, and mark and date the

Trimmed fat; bones for soup stock.

contents. (Or place the bones in double plastic freezer bags and seal with a closure.)

II. How to make pot roast stock for soup

The stock itself, along with large pieces of meat from the bones, are the main ingredients in Pot Roast Vegetable Soup. Wonderfully hearty and nutritious, with the special zesty savor of sherry, the soup—served with crusty French bread and a salad—is a favorite Sunday-night supper at our house.

Smaller bits and pieces of meat from the bones are set aside, frozen, and later on become the basis of yet another meal. (They're ideal, for example, in Pot Roast Fried Rice, page 130; Pot Roast Sloppy Joes, page 132; Pot Roast Pizza, page 128; and Pot Roast Luncheon Salad, page 131.)

Stock drained into foil; cooked bones cooling.

To Prepare the Soup Stock:

Browned bones cut from 16 pounds beef chuck blade roast*
2½ quarts (10 cups) cold water
2   teaspoons salt
¼   teaspoon black pepper
1   cup chopped onion
½   cup dry sherry wine

1. Remove browned bones from skillet and place in a large kettle.
2. Discard excess fat in skillet. Add 1 cup water and stir to loosen browned-on particles, then add to kettle along with remaining water.

* Frozen browned meat bones may be used.

3. Cover kettle and bring slowly to a boil. (The slower the water comes to a boil, the clearer the soup and the less need for skimming.)
4. Skim whenever necessary to keep the stock clear.
5. When scum no longer forms, add salt, pepper, chopped onion, and sherry. Cover and simmer for 2 hours, stirring occasionally to bring the bones to the top. (Or, if you prefer, the stock may be simmered in a 325° F. oven for the same length of time.)
6. Remove bones to a large bowl and cover to prevent the meat from drying out. Allow to cool just long enough so that the bones can be comfortably handled (between 30 and 40 minutes).
7. While meat is still quite warm, separate it from the bones.
8. Cut the larger pieces of meat into 1-inch cubes and set aside. (You should have a little over a pound of these.)

Bones with bite-sized soup pieces and small bits.

9. To handle the bits of meat at the same time, refer to instructions on *How to Freeze Small Bits and Shreds of Meat from the Soup Bones*, page 126. (Total weight of these small bits and pieces should be approximately 12 ounces.)

Now, depending on when you plan to serve the soup, you may either refrigerate the stock—for use within a day or two—or prepare it immediately for the freezer.

III. To REFRIGERATE THE STOCK

1. Strain the stock into another bowl or pan, add the 1-inch meat cubes, cover, and refrigerate until fat solidifies.
2. Discard solidified fat.
3. Cover the stock and return to refrigerator until ready for use in Pot Roast Vegetable Soup, page 121.

III-A. To PREPARE STOCK FOR THE FREEZER

If the stock is not to be made into soup within a day or so, I suggest you *immediately* prepare it for the freezer.

1. Take a large pot or kettle (the one in which the soup will be cooked) and turn it upside down. Cut a piece of 18-inch heavy-duty aluminum foil large enough to completely wrap up the pot. Mold the center of the foil over the inverted pot.
2. While the foil is in place over the pot, mark contents and date. Remove foil. Turn the pot right side up and place molded foil *inside* the pot.
3. Strain the stock into the foil-lined pot, add 1-inch cubes of meat, cover tightly and refrigerate until fat is solidified.
4. Lift off and discard solidified fat. (See p. 122.)
5. Cover the pot with a tight-fitting lid or foil and place it in the freezer.
6. When the stock is frozen solid, remove it—along with the foil liner—from the pot. (Stock and foil can be loosened by turning upside down under warm tap water

Foil shaped over pan for soup stock; contents noted.

for a few seconds. Be sure to hold on to the frozen stock with one hand to keep it from falling out into the sink.)

7. Complete the freezer wrap by bringing the long ends of the foil together over the stock. Fold down in 1-inch locked folds until the foil is drawn up tight. Next, press out as much air as possible and fold the remaining edges, pressing tightly against the food.

8. For extra protection, place the foil-wrapped stock in a regular plastic freezer bag. Squeeze out as much air as possible. Twist the top of the bag and secure with a closure. This last step is important because the foil wrapping is easily ripped. The smallest hole in the foil would expose the food to air and dry it. (See p. 124.)

9. Return stock to the freezer.

Fat removed from stock.

Pot Roast Vegetable Soup
(4 generous servings)

Once the stock is prepared, the soup itself is marvelously easy to fix—by adding vegetables and macaroni, or some other pasta product.

Both additions can be almost anything you like or happen to have on hand, and you may come up with some interesting variations depending on whim and whatever leftovers are taking up space in the refrigerator or freezer on the day you make the soup.

The vegetables may be either fresh, canned, frozen, or frozen cooked leftovers (for *How to Freeze Cooked Leftover Vegetables*, see page 268). Carrots, peas, celery, string beans, and cut corn are a few good and obvious choices, though not the only ones by any means.

Uncooked fresh and frozen vegetables should be allowed to cook in the stock for 10 or 15 minutes before serving. Canned, cooked, or frozen leftover vegetables may be added during the last few minutes of cooking.

As for the starch, I'm partial to elbow macaroni, but spaghetti in 1-inch lengths, or egg noodles, or quick-cooking rice, or leftover cooked rice, or even dumplings would do just as well.

Again, uncooked macaroni, etc., should be allowed to cook in the stock for 10 or 15 minutes. Cooked leftovers, rice, etc., may be added just a few minutes before serving.

Note: If *frozen* stock is to be used, simply take it from the freezer, remove the foil wrapping, and place over low heat in the large pot or kettle in which it was "molded." (If you have trouble removing the foil, it may be loosened

Frozen soup stock.

Frozen stock wrapped for storage.

by turning the stock upside down under warm tap water.) When the stock is thawed, proceed with the recipe.

Stock (either frozen or from the refrigerator)
1 cup diced celery and leaves
1 cup diced carrots } (or equivalent amounts of any fresh,
1 cup frozen peas   } frozen, canned or leftover vegetables)
1 scant cup elbow macaroni (or your choice of pasta, rice,
    noodles, etc.)
Salt and pepper

1. Place stock in a large pot or kettle over low heat. When liquified, bring to a medium boil.
2. Add uncooked vegetables and macaroni (if used), re-

duce heat to simmer, and cook, stirring frequently, for 10 minutes, or until vegetables and macaroni are tender.

3. Season to taste with salt and pepper. At this point add canned or leftover vegetables (if used) and cooked leftover rice, noodles, etc., (if used).

Individual Portions of Beef Pot Roast
(4 servings)

4 portions of solid meat, each about 4 inches long by 2 inches wide by 1½ inches thick. Weight about 6 ounces each
Unseasoned instant meat tenderizer (optional)
Fat trimmings from meat, or 2 tablespoons cooking fat
½ cup chopped onion, fresh or frozen
½ cup liquid—water, tomato juice, bouillon
Vegetables: carrots, potatoes, celery
Salt and pepper

1. If meat is to be tenderized, remove from refrigerator and let stand not more than 1 hour at room temperature before tenderizing. Cover meat to prevent drying out.
2. Follow manufacturer's directions to tenderize meat. Do not salt meat; correct seasoning toward end of cooking.
3. In a large skillet, heat fat trimmings until there is about 2 tablespoons, or use cooking fat. Remove trimmings and discard.
4. Brown meat slowly on all sides. (If meat is not tenderized, season with salt and pepper after browning.)
5. Remove meat to a casserole dish with a tight-fitting cover, or use a flat oven-proof container and make a lid of heavy-duty foil.
6. Remove all but 1 tablespoon of fat from skillet and

discard. Cook onion until slightly soft but not browned. Stir frequently to keep onion from burning.

7. Add ½ cup liquid to skillet and cook long enough to loosen particles. Pour over meat. (Note: Too much liquid for this amount of meat will draw out the meat juices and will take away the flavor and appearance from the meat.)

8. Cover and cook pot roast in a 325°F. oven for about 1½ to 2 hours, or until tender. (Less time is required if meat is tenderized.) Turn meat once during cooking to cook it evenly throughout. If necessary, add a small amount of liquid to serve pan juice with meat and/or vegetables.

9. Or, cook on top of the range for same length of time. Keep heat low so the liquid just simmers.

10. Add vegetables about 30 to 40 minutes before meat is done. The amount of time needed to cook the vegetables depends on the type and size of cut. Medium-size potatoes, pared and quartered; large-size carrots, scraped and cut in about 1-inch slices; and celery cut in 2-inch diagonal slices will take about 30 to 40 minutes to cook. Vegetables should not be crowded. Season vegetables with salt and pepper. Turn several times during cooking and baste with juice. If desired, remove cover during the last 5 minutes of cooking to crisp meat.

11. When meat and vegetables are done, remove meat to a platter, vegetables to a serving dish, and pour juice in a gravy boat.

IV. How to freeze small bits and shreds of meat from the soup bones

Too often, unless there's some immediate reason for saving them, small, odd-size pieces, like those from the soup bones, go to waste. But the fact is, they—or any similar bits of leftover meat—can be the basis of a kind of "bonus" meal. They're easily frozen and very handy to have on hand as the meat ingredient in recipes like the ones on the next few pages.

(I know I'm not alone in liking the idea of something for nothing. And making good use of what might otherwise be thrown out is truly like getting something for nothing.)

The procedure for freezing is as follows:

1. Remove bits of meat from the soup bones and place on a cookie tray with a rim.
2. Shape a foil "lid" for the tray. Make sure it is tightly sealed.
3. Place covered tray in coldest part of freezer.
4. When meat is frozen solid, remove from the tray. (A pancake turner is a good tool to use here.)
5. Place meat in a clear plastic bag from the supermarket; over it put a regular freezer bag. Squeeze out as much air as possible, twist the bag tops, secure with a closure and return to freezer. It's not necessary to mark the contents, since they're visible through the plastic. The loose packing makes it easy to remove any specific amount called for in a recipe.
6. Return meat to the freezer.

Something for Nothing: Bonus Meals Made with Bits and Shreds of Meat from the Soup Bones

The tiny, odd-size bits and shreds of meat removed from the soup bones can be the basis of a bonus meal. Use them in any of the six recipes that follow.

Pot Roast Pizza
(makes two 9-inch pizzzas)

Meat Topping:

1½ cups frozen pot roast bits
2   tablespoons cooking fat
½   cup chopped onion, fresh or frozen
1   can (6 ounces) tomato paste plus 1 can water
½   teaspoon salt
⅛   teaspoon black pepper
⅛   teaspoon garlic powder
1½ teaspoons oregano

Pizza Dough:

2   cups commercial biscuit mix*
¼ teaspoon salt
2   tablespoons lard
½ cup water

1   cup coarsely grated mozarella cheese

1. *To prepare topping:* in a large skillet, cook onion in fat until soft but not browned; stir occasionally. Remove from pan and set aside.
2. In the same pan, lightly brown pot roast bits, stirring frequently. (It is not necessary to thaw meat before browning.) Return onion to skillet.
3. Add tomato paste, water, salt, pepper, garlic powder, and oregano.
4. Cover and simmer for 5 minutes, stirring occasionally. Remove from heat, and cool completely.
5. *To prepare pizza dough:* measure biscuit mix into a

---

* If desired, a hot-roll mix or homemade bread dough may be substituted.

bowl and add salt. Cut in lard until mixture is crumbly. Add water and mix well with a fork.

6. Knead about 7 or 8 times on a floured board or pastry cloth.

7. Divide dough in half. Using a 9-inch layer cake pan as a guide, roll each piece into a circle ½ inch larger than the pan.

8. Place one pizza dough on a lightly greased cookie sheet and crimp edges slightly.

9. Spread ½ of meat topping evenly over dough, but within ½ inch of edge. Sprinkle ½ of mozzarella cheese over topping.

10. Bake in a preheated 400°F. oven for about 15 to 17 minutes, or until crust is golden brown and cheese is melted. If cheese starts to brown before bottom of crust is done, place a piece of foil over pizza.

How to Freeze Pizzas

A convenient way to package and freeze pizzas is to use a 9-inch round layer cake pan.

1. Cut a piece of foil 14-by-20 inches. Shape center of foil over inverted pan. Mark contents, date, and time for baking: 400°F., 15 to 17 minutes.

2. Place shaped foil inside pan. Grease foil lightly with salad oil.

3. Using another 9-inch pan as a guide, roll dough into a circle ½ inch larger than the pan. Gently transfer dough into foil-lined pan so that there will be an even edge of about ½ inch of dough.

4. Spread meat topping over dough; sprinkle mozzarella cheese over topping. Cover with foil.

5. Place pan on freezer shelf or in coldest part of freezer.

6. When frozen, remove pizza from pan. Fold over foil using the freezer wrap.

How to Bake Frozen Pizzas

1. Place frozen pizza on a cookie sheet. Uncover, but do not remove foil.
2. Bake in a preheated 400°F. oven for about 15 to 17 minutes, or until bottom of crust is brown. If cheese starts to brown before bottom of crust is done, place a piece of foil over pizza.

Pot Roast Fried Rice
(4 servings)

2 **cups or more of frozen pot roast bits**
4 **eggs, seasoned with ⅛ teaspoon salt**
4 **tablespoons cooking fat, divided**
2 **bunches green onions, including tops**
   (cut in 1 inch strips, shoestring style)
4 **cups cooked rice**
1 **package (10 ounces) frozen peas, thawed (Place peas in colander and run hot tap water over them until thawed; drain well.)**
1 **can (1 pound) bean sprouts, drained well**
¼ **teaspoon garlic powder**
⅓ **cup soy sauce (or to taste)**

1. Scramble salted eggs in a small amount of cooking fat until firm. Break up cooked eggs in small pieces. Put in a medium-size bowl and set aside.
2. In a large skillet, heat 2 tablespoons of fat. Add pot roast bits and ½ the onions. (It is not necessary to thaw meat before browning.)
3. Stir-fry until onion is soft and pot roast bits slightly browned. Remove mixture from pan and place in bowl with scrambled eggs.
4. Heat remainder of fat. Add onions, rice, and peas; stir-fry for 5 minutes, stirring frequently.

5. Add scrambled eggs, pot roast–onion mixture, bean sprouts, and garlic powder. Mix thoroughly.
6. Stir in soy sauce, a small amount at a time, tasting after each addition. Cook until all ingredients are heated through, stirring frequently.

Pot Roast Luncheon Salad
(4 servings)

1½ cups or more frozen pot roast bits, thawed
1　cup uncooked elbow macaroni
About 4 cups romaine leaves in bite-size pieces
½　cup Roquefort or blue cheese dressing, mixed with
　　½ cup salad dressing or mayonnaise
½　cup thinly sliced celery
2　hard-cooked eggs, chopped
1　tablespoon finely chopped green onion
1　cup cooked frozen green peas, chilled
¼　teaspoon salt, dash of pepper
Sliced stuffed green olives
Minced parsley

1. Cook macaroni in boiling salted water until tender. Drain, cool, and put in a large mixing bowl.
2. In a separate bowl, mix romaine leaves with a little dressing. Cover bowl and chill.
3. To macaroni, add pot roast bits, celery, chopped eggs, green onion, cooked peas, and salt and pepper.
4. Add remainder of dressing and mix thoroughly. Cover, and allow mixture to blend at least one hour in refrigerator.
5. Arrange chilled romaine on four salad plates.
6. Top with a mound of the mixture. Garnish with sliced stuffed olives and sprinkle with minced parsley.

Pot Roast Sloppy Joes, Creole Style
(makes 6 sandwiches)

2   cups or more frozen pot roast bits
2   tablespoons cooking fat
1   cup chopped onion, fresh or frozen
½ cup finely sliced celery
¼ cup finely chopped green pepper
1   can (6 ounces) tomato paste
¾ cup water
¼ cup catsup
1   teaspoon sugar
2   teaspoons Worcestershire sauce
Salt and pepper to taste
6   hamburger buns, toasted or buttered

1. In a large skillet, cook pot roast bits in 1 tablespoon fat until lightly browned. (It is not necessary to thaw meat before browning.) Remove meat from pan and set aside.
2. In remaining tablespoon of fat, cook onion, celery, and green pepper until onion is soft but not browned. Stir occasionally.
3. Return meat to pan; add remaining ingredients, except buns.
4. Bring to a boil; reduce heat. Cover and simmer for 10 minutes, stirring occasionally. If sauce is not thick enough, remove cover during the last few minutes of cooking.
5. Spoon mixture on bottom half of buns and add top half.

Hot Pot Roast Barbecued Sandwiches
(makes 3 sandwiches)

1 cup frozen pot roast bits
⅓ cup barbecue sauce, homemade or commercial (see below
**   for recipe)**
6 slices bread, or 3 buns
Softened butter or margarine

1. Heat barbecue sauce in a small pan. Add pot roast bits and mix thoroughly.
2. Bring mixture to a simmer, and cook for 5 minutes, stirring frequently.
3. Butter bread or buns; spread barbecue mixture on bottom half, add top, and serve sandwiches hot.

Note: If a smokey flavor is desired, add a few drops of liquid smoke to the barbecue sauce.

Barbecue Sauce
(makes 3 cups)

1 bottle (14 ounces) catsup
¾ cup chili sauce
1 tablespoon prepared mustard
⅓ cup brown sugar, lightly packed
⅓ cup wine vinegar
1 tablespoon instant minced onion
1 tablespoon salad oil
2 tablespoons Worcestershire sauce
1 tablespoon soy sauce
½ teaspoon coarse-ground black pepper

1. Combine all ingredients in a saucepan and mix well.
2. Cover and simmer for 5 minutes, stirring occasionally.

To Freeze Barbecue Sauce:

Pour cooled sauce into ½-pint jars. Be sure to allow ½ inch from top of jar for expansion. Mark date and contents on a strip of freezer tape and place on lid.

Pot Roast Skillet Hash
(4 servings)

2 cups of frozen pot roast bits
2 tablespoons cooking fat
½ cup chopped onion, fresh or frozen
½ cup finely chopped green pepper
½ cup catsup or chili sauce
1 tablespoon Worcestershire sauce
1 teaspoon chili powder
¾ cup water
4 cups diced cooked potatoes
Salt and pepper to taste

1. In a large skillet cook pot roast bits, onion, and green pepper in fat until meat is slightly browned; stir frequently. (It is not necessary to thaw meat before browning.)
2. Add catsup, Worcestershire sauce, chili powder, and water. Cover and simmer for 5 minutes, stirring once.
3. Add potatoes, season with salt and pepper, and mix thoroughly.
4. Cook, uncovered, over low heat, about 10 to 15 minutes, or cook longer if a brown and crusty bottom is desired.

V. HOW TO PREPARE BITE-SIZE POT ROAST PIECES

In a sense, this is the grand finale of the whole plan. Cooked and frozen, the approximately six pounds of bite-size pieces cut from the beef chuck blade roasts become the basis of *six* different budget meals of four servings each.

These pot roast pieces are wonderfully versatile and can be used in an almost unlimited number of ways. Over the years, I've developed or adapted more than one hundred 30-minute recipes in which they are the main ingredient. The best of them are collected at the end of this chapter (beginning on page 140).

To Prepare the Pot Roast Pieces:

1. In a large skillet, heat enough of the fat trimmings to make about 2 tablespoons of liquid fat. (Or use 2 tablespoons cooking fat.)
2. Brown the pot roast pieces in the skillet, making sure that individual pieces do not touch. (It is necessary to brown in three or four batches.) Season with salt and pepper.
3. As each batch is browned and seasoned, remove to a flat roasting pan or large, flat baking dish (about 2 inches deep) and cover tightly with foil. Do not have more than two layers of browned pieces in any one pan or dish.
4. If drippings adhere to the skillet, remove brown meat, add ¼ cup warm water to the skillet, and stir until drippings are liquified. Pour liquified drippings over browned meat, wipe skillet with a paper towel, and proceed with the next batch, first rendering more fat from the trimmings (about 2 tablespoons), or adding 2 tablespoons cooking fat.
5. When all the meat is browned, place it, with the drippings (there should be approximately 1 cup of these) in a baking dish or large electric skillet and cover tightly. (If there is no cover, make a snug-fitting one of aluminum foil.)
6. Braise for about 1½ hours at 325°F. Turn the meat with a spatula after about 45 minutes. (Stir frequently if using an electric skillet.) If necessary replenish the liquid with a small amount of hot water.

Cooked pieces for freezing in meal amounts.

7. When done, remove meat only. Use a slotted spoon and shake so that as much liquid as possible remains in baking dish. This liquid may be made into gravy and frozen for future use. For how to do it, see page 42.

VI. How to freeze pot roast pieces

1. Arrange meat on a large cookie tray with rim, making sure that individual pieces do not touch. Cover tightly with aluminum foil.
2. Quick-cool the meat. To do it, fill another cookie tray with ice cubes, then place the tray with the meat on top.
3. When meat feels cool to the touch, place it—still in the cookie tray—on refrigerator freezer shelf or in coldest part of freezer.
4. When meat is frozen solid, uncover and remove from tray (a pancake turner is helpful here).

Cooling pieces over ice.

5. Place in a freezer bag lined with an ordinary supermarket plastic bag. Squeeze out as much air as possible, twist the tops, secure with a closure, and return to the freezer. (It's not necessary to mark the contents since they are are easily visible through the plastic. The loose packing makes it easy to remove whatever amount may be needed.

6. Return meat to the freezer.

VI-A. How to freeze pot roast pieces in meal-size amounts

The preceding method for freezing bite-size pot roast pieces works out very nicely for me. Others, however, may prefer the convenience of freezing in meal-size amounts.

To do this, you will need six containers, either 9-inch layer cake pans, aluminum or foil, or pie pans, one for each meal you're going to freeze ahead of time. Follow the instructions for how to prepare the pot roast pieces through step #6. Then,

1. While meat is braising, cut 6 lengths of heavy-duty aluminum foil. Each should be long enough to completely wrap up the pan.
2. Shape the center of each length of foil over the bottom of each pan.
3. Date and mark the contents while foil is still shaped over the pans. Then remove foil, turn pans right side up, and place the shaped part of each length of foil inside pans.
4. When the meat is done, remove it from the baking dish. Use a slotted spoon and shake so that as much liquid as possible remains in baking dish. This liquid may be made into gravy and frozen for future use. For how to do it, see page 42.
5. Fill each of the foil-lined pans with an equal amount of meat; arrange the pieces so that they lie flat.
6. If it is necessary to have two layers of meat in any one pan, place a sheet of foil over the first layer before adding the second.
7. Complete the freezer wrap for each pan by bringing the long edges of the foil together over the meat. Fold over several times until foil is snug, but not so tight that it is drawn away from the rim of the pan. Exclude as much air as possible. Then fold the ends over several times to make a locked seam.
8. To quick-cool the meat, fill two large-rimmed cookie trays with ice cubes and place pans containing meat on top.
9. When cool to the touch, place pans containing meat on refrigerator-freezer shelf or in coldest part of freezer.
10. When frozen solid, remove each foil-wrapped block from its pan and place in individual plastic freezer bags. Squeeze out air, twist bag tops, and secure with closures. Return to freezer. (The freezer bag is necessary to

protect the foil-wrapped package from being damaged as food is shifted about within the freezer. Even the smallest hole in the foil would cause the food to dry out.)

MAKING GRAVY FROM DRIPPINGS

There are times when I'm tempted to omit this part. It usually comes last, and by the time I get around to it, I'm anxious to get myself out of the kitchen. But the gravy tastes so good and it's so very useful in so many different ways— either as an ingredient in a recipe or simply spooned over thick slices of meat—that afterward I'm always glad I've taken the few extra minutes to make it.

This recipe calls for ¼ cup flour and makes a medium-thick gravy. For a thinner gravy, use less flour; for thicker gravy, use more.

1. After cooked pot roast pieces have been removed from baking dish or skillet, pour drippings into a 2-cup measure. Let stand for about 1 minute to allow fat to rise to top.
2. Tilt measuring cup and spoon off all but 4 tablespoons (or less) of the fat.
3. Add water, milk, stock, bouillon, consommé, or vegetable juice to measure 1½ cups.
4. Pour into a saucepan.
5. In the same measuring cup, measure ½ cup cold water and blend in ¼ cup flour. Add slowly to mixture in saucepan and bring to a boil, stirring constantly. Cook until thickened (about 3 minutes).
6. Season with salt and pepper. If a richer brown color is desired, add a small amount of one of the commercial gravy-making products.

To freeze gravy, see section on *How to Prepare Cooked Food for the Freezer*, page 266.

102 Quick-and-Easy Recipes Using Frozen Cooked Pot Roast Pieces

For me, the frozen cooked pot roast pieces are a kind of built-in dinner insurance. With them on hand, I'm never at a loss as to what to serve, and even on the busiest of days I know I have the makings of a quick (30 minutes or less!) and easy, not to mention nourishing and delicious, meal. *That's* peace of mind.

Pot Roast pieces should never be thawed for the following recipes; instead go directly from freezer to skillet.

The following recipes call for frozen cooked pot roast pieces, all are based on 4 servings. Three-and-a-half to four ounces of lean cooked meat is considered one serving. The quantity of liquids, seasoning, and other ingredients may be varied. Make notes alongside the items in the recipes for changes suitable to the taste and needs of your family.

All recipes (with few exceptions) start out with a basic pattern:

Frozen cooked pot roast pieces for 4 servings
2   tablespoons cooking fat
½ cup chopped onion, fresh or frozen (or thinly sliced)
Balance of ingredients

Barbecue Pot Roast with French Fries
(4 servings)

Frozen cooked pot roast pieces for 4 servings
2   tablespoons cooking fat
½ cup chopped onion, fresh or frozen
2   cans (8 ounces each) tomato sauce
2   tablespoons cider vinegar
1   tablespoon Worcestershire sauce
¼ cup brown sugar, lightly packed
Salt and pepper
Frozen shoestring French-fried potatoes for 4 servings

1. In a large skillet, cook onion in fat until soft but not browned; stir occasionally.
2. Add pot roast pieces, tomato sauce, vinegar, Worcestershire sauce, and brown sugar. Season with salt and pepper.
3. Bring to a boil; reduce heat. Cover and simmer for 15 minutes, stirring occasionally.
4. Add potatoes and mix well with sauce.
5. Cover and simmer for 5 minutes, or until potatoes are heated through.

Budget Pot Roast Bean Soup
(4 servings)

Frozen cooked pot roast pieces for 4 servings
3   slices bacon, diced
½ cup chopped onion, fresh or frozen
½ cup chopped celery
1   can (1 pound) stewed tomatoes
2   cups water
1   can (1 pound) pork and beans
2   beef bouillon cubes
1   teaspoon Worcestershire sauce
1   teaspoon parsley flakes (optional)
1   teaspoon sugar
Salt and pepper

1. In a Dutch oven, or large pan, cook bacon until almost crisp. Remove and set aside. Pour off all but 2 tablespoons bacon fat.
2. Cook onion and celery until onion is soft but not browned; stir frequently.
3. Add stewed tomatoes. Use a potato masher to break up chunks, or whirl tomatoes in a blender for a few seconds.
4. Add pot roast pieces, water, pork and beans, bouillon cubes, Worcestershire sauce, parsley flakes, and sugar.

5. Bring to a boil; reduce heat. Cover and simmer for 15 minutes, stirring occasionally. Taste soup and correct seasoning, if necessary, with salt and pepper.
6. Serve piping hot in soup bowls.

Creole Pot Roast
(4 servings)

Frozen cooked pot roast pieces for 4 servings
2　tablespoons cooking fat
½ cup chopped onion, fresh or frozen
½ cup chopped green pepper
½ cup chopped celery
2　cans (10¾ ounces each) condensed tomato-rice soup
1　soup can water
Salt and pepper

1. In a Dutch oven, or large pan, cook onion, green pepper, and celery in fat until onion is soft but not browned; stir occasionally.
2. Add pot roast pieces, soup, and water.
3. Bring to a boil; reduce heat. Cover and simmer for 10 minutes, stirring occasionally.
4. Taste soup and correct seasoning, if necessary, with salt and pepper.

Note: Vegetables may be added to extend this dish—canned or leftover. Add during the last few minutes of cooking to heat through.

Deviled Pot Roast
(4 servings)

Frozen cooked pot roast pieces for 4 servings
2　tablespoons cooking fat
½ cup chopped onion, fresh or frozen

1   **tablespon dry mustard mixed with 1 teaspoon flour**
¼ **cup dry sherry wine**
2   **cups tomato juice**
1   **can (8 ounces) tomato sauce**
2   **tablespoons Worcestershire sauce**
1   **tablespoon brown sugar**
2   **cups thinly sliced carrots**
Salt and pepper
Hot cooked green noodles

1. In a Dutch oven, or large pan, cook onion in fat until soft but not browned; stir occasionally.
2. Blend in mustard-flour mixture and cook 1 minute.
3. Add pot roast pieces, wine, tomato juice, tomato sauce, Worcestershire sauce, brown sugar, and carrots.
4. Bring to a boil; reduce heat. Cover and simmer 10 to 15 minutes, or until carrots are done. Stir occasionally. Taste sauce and correct seasoning, if necessary, with salt and pepper.
5. If sauce is too thick, add more tomato juice.
6. Serve over green noodles, or add cooked noodles to mixture.

Hearty Pot Roast Vegetable Soup
(4 servings)

Frozen cooked pot roast pieces for 4 servings
1   **can (1 pound) stewed tomatoes**
1   **can (8 ounces) tomato sauce**
1   **cup water**
½ **package onion soup mix***
1   **package (10 ounces) frozen mixed vegetables**
Salt and pepper

* Pour contents of package on a sheet of waxpaper and mix thoroughly. Remove half of mix for recipe and reserve balance for another meal, or use in recipe Onion Soup Mix Bread, page 173.

1. Pour stewed tomatoes in a Dutch oven, or large pan. Use a potato masher to break up chunks.
2. Add tomato sauce, water, onion soup mix, pot roast pieces, and mixed vegetables; mix well.
3. Bring to a boil; reduce heat. Cover and simmer 12 to 15 minutes, or until vegetables are done.
4. Taste soup and correct seasoning, if necessary, with salt and pepper.

Note: If using canned vegetables, leftover vegetables, cooked rice, or macaroni, add during the last 5 minutes of cooking.

Italian Pot Roast Stew
(4 servings)

Frozen cooked pot roast pieces for 4 servings
2   tablespoons cooking fat
1   large onion, thinly sliced
4   cups tomato juice
1   can (6 ounces) tomato paste
1   can (4 ounces) sliced mushrooms with liquid (optional)
4   large carrots, cut in ¼-inch slices
1   can (15 ounces) garbanzo beans, drained
½ teaspoon basil
½ teaspoon oregano
Salt and pepper

1. In a Dutch oven, or large pan, cook onion in fat until soft but not browned; stir occasionally.
2. Add pot roast pieces, tomato juice, tomato paste, mushrooms and liquid, carrots, garbanzo beans, basil, and oregano.
3. Bring to a boil; reduce heat. Cover and simmer for 15 minutes or until carrots are done. Stir occasionally.
4. Taste sauce and correct seasoning, if necessary, with salt and pepper.

Pleasing Pot Roast Stew
(4 servings)

Frozen cooked pot roast pieces for 4 servings
2 **tablespoons cooking fat**
1 **medium-size onion, thinly sliced**
1 **can (No. 2) tomato juice, or 2¼ cups**
1 **cup water**
1 **beef bouillon cube**
4 **carrots, cut in ¼-inch slices**
2 **small potatoes, pared and cut in 1-inch cubes**
1 **teaspoon basil**
1 **teaspoon paprika**
4 **small zucchini, sliced ¼ inch thick**
1 **can (7 ounces) whole-kernel corn**
Salt and pepper

1. In a Dutch oven, or large pan, cook onion in fat until soft but not browned; stir occasionally.
2. Add pot roast pieces, tomato juice, water, bouillon cube, carrots, potatoes, basil, and paprika.
3. Bring to a boil; reduce heat. Cover and simmer for 5 minutes.
4. Add zucchini and corn. Simmer for about 10 minutes longer, or until vegetables are done. Stir occasionally.
5. Taste sauce and correct seasoning, if necessary, with salt and pepper.

Pot Roast with Baked Beans
(4 servings)

Frozen cooked pot roast pieces for 4 servings
2   tablespoons cooking fat
½ cup chopped onion, fresh or frozen
1   can (1 pound, 15 ounces) baked beans in tomato sauce
½ cup catsup
¼ cup water
1   tablespoon prepared mustard
1   tablespoon chili powder
Salt and pepper to taste

1. In a large skillet, cook onion in fat until soft but not browned; stir occasionally.
2. Add pot roast pieces and remaining ingredients. Taste sauce before seasoning with salt and pepper.
3. Bring to a boil; reduce heat. Cover and simmer for 15 minutes, stirring frequently.
4. If sauce is too thick, add a small amount of hot water.

Pot Roast with Barbecue Beans
(4 servings)

Frozen cooked pot roast pieces for 4 servings
2   tablespoons cooking fat
½ cup chopped onion, fresh or frozen
2   cans (1 pound each) barbecue beans (in barbecue sauce)
½ cup water
Salt and pepper

1. In a large skillet, cook onion in fat until soft but not browned; stir occasionally.

2. Add pot roast pieces, beans, and water. Season with salt and pepper.
3. Cover and simmer for 10 minutes, stirring occasionally.
4. If sauce is too thick, add a small amount of water or catsup.

Pot Roast Bean Paprikash
(4 servings)

Frozen cooked pot roast pieces for 4 servings
2   tablespoons cooking fat
½   cup chopped onion, fresh or frozen
4   teaspoons paprika
1   can (6 ounces) tomato paste
1½ cups water
2   beef bouillon cubes
⅛   teaspoon garlic powder
1   small bay leaf, crushed
2   cans (1 pound each) red kidney beans
Salt and pepper
½   cup dairy sour cream
Hot buttered noodles

1. In a Dutch oven, or large pan, cook onion in fat until soft but not browned; stir occasionally.
2. Blend in paprika and cook 1 minute.
3. Add tomato paste, water, bouillon cubes, garlic powder, crushed bay leaf, and pot roast pieces.
4. Bring to a boil; reduce heat. Cover and simmer for 10 minutes, stirring occasionally.
5. Add kidney beans. Taste sauce and correct seasoning, if necessary, with salt and pepper. Simmer for 5 minutes.
6. Remove pan from heat and blend in sour cream. Heat, but do not allow sauce to boil or it may curdle.
7. Serve over hot buttered noodles.

Pot Roast in Barbecue Wine Sauce
(4 servings)

Frozen cooked pot roast pieces for 4 servings
2 tablespoons cooking fat
½ cup chopped onion, fresh or frozen
½ cup chili sauce
1 can (8 ounces) tomato sauce
½ cup dry red wine
3 tablespoons wine vinegar
⅛ teaspoon garlic powder
1 teaspoon Worcestershire sauce
1 bay leaf
Salt and pepper

1. In a large pan or skillet, cook onion in fat until soft but not browned; stir occasionally.
2. Add chili sauce, tomato sauce, wine, vinegar, garlic powder, Worcestershire sauce, and bay leaf; blend. Add pot roast pieces.
3. Bring to a boil; reduce heat. Cover and simmer for 15 minutes, stirring occasionally. Discard bay leaf.
4. Taste sauce and correct seasoning, if necessary, with salt and pepper.

Pot Roast with Butter Beans in Tomato Sauce
(4 servings)

Frozen cooked pot roast pieces for 4 servings
2 tablespoons cooking fat
½ cup chopped onion, fresh or frozen
1 medium-size green pepper, coarsely chopped
1 can (10¾ ounces) condensed tomato soup
¼ cup dry sherry wine
2 cans (15 ounces each) butter beans, undrained
Salt and pepper

1. In a Dutch oven, or large pan, cook onion and green pepper in fat until onion is soft but not browned; stir occasionally.
2. Add pot roast pieces, soup, and wine.
3. Bring to a boil; reduce heat. Cover and simmer for 10 minutes, stirring occasionally.
4. Add butter beans and simmer for 5 minutes.
5. Taste sauce and correct seasoning, if necessary, with salt and pepper.

Pot Roast with Burgundy Sauce

(4 servings)

Frozen cooked pot roast pieces for 4 servings
2 tablespoons cooking fat
½ cup chopped onion, fresh or frozen
1 can (10¾ ounces) condensed golden mushroom soup
¼ cup burgundy, or other dry red wine
Salt and pepper
Hot buttered noodles

1. In a large skillet, cook onion in fat until soft but not browned; stir occasionally.
2. Add pot roast pieces, soup, and wine; mix well.
3. Bring to a boil; reduce heat. Cover tightly and simmer for 15 minutes, stirring occasionally.
4. Taste sauce and correct seasoning, if necessary, with salt and pepper.
5. Serve meat and sauce over hot buttered noodles.

Pot Roast with Butter Beans
(4 servings)

Frozen cooked pot roast pieces for 4 servings
2   tablespoons cooking fat
½   cup chopped onion, fresh or frozen
1   tablespoon flour
1½ cups water
¼   cup brown sugar, packed
1   tablespoon prepared mustard
2   tablespoons lemon juice
2   tablespoons tomato paste
2   cans (1 pound each) butter beans, drained
Salt and pepper

1. In a large pan, cook onion in fat until soft but not browned; stir occasionally.
2. Blend in flour; add water, pot roast pieces, brown sugar, prepared mustard, lemon juice, and tomato paste.
3. Bring to a boil; reduce heat. Cover and simmer 10 minutes, stirring occasionally.
4. Add drained butter beans and simmer for 5 minutes, stirring occasionally.
5. Taste sauce and correct seasoning, if necessary, with salt and pepper.

Pot Roast Cacciatore
(4 servings)

Frozen cooked pot roast pieces for 4 servings
2   tablespoons cooking fat
½   cup chopped onion, fresh or frozen
2   cans (8 ounces each) tomato sauce
1   can (6 ounces) tomato paste

1½ cups water

⅓   cup dry sherry wine

1   can (4 ounces) sliced mushrooms with liquid

1   teaspoon dried basil

½   teaspoon oregano

¼   teaspoon garlic powder

1   small bay leaf, crushed

Salt and pepper to taste

8   ounces or more of spaghetti, cooked and drained

1. In a large pan, cook onion in fat until soft but not browned; stir occasionally.
2. Add pot roast pieces, tomato sauce, tomato paste, water, sherry, mushrooms and liquid, and seasonings.
3. Bring to a boil; reduce heat. Cover and simmer for 20 minutes, stirring occasionally. If sauce is too thick, add a small amount of hot water.
4. Serve meat and sauce over hot cooked spaghetti.

Pot Roast and Cabbage

(4 servings)

Frozen cooked pot roast pieces for 4 servings

2   tablespoons cooking fat

½   cup chopped onion, fresh or frozen

2½ cups or more tomato juice

¼   cup dry sherry wine

8   cups coarsely chopped cabbage (1-inch-square pieces)

Salt and pepper

1. In a Dutch oven, or large pan, cook onion in fat until soft but not browned; stir occasionally.
2. Add pot roast pieces, tomato juice, and sherry.
3. Bring to a boil; reduce heat. Cover and simmer 10 minutes, stirring occasionally.

4. Cook cabbage in lightly salted water until crispy tender; drain very thoroughly.

5. Add cabbage to meat-tomato sauce; mix well. Taste sauce and correct seasoning, if necessary, with salt and pepper.

6. Continue cooking for 5 minutes longer, or until cabbage is heated through.

Pot Roast Cacciatore Stew
(4 servings)

Frozen cooked pot roast pieces for 4 servings
2 tablespoons cooking fat
1 medium-size onion, thinly sliced
1 can (16 ounces) stewed tomatoes
1 cup water
4 tablespoons tomato paste
1 teaspoon chili powder
½ teaspon oregano
¼ cup chopped parsley
4 medium-size carrots, scraped and cut into ¼-inch slices
8 ounces seashell macaroni
¼ cup grated Parmesan cheese
Salt and pepper

1. In a Dutch oven, or large pan, cook onion in fat until soft but not browned; stir occasionally.

2. Add tomatoes. Use a potato masher to break up chunks, or whirl in a blender for a few seconds.

3. Add pot roast pieces, water, tomato paste, chili powder, oregano, parsley, and carrots.

4. Bring to a boil; reduce heat. Cover and simmer for 12 to 15 minutes, or until carrots are done. Stir occasionally. Taste sauce and correct seasoning, if necessary, with salt and pepper.

5. Meanwhile, cook macaroni according to manufacturer's directions; drain well.

6. Add macaroni and Parmesan cheese to stew. Continue to cook until macaroni is heated through.

Pot Roast Casserole with Poppy Seed Biscuits
(4 servings)

Frozen cooked pot roast pieces for 4 servings
2   tablespoons cooking fat
½ cup chopped onion, fresh or frozen
¼ cup sherry wine
1   can (10¾-ounces) condensed tomato soup
1   can (1 pound) cut green beans and liquid
Salt and pepper
1   can refrigerator biscuits (10 biscuits)
1   tablespoon butter or margarine, melted
Poppy seeds, 1 teaspoon or more

1. Preheat oven to 450°F.
2. In a large skillet, cook onion in fat until soft but not browned; stir occasionally.
3. Add pot roast pieces, wine, tomato soup, and green beans and liquid.
4. Bring to a boil. Taste sauce and correct seasoning, if necessary, with salt and pepper. Pour mixture into a greased 1½-quart casserole (or 8-by-8-by-2-inch glass baking dish).
5. Brush uncooked biscuits with melted butter and sprinkle tops with poppy seeds.
6. Place biscuit dough on top of mixture and bake until biscuits are done, about 10 to 12 minutes.

Pot Roast Chili
(4 servings)

Frozen cooked pot roast pieces for 4 servings
2   tablespoons cooking fat
1   cup chopped onion, fresh or frozen
1   can (No. 2) tomatoes
1   medium-size green pepper, chopped
1   can (8 ounces) tomato sauce
4   teaspoons (or to taste) chili powder
¼ teaspoon garlic powder
1   teaspoon sugar
1   can (1 pound) red kidney beans
Salt and pepper

1. In a Dutch oven, or large pan, cook onion in fat until soft but not browned; stir occasionally.
2. Add tomatoes. To break up chunks, use a potato masher. Or whirl in a blender for a few seconds.
3. Add pot roast pieces, green pepper, tomato sauce, chili powder, garlic powder, and sugar.
4. Bring to a boil; reduce heat. Cover tightly and simmer for 15 minutes, stirring occasionally.
5. Add undrained kidney beans and continue cooking for 5 minutes.
6. Taste sauce and correct seasoning, if necessary, with salt and pepper.

Pot Roast with Chili Limas
(4 servings)

Frozen cooked pot roast pieces for 4 servings
2 tablespoons cooking fat
½ cup chopped onion, fresh or frozen
3 cups tomato juice
1 cup thinly sliced carrots
1 cup thinly sliced celery
1 tablespoon (or to taste) chili powder
1 teaspoon sugar
½ teaspoon oregano
1 package (10 ounces) frozen baby lima beans,
   or 1-pound can baby lima beans, drained
Salt and pepper

1. In a large pan, or skillet, cook onion in fat until soft but not browned; stir occasionally.
2. Add tomato juice, carrots, celery, chili powder, sugar, oregano, and pot roast pieces.
3. *For frozen lima beans*: Add frozen beans to mixture. Bring to a boil; reduce heat. Cover and simmer for 10 to 15 minutes or until vegetables are done. Stir several times during cooking.
4. *For canned lima beans*: Follow steps #1 and 2. Bring to a boil; reduce heat. Cover and simmer 10 minutes, stirring occasionally. Add lima beans and simmer for about 5 minutes, or until beans are heated through.
5. Taste sauce and correct seasoning, if necessary, with salt and pepper.
6. If a thicker sauce is desired, remove cover during the last few minutes of cooking.

Pot Roast Chili with Mushroom Soup Sauce
(4 servings)

Frozen cooked pot roast pieces for 4 servings
2   tablespoons cooking fat
1   cup chopped onion, fresh or frozen
1   cup thinly sliced celery
1   can (10½ ounces) condensed cream of mushroom soup
1   can (15 ounces) tomato sauce with tomato bits
2   tablespoons (or to taste) chili powder
1   can (15¼ ounces) red kidney beans
Salt and pepper

1. In a Dutch oven, or large pan, cook onion in fat until soft but not browned; stir occasionally.
2. Add celery, soup, tomato sauce with tomato bits, and chili powder; mix well.
3. Add pot roast pieces and kidney beans.
4. Bring to a boil; reduce heat. Cover tightly and simmer for 15 minutes, stirring occasionally.
5. Taste sauce and correct seasoning, if necessary, with salt and pepper.

Pot Roast Chili with Red Wine–Herb Sauce
(4 servings)

Frozen cooked pot roast pieces for 4 servings
2   tablespoons cooking fat
½ cup chopped onion, fresh or frozen
1   can (No. 2) tomatoes, or 2½ cups
4   teaspoons (or to taste) chili powder
⅛ teaspoon garlic powder
1   teaspoon oregano
½ teaspoon basil
½ cup dry red wine
1   can (1 pound) red kidney beans
Salt and pepper

1. In a Dutch oven, or large pan, cook onion in fat until soft but not browned; stir occasionally.
2. Add tomatoes. Use a potato masher to break up chunks, or whirl tomatoes in a blender for a few seconds.
3. Add pot roast pieces, chili powder, garlic powder, oregano, basil, and red wine.
4. Bring to a boil; reduce heat. Cover and simmer for 15 minutes, stirring occasionally.
5. Add kidney beans and continue cooking until beans are heated through.
6. Taste sauce and correct seasoning, if necessary, with salt and pepper.

Pot Roast Chili Rice
(4 servings)

Frozen cooked pot roast pieces for 4 servings
2 tablespoons cooking fat
½ cup chopped onion, fresh or frozen
1 medium-size green pepper, chopped
1 can (6 ounces) tomato paste
3 cups water
¼ teaspoon garlic powder
1 tablespoon or more chili powder
Salt and pepper
2 cups packaged instant rice

1. In a Dutch oven, or large pan, cook onion and green pepper in fat until onion is soft but not browned; stir occasionally.
2. Add pot roast pieces, tomato paste, water, garlic powder, and chili powder.
3. Add rice; bring to boil and reduce heat. Cover and simmer for 10 minutes, or until rice is done. Stir frequently.

4. Taste sauce and correct seasoning, if necessary, with salt and pepper.

Pot Roast and Chinese Chop Suey Vegetables
(4 servings)

Frozen cooked pot roast pieces for 4 servings
2 tablespoons cooking fat
½ cup chopped onion, fresh or frozen
2 cans (10½ ounces each) condensed golden mushroom soup
½ cup water (or liquid from vegetables)
1 tablespoon soy sauce
2 cans (1 pound each) Chinese chop suey vegetables,
   well drained
Salt and pepper
Hot cooked rice

1. In a Dutch oven, or large pan, cook onion in fat until soft but not browned; stir occasionally.
2. Add pot roast pieces, soup, water, and soy sauce.
3. Bring to a boil; reduce heat. Cover and simmer for 10 minutes, stirring occasionally.
4. Add vegetables and simmer for 5 minutes more. Taste sauce and correct seasoning, if necessary, with salt and pepper.
5. Serve over hot cooked rice.

Pot Roast Chop Suey
(4 servings)

Frozen cooked pot roast pieces for 4 servings
2 tablespoons cooking fat
1 can (10½ ounces) condensed beef broth
3 tablespoons soy sauce
1 large onion, thinly sliced

**2 cans (1 pound each) chop suey vegetables, drained
(save ¼ cup liquid for step #4)**
1 tablespoon cornstarch
¼ teaspoon ginger
1 tablespoon molasses
Salt to taste
Hot cooked rice, or crisp chow mein noodles

1. Heat fat in a large pan, or skillet. Add pot roast pieces, bouillon, and soy sauce.
2. Bring to a boil; reduce heat. Cover and simmer for 2 minutes.
3. Add sliced onion and chop suey vegetables. Cover and simmer for 8 minutes, stirring occasionally.
4. Mix together ¼ cup liquid from vegetables, cornstarch, ginger, and molasses.
5. Add this to pan mixture and stir until thickened. Simmer for 3 minutes, stirring frequently.
6. Taste sauce and correct seasoning, if necessary, with salt. If desired, add more soy sauce and molasses, a small amount at a time, and taste sauce after each addition.
7. Serve over hot rice or crisp chow mein noodles.

Pot Roast Chuck Wagon Chowder
(4 servings)

Frozen cooked pot roast pieces for 4 servings
2 tablespoons cooking fat
½ cup chopped onion, fresh or frozen
1 can (1 pound) stewed tomatoes
¼ cup chopped green pepper
¼ cup chopped celery
1 can (15½ ounces) chili beans
Salt and pepper
Chili powder (optional)

1. In a large pan, or skillet, cook onion in fat until soft but not browned; stir occasionally.
2. Add stewed tomatoes. Use a potato masher to break up chunks.
3. Add pot roast pieces, green pepper, celery, and chili beans.
4. Season to taste with salt, pepper, and additional chili powder, if desired.
5. Bring to a boil; reduce heat. Cover and simmer for 15 minutes, stirring occasionally.

Pot Roast Circus Mulligan
(4 servings)

Frozen cooked pot roast pieces for 4 servings
2   tablespoons cooking fat
½ cup chopped onion, fresh or frozen
1   cup chopped celery
½ cup chopped green pepper
1   can (1 pound) cream-style corn
1   can (15 ounces) tomato sauce
1   tablespoon chopped pimiento (optional)
Salt and pepper

1. In a Dutch oven, or large pan, cook onion, celery, and green pepper in fat until onion is soft but not browned; stir frequently.
2. Add pot roast pieces, corn, tomato sauce, and pimiento.
3. Bring to a boil; reduce heat. Cover and simmer 15 minutes, stirring occasionally. Taste sauce and correct seasoning, if necessary, with salt and pepper.

Pot Roast Company Fare
(4 servings)

Frozen cooked pot roast pieces for 4 servings
2 tablespoons cooking fat
1 medium-size onion, thinly sliced
2 medium-size green peppers, cut in thin strips
1 can (10½ ounces) condensed cream of celery soup
½ cup salad dressing
1 can (4 ounces) sliced mushrooms, drained (save liquid)
Salt and pepper
Hot cooked noodles

1. In a large skillet, or pan, cook onion in fat until soft but not browned; stir occasionally.
2. Add pot roast pieces, pepper strips, celery soup, salad dressing, and mushrooms; mix well.
3. Bring to a boil; reduce heat. Cover and simmer for 15 minutes, or until green pepper strips are crisply tender. Stir frequently.
4. Taste sauce and correct seasoning, if necessary, with salt and pepper. If sauce is too thick, gradually add liquid from mushrooms.
5. Serve over hot cooked noodles.

Pot Roast and Corn Chips
(4 servings)

Frozen cooked pot roast pieces for 4 servings
2 tablespoons cooking fat
½ cup chopped onion, fresh or frozen
½ cup chopped celery
½ cup chopped green pepper
1 can (6 ounces) tomato paste
1 can (8 ounces) tomato sauce
½ cup catsup
1¼ cups water
2 teaspoons chili powder
1 tablespoon Worcestershire sauce
Salt and pepper
2 packages (6 ounces each) corn chips
Medium or sharp Cheddar cheese, shredded (optional)

1. In a Dutch oven, or large pan, cook onion, celery, and green pepper in fat until onion is soft but not browned; stir frequently.
2. Add tomato paste, tomato sauce, catsup, water, chili powder, Worcestershire sauce, and pot roast pieces.
3. Bring to a boil; reduce heat. Cover and simmer for 15 minutes, stirring occasionally. Taste sauce and correct seasoning, if necessary, with salt and pepper. If sauce is too thick, add a small amount of hot water.
4. Serve over corn chips and sprinkle with cheese.

Pot Roast with Corn Niblets and Corn Chips
(4 servings)

Frozen cooked pot roast pieces for 4 servings
2 tablespoons cooking fat
½ cup chopped onion, fresh or frozen

½ cup chopped green pepper
1   can (10¾ ounces) condensed tomato soup
1   can (12 ounces) corn niblets, undrained
1   teaspoon chili powder
Salt and pepper
1   package (6 ounces) corn chips, slightly crushed

1. In a large skillet, or pan, cook onion and green pepper in fat until onion is soft but not browned; stir occasionally.
2. Add pot roast pieces, soup, corn niblets, and chili powder; mix well.
3. Bring to a boil, reduce heat. Cover and simmer for 15 minutes, stirring occasionally.
4. Taste sauce and correct seasoning, if necessary, with salt and pepper.
5. Serve over corn chips.

Pot Roast Country-Style Stew
(4 servings)

Frozen cooked pot roast pieces for 4 servings
2   tablespoons cooking fat
½ cup chopped onion, fresh or frozen
1   can (10¾ ounces) condensed tomato soup
1   can (11½ ounces) condensed bean-with-bacon soup
½ cup milk
1   can (16 ounces) mixed vegetables and liquid
Salt and pepper

1. In a Dutch oven, or large pan, cook onion in fat until soft but not browned; stir occasionally.
2. Add pot roast pieces, soups, and milk. Bring to a boil; reduce heat. Cover and simmer for 10 minutes, stirring occasionally.

3. Add vegetables and liquid. Cover and simmer for 5 minutes.
4. Taste sauce and correct seasoning, if necessary, with salt and pepper.
5. If sauce seems too thick, add more milk.

Pot Roast Creamy Herbed Stew
(4 servings)

Frozen cooked pot roast pieces for 4 servings
2   tablespoons cooking fat
½   cup chopped onion, fresh or frozen
1   cup water
1   beef bouillon cube
4   medium-size carrots, scraped and cut in ¼-inch slices
2   medium-size potatoes, pared and cut in ½-inch cubes
1   package (10 ounces) frozen peas
¼   teaspoon marjoram
¼   teaspoon thyme
1   can (10½ ounces) condensed cream of celery soup
1½ cups milk
Salt and pepper

1. In a Dutch oven, or large pan, cook onion in fat until soft but not browned; stir occasionally.
2. Add water, bouillon cube, carrots, potatoes, peas, marjoram, thyme, and pot roast pieces.
3. Bring to a boil; reduce heat. Cover tightly and simmer for 10 minutes, or until vegetables are done. Stir once during cooking.
4. Add soup and milk. Taste sauce and correct seasoning, if necessary, with salt and pepper. Simmer until heated through.

Pot Roast Curry Sauce and Macaroni
(4 servings)

Frozen cooked pot roast pieces for 4 servings
2 tablespoons cooking fat
½ cup chopped onion, fresh or frozen
2 tablespoons flour
1 teaspoon or more curry powder
2 cups milk
½ cup diced Cheddar cheese
Salt and pepper
8 ounces elbow macaroni

1. In a Dutch oven, or large pan, cook onion in fat until soft but not browned; stir occasionally.
2. Blend in flour and curry powder; cook 1 minute.
3. Add milk slowly, then cheese. Cook until thickened, stirring constantly. Season with salt and pepper.
4. Add pot roast pieces. Cover and simmer for 10 minutes, stirring occasionally.
5. Meanwhile cook macaroni and drain. Add to sauce and simmer for a few minutes, or until heated through.
6. If sauce is too thick, add a small amount of milk.

Pot Roast Curry with Fruit
(4 servings)

Frozen cooked pot roast pieces for 4 servings
2 tablespoons cooking fat
½ cup chopped onion, fresh or frozen
1 tablespoon curry powder (more or less)
1 beef bouillon cube dissolved in 1 cup hot water
1 can (No. 211) pineapple tidbits, drained
2 tablespoons raisins
2 medium-size apples, pared and diced
1 banana, cut in ¼-inch slices
Salt and pepper
Hot cooked rice

1. In a large pan, or skillet, cook onion in fat until soft but not browned; stir occasionally.
2. Add curry powder and blend. Add bouillon mixture, pot roast pieces, pineapple tidbits, and raisins.
3. Bring to a boil; reduce heat. Cover and simmer for 5 minutes, stirring occasionally.
4. Add diced apple and sliced banana. Cover and simmer 3 minutes. Taste sauce and correct seasoning, if necessary, with salt and pepper.
5. If a thicker sauce is desired, remove cover during the last few minutes of cooking.
6. Serve over hot fluffy rice.

Pot Roast with Curry-Mushroom Sauce
(4 servings)

Frozen cooked pot roast pieces for 4 servings
2 tablespoons cooking fat
½ cup chopped onion, fresh or frozen
2 teaspoon curry powder mixed with 1 tablespoon flour

¼ cup dry sherry wine
1 can (10½ ounces) condensed cream of mushroom soup
1 can (4 ounces) sliced mushrooms and liquid
½ cup or more dairy sour cream
Salt and pepper
Hot cooked rice or fine noodles

1. In a large pan, or skillet, cook onion in fat until soft but not browned; stir occasionally.
2. Blend in curry-flour mixture and cook 1 minute.
3. Add pot roast pieces, sherry, mushroom soup, and sliced mushrooms and liquid.
4. Bring to a boil; reduce heat. Cover and simmer for 10 minutes, stirring occasionally.
5. Remove pan from heat and blend in sour cream. Taste sauce and correct seasoning, if necessary, with salt and pepper.
6. Heat, but do not allow sauce to boil or it may curdle.
7. Serve over hot rice or noodles.

Pot Roast with Curry–Sour Cream Sauce
(4 servings)

Frozen cooked pot roast pieces for 4 servings
2 tablespoons cooking fat
½ cup chopped onion, fresh or frozen
2 teaspoons curry powder, mixed with 1 tablespoon flour
¼ cup dry sherry wine
2 beef bouillon cubes dissolved in 1 cup hot water
1 teaspoon grated fresh ginger root*
   or ½ teaspoon ground ginger
2 tablespoons Worcestershire sauce
1 cup dairy sour cream
Salt and pepper
Hot cooked rice or noodles

* See instructions on How to Freeze Fresh Ginger, next page.

1. In a large pan, or skillet, cook onion in fat until soft but not browned; stir occasionally.
2. Add curry powder-flour mixture and mix well. Add pot roast pieces, sherry, bouillon, ginger, and Worcestershire sauce.
3. Bring to a boil; reduce heat. Cover and simmer for 10 minutes, stirring occasionally.
4. Remove pan from heat and blend in sour cream. Taste sauce and correct seasoning, if necessary, with salt and pepper.
5. Heat, but do not allow sauce to boil or it may curdle.
6. Serve over hot rice or noodles.

How to Freeze Fresh Ginger

1. Cut ginger in about 2-inch pieces, and pare.
2. Wrap pieces individually in foil.
3. Place wrapped ginger in a plastic bag. Write the word *GINGER* and the date on a small piece of paper, and place inside plastic bag for easy identification.
4. Twist plastic bag and fasten with a closure. Place bag on freezer shelf.

How to Use Frozen Fresh Ginger

1. Remove foil from piece of frozen ginger. DO NOT THAW.
2. Grate amount needed, or chop fine.
3. Wrap any remainder of ginger in foil and return to freezer.

Pot Roast Goulash Supreme
   (4 servings)

Frozen cooked pot roast pieces for 4 servings
2   tablespoons cooking fat
½ cup chopped onion, fresh or frozen
½ cup green pepper
1   cup diced celery

1 can (10¾ ounces) condensed tomato soup
1 can (10½ ounces) condensed cream of mushroom soup
¼ cup dry sherry wine
½ cup water
1 package (10 ounces) frozen cut corn
1 teaspoon paprika
¼ teaspoon garlic powder (or 1 clove, minced)
Salt and pepper to taste
4 ounces thin spaghetti, cut in 1-inch pieces, cooked and drained

1. In a Dutch oven, or large pan, cook onion, green pepper, and celery in fat until onion is soft but not browned; stir frequently.
2. Add pot roast pieces, tomato and mushroom soups, sherry, water, corn, and seasonings.
3. Bring to a boil; reduce heat. Cover and simmer for 10 minutes, stirring occasionally.
4. Add cooked spaghetti, mix thoroughly, and cook for about 3 minutes, or until spaghetti is heated through.

Pot Roast Goulash with Poppy Seed Noodles
(4 servings)

Frozen cooked pot-roast pieces for 4 servings
2 tablespoons cooking fat
½ cup chopped onion, fresh or frozen
1 tablespoon flour
1 tablespoon paprika
1 can (8 ounces) tomato sauce
1 can (1 pound) stewed tomatoes, or 2 cups canned tomatoes
⅛ teaspoon each oregano, basil, thyme, and marjoram
¼ teaspoon garlic powder (or 1 clove, minced)
Salt and pepper to taste
6 ounces noodles
2 tablespoons butter or margarine
2 teaspoons poppy seed

1. In a large pan, or skillet, cook onion in fat until soft but not browned; stir occasionally.
2. Add flour and paprika; mix thoroughly and cook for 1 minute.
3. Add pot roast pieces, tomato sauce, stewed tomatoes, and seasonings.
4. Bring to a boil; reduce heat. Cover and simmer for 15 minutes, stirring frequently. If sauce is too thick, add a small amount of hot water.
5. Cook noodles according to package directions; drain. Add butter and poppy seed; mix thoroughly.
6. Serve goulash over noodles.

Pot Roast with Garbanzo Bean Curry Sauce
(4 servings)

Frozen cooked pot roast pieces for 4 servings
2   tablespoons cooking fat
½ cup chopped onion, fresh or frozen
2   teaspoons curry powder
2   cans (10¾ ounces each) condensed tomato soup,
     plus 1 can water
1   can (15 ounces) garbanzo beans, drained
Salt and pepper
Hot cooked noodles, macaroni, or rice

1. In a Dutch oven, or large pan, cook onion in fat until soft but not browned; stir occasionally.
2. Add curry powder; blend. Cook for 1 minute.
3. Add tomato soup, water, garbanzo beans, and pot roast pieces.
4. Bring to a boil; reduce heat. Cover and simmer for 15 minutes, stirring occasionally. Taste sauce and correct seasoning, if necessary, with salt and pepper.
5. If sauce is too thick, add a small amount of hot water.
6. Serve over hot cooked noodles, macaroni, or rice.

Pot Roast with Green Pepper Sauce
(4 servings)

Frozen cooked pot roast pieces for 4 servings
2 tablespoons cooking fat
1 medium-size onion, thinly sliced
2 medium-size green peppers, cut in ½-inch strips
1 can (15 ounces) tomato sauce
1 teaspoon prepared mustard
2 tablespoons Worcestershire sauce
Salt and pepper
Hot cooked noodles or rice

1. In a large skillet, or pan, cook onion in fat until soft but not browned; stir occasionally.
2. Add sliced peppers, tomato sauce, mustard, Worcestershire sauce, and pot roast pieces.
3. Bring to a boil; reduce heat. Cover and simmer for 15 minutes, or until pepper strips are crisply tender. Stir occasionally.
4. Taste sauce and correct seasoning, if necessary, with salt and pepper.
5. Serve over hot cooked noodles or rice.

Pot Roast Indienne
(4 servings)

Frozen cooked pot roast pieces for 4 servings
2   tablespoons cooking fat
½ cup chopped onion, fresh or frozen
2   teaspoons curry powder mixed with 1 tablespoon flour
2½ cups water
2   beef bouillon cubes
2   cups thinly sliced carrots
1   cup thinly sliced celery
Salt and pepper
Hot cooked rice or noodles

1. In a large skillet, or pan, cook onion in fat until soft but not browned; stir occasionally.
2. Blend in curry-flour mixture with onion and cook 1 minute.
3. Add water, bouillon cubes, pot roast pieces, carrots, and celery.
4. Bring to a boil; reduce heat. Cover and simmer 15 minutes, or until vegetables are done, stirring occasionally.
5. Taste sauce and correct seasoning, if necessary, with salt and pepper.
6. Serve over hot rice or noodles.

Pot Roast with Onion Soup Mix Sauce, Italiano Style

Frozen cooked pot roast pieces for 4 servings
2 tablespoons cooking fat
1 can (1 pound) tomato puree
1 can (15 ounces) tomato sauce
½ cup water
¼ cup dry red wine
1 package onion soup mix, less 3 tablespoons*
⅛ teaspoon garlic powder
½ teaspoon basil
¼ teaspoon oregano
¼ cup chopped parsley
½ teaspoon sugar
Salt and pepper
Cooked spaghetti, drained
Parmesan cheese

1. In a Dutch oven, or large pan, heat fat. Add tomato puree, tomato sauce, water, wine, soup mix, garlic powder, basil, oregano, parsley, sugar, and pot roast pieces.

---

* Pour contents of package on a sheet of wax paper and mix thoroughly. Remove 3 tablespoons for Onion Soup Mix Bread (recipe follows).

2. Bring to a boil; reduce heat. Cover and simmer for 15 minutes, stirring occasionally. Taste sauce and correct seasoning, if necessary, with salt and pepper.
3. Serve over spaghetti and sprinkle with Parmesan cheese.

Onion Soup Mix Bread
(4 to 6 servings)

3 tablespoons onion soup mix
6 tablespoons softened butter or margarine
⅛ teaspoon garlic powder
1 loaf (1 pound) Italian bread
Aluminum foil

1. Preheat oven to 375°F.
2. Combine butter or margarine, soup mix, and garlic powder in a small bowl. Cover and let stand so that flavors will blend.
3. Slice bread without cutting through lower crust. Spread mixture generously between slices.
4. Wrap in foil, leaving top partially open.
5. Bake for 15 to 20 minutes.

Pot Roast with Canned Italienne Zucchini
(4 servings)

Frozen cooked pot roast pieces for 4 servings
2   tablespoons cooking fat
½   cup chopped onion, fresh or frozen
1½ cups tomato juice
¼   cup dry sherry wine
1   can (1 pound) cut Italienne zucchini
Salt and pepper

1. In a large pan, cook onion in fat until soft but not browned; stir occasionally.

2. Add pot roast pieces, tomato juice, and sherry.
3. Bring to a boil; reduce heat. Cover pan and simmer for 10 minutes, stirring occasionally.
4. Add zucchini and liquid; cook for 5 minutes, or until vegetable is heated through. Taste sauce and correct seasoning, if necessary, with salt and pepper.
5. If a thicker sauce is desired, remove cover during the last few minutes of cooking.

Pot Roast Jamboree
(4 servings)

Frozen cooked pot roast pieces for 4 servings
2 tablespoons cooking fat
½ cup chopped onion, fresh or frozen
1 medium-size green pepper, chopped
1 can (15 ounces) tomato sauce
1 can (No. 303, or 2 cups) whole-kernel corn and liquid
½ teaspoon oregano
¼ teaspoon garlic powder
¼ teaspoon allspice
Salt and pepper
1 cup sliced ripe olives
1 cup grated Cheddar cheese
Hot cooked fine noodles

1. In a Dutch oven, or large pan, cook onion and green pepper in fat until onion is soft but not browned; stir frequently.
2. Add pot roast pieces, tomato sauce, corn and liquid, oregano, garlic powder, and allspice.
3. Bring to a boil; reduce heat. Cover and simmer for 10 minutes, stirring occasionally. Taste sauce and correct seasoning, if necessary, with salt and pepper.

4. Add olives and grated Cheddar cheese. Cook until cheese is melted.
5. Serve over hot noodles; or add cooked noodles to mixture.

Pot Roast Jumble

(4 servings)

Frozen cooked pot roast pieces for 4 servings
2   tablespoons cooking fat
½ cup chopped onion, fresh or frozen
1   cup chopped celery and leaves
1   can (10¾ ounces) condensed minestrone soup
1   can (16 ounces) pork and beans in tomato sauce
1   can (8 ounces) tomato sauce
1   teaspoon Worcestershire sauce
¼ teaspoon basil, crushed
Salt and pepper

1. In a Dutch oven, or large pan, cook onion and celery in fat until onion is soft but not browned; stir occasionally.
2. Add pot roast pieces, soup, pork and beans in tomato sauce, Worcestershire sauce, and basil; mix well.
3. Bring to a boil; reduce heat. Cover tightly and simmer for 15 minutes, stirring occasionally.
4. If sauce is too thick, add a small amount of hot water.
5. Taste sauce and correct seasoning, if necessary, with salt and pepper.

Pot Roast with Kidney Beans and Red Wine
(4 servings)

Frozen cooked pot roast pieces for 4 servings
2   tablespoons cooking fat
½ cup chopped onion, fresh or frozen
2   cans (15 ounces each) kidney beans and liquid
⅔ cup dry red wine
Salt and pepper

1. In a large skillet, cook onion in fat until soft but not browned; stir occasionally.
2. Add pot roast pieces, kidney beans, and wine. Season with salt and pepper.
3. Bring to a boil; reduce heat. Cover and simmer for 15 minutes, stirring frequently.
4. If sauce is too thin, remove cover during the last few minutes of cooking.

Pot Roast Kidney Bean Stew
(4 servings)

Frozen cooked pot roast pieces for 4 servings
2   tablespoons cooking fat
½   cup chopped onion, fresh or frozen
1   can (15 ounces) tomato sauce
½   cup water
1½ cups thinly sliced celery
1½ cups carrots, sliced ¼-inch thick
1   can (15 ounces) red kidney beans, undrained
1   small bay leaf, crushed
⅛   teaspoon thyme
Salt and pepper to taste

1. In a Dutch oven, or large pan, cook onion in fat until soft but not browned; stir occasionally.
2. Add pot roast pieces and remaining ingredients.
3. Bring to a boil; reduce heat. Cover and simmer for 15 minutes, or until vegetables are done. Stir occasionally.

Pot Roast with Lima Beans in Mustard Sauce
(4 servings)

Frozen cooked pot roast pieces for 4 servings
2   **tablespoons cooking fat**
½   **cup chopped onion, fresh or frozen**
1   **tablespoon flour**
1½ cups water
¼   **cup dry sherry wine**
1   **tablespoon brown sugar**
1   **tablespoon prepared mustard**
¼   **teaspoon salt**
Dash of pepper and paprika
2   **packages (10 ounces each) frozen baby lima beans, cooked and drained**

1. In a large pan, or skillet, cook onion in fat until soft but not browned; stir occasionally.
2. Blend in flour; add water, pot roast pieces, sherry, brown sugar, mustard, and seasonings.
3. Bring to a boil; reduce heat. Cover and simmer for 10 minutes, stirring occasionally.
4. Add lima beans and cook until heated through.

Pot Roast Lima Bean Stew
(4 servings)

Frozen cooked pot roast pieces for 4 servings
2   tablespoons cooking fat
½   cup chopped onion, fresh or frozen
2½ cups tomato juice
4   carrots, scraped and cut in ¼-inch slices
4   stalks celery, thinly sliced
1   small bay leaf
1   can (15 ounces) cooked dry butter (large lima)
      beans and liquid
Salt and pepper

1. In a Dutch oven, or large pan, cook onion in fat until soft but not browned; stir occasionally.
2. Add pot roast pieces, tomato juice, carrots, celery, and bay leaf.
3. Bring to a boil; reduce heat. Cover and simmer for 10 minutes, stirring occasionally.
4. Add butter beans and liquid. Simmer for 5 minutes, or until carrots and celery are done. Taste sauce and correct seasoning, if necessary, with salt and pepper.
5. Remove bay leaf before serving.

Pot Roast Macaroni and Bean Dinner
(4 servings)

Frozen cooked pot roast pieces for 4 servings
2 tablespoons cooking fat
½ cup chopped onion, fresh or frozen
¼ cup chopped green pepper
1 can (10¾ ounces) condensed tomato soup,
    plus ½ can water

1 can (15 ounces) red kidney beans and liquid
½ cup catsup
Salt and pepper
1 cup uncooked elbow macaroni

1. In a Dutch oven, or large pan, cook onion in fat until soft but not browned; stir occasionally.
2. Add pot roast pieces, green pepper, tomato soup, water, kidney beans and liquid, and catsup.
3. Bring to a boil; reduce heat. Cover and simmer for 10 minutes, stirring occasionally. Taste sauce and correct seasoning, if necessary, with salt and pepper.
4. Cook macaroni according to manufacturer's directions; drain.
5. Add macaroni to meat mixture and cook until macaroni is heated through.

Pot Roast Minestrone Soup
(4 servings)

Frozen cooked pot roast pieces for 4 servings
4 slices bacon, chopped
1 cup chopped onion, fresh or frozen
2 stalks celery, chopped (include leaves for flavor)
2 cans (8 ounces each) tomato sauce, plus 2 cans of water
1 can (1 pound) tiny new potatoes, halved, plus liquid
1 package (10 ounces) frozen mixed vegetables
3 cups chopped cabbage (do not include thick part of leaves)
1 can (1 pound) red kidney beans
1 cup uncooked elbow macaroni
Salt and pepper to taste

1. In a large pan, cook bacon, onion, celery and leaves, until onion is soft but not browned; stir occasionally. Remove all but 2 tablespoons of fat.

2. Add pot roast pieces and remaining ingredients.
3. Bring to a boil; reduce heat. Cover pan and simmer for 15 minutes, or until vegetables are crisply tender and macaroni is cooked. If necessary, add a small amount of hot water.
4. Stir minestrone often, as macaroni tends to stick to bottom of pan.
5. Macaroni can be cooked separately and added to mixture.

Pot Roast in Mushroom Gravy
(4 servings)

Frozen cooked pot roast pieces for 4 servings
2 tablespoons cooking fat
1 medium-size onion, thinly sliced
⅛ teaspoon garlic powder, or 1 small clove garlic, minced
1 can (10½ ounces) mushroom gravy
2 tablespoons dry sherry wine
1 cup thinly sliced carrots
1 can (8 ounces or larger) cut green beans, drained
Salt and pepper
Hot cooked noodles

1. In a large skillet, or pan, cook onion in fat until soft but not browned; stir occasionally. (If using fresh garlic, cook with onion.)
2. Add garlic powder, mushroom gravy, sherry, carrots, and pot roast pieces.
3. Bring to a boil; reduce heat. Cover and simmer for 15 minutes, stirring occasionally.
4. Add green beans and cook until heated through.
5. Taste gravy and correct seasoning, if necessary, with salt and pepper.
6. Serve over hot cooked noodles.

Pot Roast with Mushrooms and Herb Gravy
(4 servings)

Frozen cooked pot roast pieces for 4 servings
2 tablespoons cooking fat
½ cup chopped onion, fresh or frozen
1 can (15 ounces) tomato sauce
¼ cup catsup
¼ cup dry sherry wine
1 can (4 ounces) sliced mushrooms and liquid
2 teaspoons Worcestershire sauce
¼ teaspoon oregano
½ cup applesauce
Salt and pepper
1 can (1 pound) cut green beans, drained (save liquid)
Hot cooked rice or noodles

1. In a Dutch oven, or large pan, cook onion in fat until soft but not browned; stir occasionally.
2. Add tomato sauce, catsup, sherry, mushrooms and liquid, Worcestershire sauce, oregano, applesauce, and pot roast pieces.
3. Bring to a boil; reduce heat. Cover and simmer for 10 minutes, stirring occasionally.
4. Add green beans and cook until heated through. If sauce is too thick, add a small amount of liquid from beans.
5. Taste sauce and correct seasoning, if necessary, with salt and pepper.
6. Serve over cooked rice or noodles.

Pot Roast with Mushroom Soup Sauce and Green Pepper
(4 servings)

Frozen cooked pot roast pieces for 4 servings
2 tablespoons cooking fat
½ cup chopped onion, fresh or frozen
2 cans (10½ ounces each) condensed cream of mushroom soup
2 tablespoons dry sherry wine
1 can (4 ounces) sliced mushrooms and liquid
1 medium-size green pepper, cut in thin strips
Salt and pepper
1 cup or more small seashell macaroni, cooked and drained

1. In a Dutch oven, or large pan, cook onion in fat until soft but not browned; stir occasionally.
2. Add mushroom soup, wine, mushrooms and liquid, and green pepper. Mix well. Add pot roast pieces.
3. Bring to a boil; reduce heat. Cover and simmer for 15 minutes, stirring occasionally. Taste sauce and correct seasoning, if necessary, with salt and pepper.
4. Add cooked macaroni and cook for a few minutes, or until heated through.

Pot Roast with Noodles in Catsup Sauce
(4 servings)

Frozen cooked pot roast pieces in 4 servings
2 tablespoons cooking fat
½ cup chopped onion, fresh or frozen
1 cup chopped celery
1 bottle (14 ounces) catsup

1 tablespoon Worcestershire sauce
¼ teaspoon garlic powder
Salt and pepper
Hot cooked noodles

1. In a Dutch oven, or large pan, cook onion in fat until soft but not browned; stir occasionally.
2. Add pot roast pieces, celery, catsup, Worcestershire sauce, garlic powder.
3. Bring to a boil; reduce heat. Cover and simmer for 10 minutes, stirring occasionally. If sauce is too thick, add a small amount of hot water. Taste sauce and correct seasoning, if necessary with salt and pepper.
4. Add cooked noodles, mix thoroughly, and cook for about 3 minutes, or until heated through.

Pot Roast Noodle Chili

(4 servings)

Frozen cooked pot roast pieces for 4 servings
2 tablespoons cooking fat
½ cup chopped onion, fresh or frozen
1 can (16 ounces) stewed tomatoes
1 tablespoon sugar
2 tablespoons chili powder (or to taste)
1 can (15 ounces) red kidney beans
2 tablespoons tomato paste
Salt and pepper
6 ounces or more thin noodles

1. In a large pan, cook onion in fat until soft but not browned; stir occasionally.
2. Add stewed tomatoes and break chunks with a potato masher.

3. Add pot roast pieces, sugar, chili powder, kidney beans, and tomato paste.
4. Bring to a boil; reduce heat. Cover and simmer 10 minutes, stirring occasionally. Taste sauce and correct seasoning, if necessary, with salt and pepper.
5. Meanwhile, cook noodles according to package directions. Drain and reserve 1 cup of cooking water.
6. Add noodles to meat mixture. Gradually add cooking water to desired thickness of sauce. Mix well and simmer for a few minutes.
7. Serve piping hot.

Pot Roast Noodle Quickie

(4 servings)

Frozen cooked pot roast pieces for 4 servings
4　cups tomato juice
¼ cup dry sherry wine
1　package onion soup mix
6　ounces very thin noodles, cooked and drained
½ cup or more shredded Cheddar cheese
Salt and pepper

1. In a Dutch oven, or large pan, heat tomato juice to boiling point; reduce heat. Add sherry and blend in soup mix.
2. Add pot roast pieces. Cover and simmer for 10 minutes, stirring occasionally.
3. Add cooked noodles, mix thoroughly, and cook for about 3 minutes, or until noodles are heated through.
4. Taste sauce and correct seasoning, if necessary, with salt and pepper.
5. To serve, sprinkle Cheddar cheese over mixture.

Pot Roast Noodle Soup
(4 servings)

Frozen cooked pot roast pieces for 4 servings
2 tablespoons cooking fat
½ cup chopped onion, fresh or frozen
2 packages Beef Noodle Soup Mix
6 cups water
¼ cup dry sherry wine
Salt and pepper to taste
Frozen vegetables for 4 servings (carrots and peas;
**   mixed vegetables; succotash)**
**   or**
Canned vegetables for 4 servings (use liquid from
**   vegetables plus water to measure 6 cups)**

1. *For frozen vegetables:* In a Dutch oven, or large pan, cook onion in fat until soft but not browned; stir occasionally. Add pot roast pieces, soup mix, water, and sherry. Season with salt and pepper.
2. Bring to a boil; add vegetables. Bring to a boil again; reduce heat. Cover and simmer until vegetables are done. Check number of minutes to cook vegetables on package.
3. *For canned vegetables:* Drain vegetables and add enough water to liquid to measure 6 cups.
4. In a Dutch oven, or large pan, cook onion in fat until soft but not browned; stir occasionally. Add pot roast pieces, soup mix, liquid and wine. Season with salt and pepper.
5. Bring to a boil; reduce heat. Cover and simmer for 10 minutes.
6. Add vegetables and cook long enough to heat vegetables.

Pot Roast Omar Khayyam
(4 servings)

Frozen cooked pot roast pieces for 4 servings
2   tablespoons cooking fat
½ cup chopped onion, fresh or frozen
3   cups tomato juice
¼ cup dry sherry wine
Salt and pepper to taste
Frozen vegetables for 4 servings (peas; green beans;
**   peas and carrots)**
**   or**
Canned vegetables for 4 servings (peas; green beans; canned
**   potatoes)—drain, and save liquid**

1. In a large skillet, cook onion in fat until soft but not browned; stir occasionally.
2. Add pot roast pieces, tomato juice, and sherry; season with salt and pepper.
3. Bring to a boil; reduce heat. Cover and simmer for 5 minutes, stirring occasionally.
4. *For frozen vegetables:* After sauce has simmered for 5 minutes, add vegetables and cook 10 to 12 minutes, or until vegetables are done.
5. *For canned vegetables:* Simmer sauce for 10 minutes. Add drained vegetables and cook for about 5 minutes, or until vegetables are heated through.
6. If sauce is too thick, add more tomato juice or water. If canned vegetables are used, add liquid from this source.

Pot Roast with Onion-Tomato Sauce
(4 servings)

Frozen cooked pot roast pieces for 4 servings
2   tablespoons cooking fat
1   large onion, thinly sliced
¼ cup dry sherry wine

1   can (10³⁄₄ ounces) condensed tomato soup
¹⁄₄ teaspoon basil
1   cup dairy sour cream
Salt and pepper
Cooked green noodles

1. In a large skillet, cook onion in fat until soft but not browned; stir occasionally.
2. Add pot roast pieces, sherry, tomato soup, and basil.
3. Bring to a boil; reduce heat. Cover and simmer for 10 minutes, stirring occasionally.
4. Remove pan from heat and blend in sour cream. Taste sauce and correct seasoning, if necessary, with salt and pepper.
5. Heat, but do not allow sauce to boil or it may curdle.
6. Serve over hot green noodles.

Pot Roast Orientale

(4 servings)

Frozen cooked pot roast pieces for 4 servings
1   can (No. 211) pineapple tidbits
¹⁄₂ teaspoon salt
2   tablespoons brown sugar
¹⁄₃ cup white vinegar
1   tablespoon soy sauce
2   tablespoons cornstarch
1   can (4 ounces) sliced mushrooms and liquid
1   medium-size green pepper, sliced in thin strips
1   medium-size onion, thinly sliced
1   tablespoon toasted sesame seeds*
Hot cooked rice

* *To Toast Sesame Seeds:*
1. Place sesame seeds in a small saucepan.
2. Cook over medium heat until toasted, about 5 minutes. Shake pan frequently to stir seeds. Watch carefully or seeds will burn.
3. DO NOT USE OIL, BUTTER, OR ANY FAT TO TOAST SEEDS.

1. Drain syrup from pineapple tidbits and add enough water to measure 1½ cups.
2. In a large skillet, heat syrup to boiling; reduce to a simmer. Add salt and brown sugar.
3. In a cup, combine vinegar, soy sauce, and cornstarch. Add to mixture, stirring constantly until sauce thickens.
4. Add pineapple tidbits, mushrooms and liquid, green pepper strips, onion, toasted sesame seeds, and pot roast pieces.
5. Bring to a boil; reduce heat. Cover and simmer over low heat for 10 minutes, stirring frequently. If necessary, remove cover during the last few minutes to thicken sauce.
6. Serve over fluffy steamed rice.

Pot Roast and Peas in Tomato Sauce
(4 servings)

Frozen cooked pot roast pieces for 4 servings
2   tablespoons cooking fat
½ cup chopped onion, fresh or frozen
2   teaspoons curry powder
1   teaspoon paprika
¼ teaspoon garlic powder
1   can (15 ounces) tomato sauce
1   can (1 pound) peas and liquid
Salt and pepper
Hot cooked noodles or rice

1. In a large pan, or skillet, cook onion in fat until soft but not browned; stir occasionally.
2. Blend in curry powder, paprika, and garlic powder. Cook 1 minute.
3. Add pot roast pieces, tomato sauce, peas and liquid.

4. Bring to a boil; reduce heat. Cover and simmer for 10 minutes stirring occasionally. Taste sauce and correct seasoning, if necessary, with salt and pepper.
5. Serve over hot cooked noodles or rice.

Pot Roast in Pepper Tomato Sauce with Cheddar Noodles
(4 servings)

Frozen cooked pot roast pieces for 4 servings
2 tablespoons cooking fat
½ cup chopped onion, fresh or frozen
1 large green pepper, cut in thin strips
1 can (1 pound, 12 ounces) tomatoes
1 beef bouillon cube
2 tablespoons water
2 tablespoons soy sauce
1 teaspoon sugar
1 tablespoon cornstarch
Salt and pepper
3 cups medium noodles
1 cup (4 ounces) finely grated Cheddar cheese

1. In a Dutch oven, or large pan, cook onion and green pepper in fat until onion is soft but not browned; stir occasionally. Push to one side of pan.
2. Add tomatoes. Break up lumps with a potato masher, or whirl tomatoes in a blender for a few seconds.
3. Add beef bouillon cube and pot roast pieces. Bring to a boil; reduce heat. Cover and simmer for 10 minutes, stirring occasionally.
4. Blend together water, soy sauce, sugar, and cornstarch.
5. Add to meat mixture and cook, stirring constantly, until thickened, about 3 minutes. Taste sauce and correct seasoning, if necessary, with salt and pepper.

6. Meanwhile cook noodles according to package directions; drain. Mix with Cheddar cheese.
7. Serve meat and sauce over hot noodles.

Pot Roast Pepper Steak, Chinese Style
(4 servings)

Frozen cooked pot roast pieces for 4 servings
2 tablespoons cooking fat
1 medium-size onion, thinly sliced
1 can (10½ ounces) condensed consommé
2 medium-size green peppers, cut in ½-inch strips
1 large tomato, diced
¼ cup dry sherry wine
¼ cup soy sauce
⅛ teaspoon garlic powder
1 teaspoon sugar
¼ teaspon ground ginger
2 tablespoons cornstarch
⅓ cup water
Hot cooked rice

1. In a large skillet or pan, cook onion in fat until soft but not browned; stir occasioanlly.
2. Add pot roast pieces, consommé, pepper strips, tomato, sherry, soy sauce, garlic powder, sugar, and ginger.
3. Bring to a boil; reduce heat. Cover and simmer for 10 minutes, stirring occasionally.
4. Mix together cornstarch and water; add to meat mixture. Simmer for 5 minutes, stirring constantly. Taste sauce and correct seasoning, if necessary, with salt and pepper.
5. Serve over hot cooked rice.

Pot Roast Pork and Beans Chili
(4 servings)

Frozen cooked pot roast pieces for 4 servings
2   tablespoon cooking fat
½ cup chopped onion, fresh or frozen
1   medium-size green pepper, chopped
2   cans (10¾ ounces each) condensed tomato soup
½ soup can water
1   tablespoon (or to taste) chili powder
½ teaspoon cumin (optional)
1   can (1 pound) pork and beans
Salt and pepper

1. In a Dutch oven, or large pan, cook onion and green pepper in fat until onion is soft, but not browned; stir occasionally.
2. Add pot roast pieces, tomato soup, water, chili powder, and cumin; mix well.
3. Bring to a boil; reduce heat. Cover tightly and simmer for 10 minutes, stirring occasionally.
4. Add pork and beans; continue cooking for 5 minutes.
5. Taste sauce and correct seasoning, if necessary, with salt and pepper.
6. If sauce is too thick, add a small amount of hot water.

Pot Roast Ratatouille
(4 servings)

Frozen cooked pot roast pieces for 4 servings
3 tablespoons cooking fat
1/2 cup chopped onion, fresh or frozen
1 medium-size eggplant, cut in 1-inch cubes
2 small zucchini, cut in 3/4-inch slices
1 medium-size green pepper, cut in 1/2-inch slices
1/4 cup minced parsley
1 teaspoon basil
1/2 teaspoon garlic powder
2 medium-size tomatoes, cut into wedges
   (or 2 cups canned tomatoes; break up chunks with
   potato masher)
Salt and pepper

1. In a Dutch oven, or large pan, cook onion in fat until soft but not browned; stir occasionally.
2. Add eggplant, zucchini, green pepper, parsley, basil, and garlic powder. Cook for 3 minutes, stirring often.
3. Add pot roast pieces and tomatoes. Season with salt and pepper.
4. Cover and simmer 15 to 20 minutes, or until vegetables are done. Stir occasionally, turning vegetables with a large spoon to keep their shape.
5. If sauce is too thin, remove cover during the last 5 minutes of cooking.

Pot Roast with Red Wine and Vegetables
(4 servings)

Frozen cooked pot roast pieces for 4 servings
2 tablespoons cooking fat
1/2 cup chopped onion, fresh or frozen

1   **tablespoon flour**
½   **cup dry red wine**
1   **can (10½ ounces) condensed consommé (beef)**
1   **medium-size green pepper, thinly sliced**
2   **cups thinly sliced celery**
1½ **cups thinly sliced carrots**
Salt and pepper

1. In a Dutch oven, or large pan, cook onion in fat until soft but not browned; stir occasionally.
2. Blend in flour and cook for 1 minute.
3. Add pot roast pieces, wine, consommé, green pepper, celery, and carrots.
4. Bring to a boil; reduce heat. Cover and simmer for 12 to 15 minutes or until vegetables are done. Stir occasionally.
5. Taste sauce and correct seasoning, if necessary, with salt and pepper.

Pot Roast with Ripe Olives in Tomato Sauce
(4 servings)

Frozen cooked pot roast pieces for 4 servings
2   **tablespoons cooking fat**
½   **cup chopped onion, fresh or frozen**
1   **tablespoon flour**
2   **beef bouillon cubes dissolved in 2 cups hot water**
¼   **cup dry sherry wine**
2   **tablespoons tomato paste**
2   **teaspoons chili powder**
¼ **teaspoon garlic powder**
Salt and pepper
1   **cup sliced ripe olives**
Hot cooked noodles

1. In a large pan, or skillet, cook onion in fat until soft but not browned; stir occasionally.

2. Blend in flour and cook 1 minute.
3. Add pot roast pieces, bouillon, sherry, tomato paste, and chili and garlic powder.
4. Bring to a boil; reduce heat. Cover and simmer for 10 minutes, stirring occasionally. Taste sauce and correct seasoning, if necessary, with salt and pepper.
5. Add olives and simmer for about 5 minutes.
6. Serve over hot noodles.

Pot Roast and Sausage in Green Pepper Sauce
(4 servings)

Frozen cooked pot roast pieces for 4 servings
3   links of Italian sausage, cut into 1-inch pieces
½ cup chopped onion, fresh or frozen
2   medium-size green peppers, thinly sliced
2   cups tomato juice
¼ cup dry sherry wine
2   beef bouillon cubes, dissolved in ½ cup hot water
¼ teaspoon garlic powder
Salt and pepper
Frozen shoestring French-fried potatoes for 4 servings

1. In a Dutch oven, brown sausage in fat. Remove sausage and all but 2 tablespoons of fat.
2. Cook onion and green pepper until onion is soft but not browned; stir occasionally.
3. Add pot roast pieces, sausage, tomato juice, sherry, bouillon, and garlic powder.
4. Bring to a boil; reduce heat. Cover and simmer for 10 minutes, stirring occasionally. Taste sauce and correct seasoning, if necessary, with salt and pepper.
5. Add frozen potatoes and mix thoroughly. Cover and cook for 5 minutes, stirring several times.
6. If a thicker sauce is desired, remove cover during the last few minutes of cooking.

Pot Roast Shepherd's Pie

(4 servings)

Frozen cooked pot roast pieces for 4 servings
2   **tablespoons cooking fat**
½ **cup chopped onion, fresh or frozen**
¼ **cup dry sherry wine**
2   **cans (10¾ ounces each) beef gravy, plus 1 can of water***
1   **package (10 ounces) frozen peas and carrots**
Salt and pepper
Refrigerator biscuits or mashed potatoes

1. Heat oven to 425°F.
2. In a large pan, or skillet, cook onion in fat until soft but not browned; stir occasionally.
3. Add pot roast pieces, sherry, gravy, water, and peas and carrots.
4. Bring to a boil. Taste gravy and correct seasoning, if necessary, with salt and pepper. Pour mixture into a well-greased casserole. A flat baking dish (8-by-8-by-2-inch) is preferred because mixture will cook more evenly and faster.
5. *For refrigerator biscuits:* Place dough on top of mixture and bake for 10 to 12 minutes, or until biscuits are done.
6. *For mashed potatoes:* Place layer of mashed potatoes on top of mixture and bake for 12 to 15 minutes, or until top is lightly browned.

* Packaged gravy mix may be used in place of canned gravy. Follow manufacturer's directions to make about 3 cups of gravy.

Pot Roast Sloppy Joe Stew
(4 servings)

Frozen cooked pot roast pieces for 4 servings
2   tablespoons cooking fat
½ cup chopped onion, fresh or frozen
1   can (8 ounces) tomato sauce
2   cups water
1   package Sloppy Joe seasoning mix
1   package (10 ounces) frozen peas and carrots,
    partially thawed*
1   cup elbow macaroni, cooked and drained
Salt and pepper

1. In a Dutch oven, or large pan, cook onion in fat until soft but not browned; stir occasionally.
2. Add tomato sauce, water, seasoning mix, and pot roast pieces; mix well.
3. Bring to a boil; reduce heat. Cover and simmer for 10 minutes, stirring occasionally.
4. Add peas and carrots and simmer 5 to 8 minutes, or until vegetables are done.
5. Add cooked macaroni and cook until heated through. Taste sauce and correct seasoning, if necessary, with salt and pepper.
6. If more sauce is desired, use 2 cans of tomato sauce, or tomato juice.

Note: This is excellent recipe for leftover vegetables.

* Place frozen peas and carrots in a colander and hold under lukewarm running tap water until partially thawed.

Pot Roast Smothered with Onions
(4 servings)

Frozen cooked pot roast pieces for 4 servings
3 tablespoons cooking fat
2 large onions, thinly sliced
2 cans (10½ ounces each) condensed consommé (beef)
1 can water
1 can (4 ounces) sliced mushrooms, drained (save liquid)
¼ teaspoon basil
¼ teaspoon oregano
2 tablespoons chopped parsley
3 tablespoons cornstarch mixed with mushroom liquid
Salt and pepper
½ cup or more dairy sour cream (optional)
Cooked buttered noodles

1. In a large skillet, or pan, cook onion in fat until soft but not browned; stir occasionally.
2. Add pot roast pieces, consommé, water, mushrooms, basil, oregano, and parsley.
3. Bring to a boil; reduce heat. Cover and simmer for 5 minutes, stirring occasionally.
4. Add cornstarch mixture, bring to a boil, stirring constantly, and cook until thickened, about 3 minutes.
5. Taste sauce and correct seasoning, if necessary, with salt and pepper.
6. *If using sour cream:* Add dollops of sour cream, cover pan, and cook gently for 1 minute, or until sour cream is heated through.
7. Serve over hot buttered noodles.

Pot Roast with Sour Cream–Tomato Sauce
(4 servings)

Frozen cooked pot roast pieces for 4 servings
2 tablespoons cooking fat
½ cup chopped onion, fresh or frozen
¼ cup dry sherry wine
2 cans (8 ounces each) tomato sauce
1 tablespoon prepared mustard
1 package (10 ounces) frozen peas or cut green beans
1 cup dairy sour cream
Salt and pepper
Hot cooked noodles

1. In a large skillet, cook onion in fat until soft but not browned; stir occasionally.
2. Add pot roast pieces, wine, tomato sauce, mustard, and peas.
3. Bring to a boil; reduce heat. Cover and simmer for 10 minutes, or until peas are done, stirring occasionally.
4. Remove pan from heat and blend in sour cream. Taste sauce and correct seasoning, if necessary, with salt and pepper.
5. Heat, but do not allow sauce to boil or it may curdle.
6. Serve over cooked noodles.

Pot Roast Stew
(4 servings)

Frozen cooked pot roast pieces for 4 servings
2 tablespoons cooking fat
½ cup chopped onion, fresh or frozen
4 cups water
1 package beef stew seasoning mix

2 medium-size potatoes, pared and cut in about 1-inch cubes
4 or more carrots, sliced ¼-inch thick
Salt and pepper

1. In a Dutch oven, or large pan, cook onion in fat until soft but not browned; stir occasionally.
2. Add water and beef stew seasoning mix; mix well.
3. Add pot roast pieces, potatoes, and carrots. Bring to a boil; reduce heat. Cover tightly and simmer 10 to 12 minutes, or until vegetables are done. Stir occasionally.
4. Taste sauce and correct seasoning, if necessary, with salt and pepper.

Pot Roast Beer Stroganoff
(4 servings)

Frozen cooked pot roast pieces for 4 servings
2 tablespoons cooking fat
1 medium-size onion, thinly sliced
3 tablespoons flour
½ teaspoon paprika
1 can (12 ounces) beer
1 can (4 ounces) sliced mushrooms and liquid
1 teaspoon Worcestershire sauce
¼ teaspoon salt, dash of pepper
½ cup or more dairy sour cream
Hot buttered noodles

1. In a Dutch oven, or large pan, cook onion in fat until soft but not browned; stir occasionally.
2. Push onion to one side of pan. Blend flour and paprika in pan drippings. Add beer, mushrooms and liquid, Worcestershire sauce, salt and pepper. Cook until thickened.
3. Add pot roast pieces. Cover tightly and simmer for 15 minutes, stirring occasionally.

4. Remove pan from heat and blend in sour cream. Taste sauce and correct seasoning, if necessary, with salt and pepper.
5. Heat, but do not allow sauce to boil or it may curdle.
6. Serve meat and sauce over hot buttered noodles.

Pot Roast Stroganoff with Brown Gravy Mix
(4 servings)

Frozen cooked pot roast pieces for 4 servings
1   package Brown Gravy Mix
2   tablespoons cooking fat
½ cup chopped onion, fresh or frozen
1   tablespoon flour
¼ cup dry sherry wine
1   can (4 ounces) sliced mushrooms, drained (save liquid)
½ teaspoon caraway seeds (optional)
1   cup dairy sour cream
Salt and pepper
Hot buttered noodles

1. Prepare brown gravy mix according to manufacturer's directions. Set aside.
2. In a large skillet, cook onion in fat until soft but not browned; stir occasionally.
3. Add flour, sherry, pot roast pieces, gravy, mushrooms, and caraway seeds.
4. Bring to a boil; reduce heat. Cover and simmer for 10 minutes, stirring occasionally.
5. Remove pan from heat and blend in sour cream. If sauce is too thick, add liquid from mushrooms. Taste sauce and correct seasoning, if necessary, with salt and pepper.
6. Heat, but do not allow sauce to boil or it may curdle.
7. Serve over hot buttered noodles.

Pot Roast Stroganoff with Canned Gravy
(4 servings)

Frozen cooked pot roast pieces for 4 servings
2   tablespoons cooking fat
½ cup chopped onion, fresh or frozen
1   can (10¾ ounces) beef gravy
¼ cup dry sherry wine
1   can (4 ounces) sliced mushrooms and liquid
½ teaspoon caraway seeds (optional)
1   cup dairy sour cream
Salt and pepper
Hot buttered noodles

1. In a large skillet, cook onion in fat until soft but not browned; stir occasionally.
2. Add gravy, sherry, pot roast pieces, mushrooms and liquid, and caraway seeds.
3. Bring to a boil; reduce heat. Cover and simmer for 10 minutes, stirring occasionally.
4. Remove pan from heat and blend in sour cream. Taste sauce and correct seasoning, if necessary, with salt and pepper.
5. Heat, but do not allow sauce to boil or it may curdle.
6. Serve over hot buttered noodles.

Pot Roast Stroganoff with Mushroom Soup
(4 servings)

Frozen cooked pot roast pieces for 4 servings
2   tablespoons cooking fat
½ cup chopped onion, fresh or frozen
1   can (10½ ounces) condensed cream of mushroom soup
¼ cup dry sherry wine
1   can (4 ounces) sliced mushrooms, drained
½ teaspoon caraway seeds (optional)
1   cup dairy sour cream
Salt and pepper
Hot buttered noodles

1. In a large skillet, cook onion in fat until soft but not browned; stir occasionally.
2. Add soup, sherry, mushrooms, caraway seeds, and pot roast pieces.
3. Bring to a boil; reduce heat. Cover and simmer for 10 minutes, stirring occasionally.
4. Remove pan from heat and blend in sour cream. Taste sauce and correct seasoning, if necessary, with salt and pepper.
5. Heat, but do not allow sauce to boil or it may curdle.
6. Serve over hot buttered noodles.

Pot Roast Stroganoff with Onion Soup Mix
(4 servings)

Frozen cooked pot roast pieces for 4 servings
1   package onion soup mix
3   tablespoons flour
2½ cups water
2   tablespoons tomato paste

 2 **tablespoons dry sherry wine**
 1 **can (4 ounces) sliced mushrooms, drained (save liquid)**
 ½ **cup dairy sour cream**
 Hot cooked noodles

1. In a large skillet, or pan, blend soup mix with flour. Add water, tomato paste, and sherry; mix well.
2. Bring to a boil; reduce heat. Cover and simmer for 5 minutes.
3. Add pot roast pieces and sliced mushrooms. Cover and simmer for 10 minutes, stirring occasionally.
4. Remove pan from heat and blend in sour cream. If sauce is too thick, add some of the liquid from mushrooms. Taste sauce and correct seasoning, if necessary, with salt and pepper.
5. Heat, but do not allow sauce to boil or it may curdle.
6. Serve over hot cooked noodles.

Pot Roast with Stroganoff Sauce Mix
 (4 servings)

 Frozen cooked pot roast pieces for 4 servings
 2 **tablespoons cooking fat**
 ½ **cup chopped onion, fresh or frozen**
 1 **package Stroganoff sauce mix**
 ¼ **cup dry sherry wine**
 1 **can (4 ounces) sliced mushrooms, drained (save liquid)**
 1 **cup dairy sour cream**
 Salt and pepper
 Hot buttered noodles

1. In a large skillet, cook onion in fat until soft but not browned; stir occasionally.
2. Add amount of water called for in sauce mix. Add sauce mix and blend.

3. Add sherry, pot roast pieces, and mushrooms.
4. Bring to a boil; reduce heat. Cover and simmer for 10 minutes, stirring occasionally.
5. Remove pan from heat and blend in sour cream. If sauce is too thick, add liquid from mushrooms. Taste sauce and correct seasoning, if necessary, with salt and pepper.
6. Heat, but do not allow sauce to boil or it may curdle.
7. Serve over hot buttered noodles.

Pot Roast Stroganoff with Tomato Juice Sauce
(4 servings)

Frozen cooked pot roast pieces for 4 servings
2 tablespoons cooking fat
½ cup chopped onion, fresh or frozen
2 tablespoons flour
2 cups tomato juice
¼ cup dry sherry wine
1 can (4 ounces) sliced mushrooms and liquid
1 cup dairy sour cream
Salt and pepper
Hot buttered noodles

1. In a large skillet, cook onion in fat until soft but not browned; stir occasionally.
2. Blend in flour; add tomato juice, wine, pot roast pieces, and mushrooms and liquid.
3. Bring to a boil; reduce heat. Cover and simmer for 10 minutes, stirring occasionally.
4. Remove pan from heat and blend in sour cream. Taste sauce and correct seasoning, if necessary, with salt and pepper.
5. Heat, but do not allow sauce to boil or it may curdle.
6. Serve over hot buttered noodles.

Pot Roast Stroganoff with Vegetables
(4 servings)

Frozen cooked pot roast pieces for 4 servings
2 tablespoons cooking fat
½ cup chopped onion, fresh or frozen
1 package Stroganoff sauce mix
2 cups water
Salt and pepper
1 cup or more cooked vegetables
Hot cooked noodles

1. In a large skillet, or pan, cook onion in fat until soft but not browned; stir occasionally.
2. Add Stroganoff mix and water; mix well. Bring to a boil; reduce heat. Cook until thickened, stirring constantly.
3. Add pot roast pieces. Cover and simmer for 10 minutes, stirring frequently. Add more water if sauce is too thick. Taste sauce and correct seasoning, if necessary, with salt and pepper.
4. Add vegetables and cook only until heated through.
5. Serve over hot cooked noodles.

Pot Roast with Green Beans and Corn
(4 servings)

Frozen cooked pot roast pieces for 4 servings
2 tablespoons cooking fat
½ cup chopped onion, fresh or frozen
2 tablespoons chopped green pepper
¼ cup dry sherry wine
1 can (15 ounces) tomato sauce
1 package (10 ounces) frozen cut green beans
1 package (10 ounces) frozen cut corn
¼ teaspoon each basil and oregano
Salt and pepper to taste
Hot cooked rice or noodles

1. In a large skillet, cook onion in fat until soft but not browned; stir occasionally.
2. Add pot roast pieces and remaining ingredients, except rice.
3. Bring to a boil; reduce heat. Cover and simmer for 10 to 12 minutes, or until vegetables are done. Stir occasionally.
4. Serve over rice or noodles.

Pot Roast Supper Chili
(4 servings)

Frozen cooked pot roast pieces for 4 servings
2 tablespoons cooking fat
½ cup chopped onion, fresh or frozen
1 medium-size green pepper, chopped
1 tablespoon (or to taste) chili powder
2 cans (10¾ ounces each) condensed tomato soup
2 soup cans water

½ cup regular raw rice*
½ cup grated Cheddar cheese
1 can (8 ounces) corn niblets
Salt and pepper to taste

1. In a Dutch oven, or large pan, cook onion and green pepper in fat until onion is soft but not browned; stir occasionally.
2. Add remaining ingredients.
3. Bring to a boil; reduce heat. Cover and simmer for 20 minutes, or until rice is done. Stir frequently to prevent rice from sticking to pan.

Pot Roast with Sweet and Sour Barbecue Sauce
(4 servings)

Frozen cooked pot roast pieces for 4 servings
2 tablespoons cooking fat
½ cup chopped onion, fresh or frozen
1 medium-size green pepper, chopped
2 cans (15 ounces each) tomato sauce
¼ cup vinegar
1 tablespoon Worcestershire sauce
1 can (No. 211) pineapple tidbits and syrup
1 teaspoon prepared mustard
2 tablespoons brown sugar
Salt and pepper to taste
Hot cooked noodles

1. In a large pan, cook onion in fat until soft but not browned; stir occasionally.
2. Add pot roast pieces and remaining ingredients, except noodles.

* Or use 2 cups cooked rice and add during the last 5 minutes of cooking.

3. Bring to a boil; reduce heat. Cover and simmer for 15 minutes, stirring occasionally.
4. Serve over hot noodles.

Pot Roast with Sweet and Sour Sauce, Chinese Style
(4 servings)

Frozen cooked pot roast pieces for 4 servings
2   tablespoons cooking fat
½ cup chopped onion, fresh or frozen
1   green pepper, cut in ½-inch strips
1   can (No. 211) pineapple tidbits and syrup
1   tablespoon brown sugar
¼ cup dry sherry wine
¼ cup vinegar
2   tablespoons lemon juice
¼ cup catsup
1   tomato, skinned and diced
¾ cup water, ¼ cup soy sauce, 3 tablespoons cornstarch, mixed together
Salt and pepper
Hot cooked rice

1. In a large pan, or skillet, cook onion in fat until soft but not browned; stir occasionally.
2. Add pot roast pieces and remaining ingredients, except rice. Taste sauce before seasoning with salt and pepper.
3. Bring to a boil; reduce heat. Cover and simmer for 15 minutes, stirring occasionally.
4. Serve over hot rice.

Pot Roast with Taco Seasoning Mix
(4 servings)

Frozen cooked pot roast pieces for 4 servings
2 tablespoons cooking fat
½ cup chopped onion, fresh or frozen
1 medium-size green pepper, chopped
1 can (15 ounces) tomato sauce
1 cup water
1 package taco seasoning mix
Salt and pepper
Hot cooked rice or noodles

1. In a large skillet, or pan, cook onions and green pepper in pot until onion is soft but not browned; stir occasionally.
2. Add tomato sauce, water, taco seasoning mix, and pot roast pieces.
3. Bring to a boil; reduce heat. Cover tightly and simmer for 15 minutes, stirring occasionally. Taste sauce and correct seasoning, if necessary, with salt and pepper.
4. If sauce is too thin, remove cover during the last five minutes of cooking.
5. Serve meat and sauce over cooked rice or noodles.

Pot Roast with Tomatoes and Beef Stew Seasoning Mix
(4 servings)

Frozen cooked pot roast pieces for 4 servings
2 tablespoons cooking fat
½ cup chopped onion, fresh or frozen
1 can (14½ ounces) stewed tomatoes
2 cups water
1 package (1½ ounces) beef stew seasoning mix
1 package (10 ounces) frozen mixed vegetables
Salt and pepper

1. In a Dutch oven, or large pan, cook onion in fat until soft but not browned; stir occasionally.
2. Add stewed tomatoes and break up large chunks with a potato masher.
3. Add water, stew seasoning mix, pot roast pieces, and mixed vegetables.
4. Bring to a boil; reduce heat. Cover tightly and simmer for 15 minutes, or until vegetables are done. Stir occasionally.
5. Taste sauce and correct seasoning, if necessary, with salt and pepper.

Pot Roast in Tomato–Curry Sauce
(4 servings)

Frozen browned pot roast pieces for 4 servings
2 tablespoons cooking fat
1 cup chopped onion, fresh or frozen
1 medium-size apple, pared and diced
2 teaspoons curry powder
1 tablespoon flour
2 teaspoons sugar

2   **beef bouillon cubes dissolved in 1½ cups hot water**
1½ **cups tomato juice**
Salt and pepper
Hot cooked rice

1. In a Dutch oven, or large pan, cook onion, apple, and curry powder in fat until onion is soft but not browned; stir frequently.
2. Blend in flour and sugar; cook 1 minute.
3. Add pot roast pieces, bouillon, and tomato juice.
4. Bring to a boil; reduce heat. Cover and simmer for 15 minutes, stirring occasionally. Taste sauce and correct seasoning, if necessary, with salt and pepper.
5. If a thicker sauce is desired, remove cover during the last 5 minutes of cooking.
6. Serve over hot cooked rice.

Pot Roast with Tomato Sauce and Mushrooms
(4 servings)

Frozen cooked pot roast pieces for 4 servings
2   **tablespoons cooking fat**
½ **cup chopped onion, fresh or frozen**
2   **cans (8 ounces each) tomato sauce**
1   **can (10½ ounces) condensed consommé**
2   **tablespoons tomato paste***
¼ **cup dry red wine**
1   **can (4 ounces) sliced mushrooms and liquid**
½ **teaspoon basil**
½ **teaspoon oregano**
1   **small bay leaf, crushed**
Salt and pepper
Hot cooked spaghetti or macaroni
Grated Parmesan cheese

* *Note:* See instructions on How to Freeze Tomato Paste, p. 212.

1. In a large pan, cook onion in fat until soft but not browned; stir occasionally.
2. Add tomato sauce, consommé, tomato paste, wine, mushrooms and liquid, basil, oregano, bay leaf, and pot roast pieces.
3. Bring to a boil; reduce heat. Cover and simmer for 15 minutes, stirring occasionally. Taste sauce and correct seasoning, if necessary, with salt and pepper.
4. Serve over hot cooked spaghetti and sprinkle with Parmesan cheese.
5. If a thicker sauce is desired, add more tomato paste, or remove cover during the last few minutes of cooking.

How to Freeze Tomato Paste in Tablespoon Amounts

1. Before opening a 6-ounce can of tomato paste, shape (individually) eight 4-inch squares of foil around can.
2. Mark contents while foil is shaped around can.
3. Put 1 tablespoon of tomato paste in each foil container or packet.
4. Place packets on a small tray (with rim) and freeze.
5. When frozen, fold over foil to exclude air.
6. Place frozen packets in a small plastic bag. Twist bag and fasten with a closure.

Note: Instead of marking contents of each packet, write the words *TOMATO PASTE* on a small piece of paper for identification and slip into plastic bag.

Pot Roast with Vegetables, Chinese Style

(4 servings)

Frozen cooked pot roast pieces for 4 servings
2 tablespoons cooking fat
1 medium-size onion, thinly sliced
Liquid from bean sprouts, mushrooms, and water
**   to measure 2 cups**
¼ cup soy sauce
2 tablespoons cornstarch
2 cups celery, sliced diagonally, about ½ inch wide
1 package (10 ounces) French-cut frozen green beans,
**   partially thawed***
1 can (1 pound) bean sprouts (drained, save liquid)
1 can (4 ounces) sliced mushrooms (drained, save liquid)
Salt and pepper
Hot cooked rice

1. In a large skillet, cook onion in fat until soft but not browned; stir occasionally.
2. Combine 2 cups liquid, soy sauce, and cornstarch in a bowl. Add to onion and cook until thick, stirring frequently.
3. Add pot roast pieces, celery, green beans, bean sprouts, and mushrooms.
4. Bring to a boil; reduce heat. Cover and simmer for 10 minutes, or until vegetables are done, stirring occasionally. Taste sauce and correct seasoning, if necessary, with salt and pepper.
5. Serve with hot rice and additional soy sauce.

* Empty into colander and run hot tap water over beans to thaw partially.

Pot Roast with Vegetables
(4 servings)

Frozen cooked pot roast pieces for 4 servings
2 tablespoons cooking fat
½ cup chopped onion, fresh or frozen
2 cups canned tomatoes
1 medium-size green pepper, chopped
½ cup water
¼ teaspoon basil
2 medium-size potatoes, pared and cut in 1-inch cubes
1 package (10 ounces) frozen cut green beans
Salt and pepper

1. In a large pan, or skillet, cook onion in fat until soft but not browned; stir occasionally.
2. Add tomatoes. (Use a potato masher to break up chunks, or whirl in a blender for a few seconds.)
3. Add pot roast pieces, green pepper, and water.
4. Bring to a boil; reduce heat. Cover and simmer for 10 minutes, stirring occasionally.
5. Add basil, potatoes, and cut green beans. Season with salt and pepper. Cover and simmer until vegetables are done, about 8 to 10 minutes.
6. If sauce is too thin, remove cover during the last few minutes of cooking.

Pot Roast and Vegetables in Curry Sauce
(4 servings)

Frozen cooked pot roast pieces for 4 servings
2 tablespoons cooking fat
½ cup chopped onion, fresh or frozen
4 cups water
2 beef bouillon cubes
2 tablespoons dry sherry wine
4 medium-size carrots, scraped and cut in ¼-inch slices
1 package (10 ounces) frozen peas
2 teaspoons curry powder
3 tablespoons cornstarch
⅓ cup cold water
Salt and pepper
1 cup small seashell macaroni, cooked and drained

1. In a Dutch oven, or large pan, cook onion in fat until soft but not browned; stir occasionally.
2. Add water, bouillon cubes, sherry, carrots, and pot roast pieces.
3. Bring to a boil; reduce heat. Cover and simmer for 5 minutes.
4. Add peas; cover pan and continue to simmer for 5 minutes.
5. Mix curry powder and cornstarch; dissolved in cold water.
6. Add mixture to meat and vegetables and cook until thickened, stirring constantly. Continue simmering for 3 minutes, or until vegetables are done.
7. Add cooked seashell macaroni and cook until heated through. Taste sauce and correct seasoning, if necessary, with salt and pepper.
8. Serve hot in soup bowls.

Pot Roast Vegetable Soup, Italian Style
(4 servings)

Frozen cooked pot roast pieces for 4 servings
2 tablespoons cooking fat
½ cup chopped onion, fresh or frozen
1 can (No. 2) tomatoes
1 beef bouillon cube dissolved in ½ cup hot water
1 cup chopped celery
1 cup chopped cabbage
1 cup thinly sliced carrots
1 small bay leaf, crushed
⅛ teaspoon oregano
Salt and pepper to taste

1. In a Dutch oven, or pan, cook onion in fat until soft but not browned; stir occasionally.
2. Add tomatoes. (Use a potato masher to break up chunks of tomatoes, or whirl in a blender for a few seconds.)
3. Add pot roast pieces and remaining ingredients.
4. Bring to a boil; reduce heat. Cover and simmer for 12 to 15 minutes, or until vegetables are done. Stir occasionally.

Pot Roast in Wine Sauce
(4 servings)

Frozen cooked pot roast pieces for 4 servings
2 tablespoons cooking fat
½ cup chopped onion, fresh or frozen
1 can (10¾ ounces) beef gravy
1 can (4 ounces) sliced mushrooms, drained
¼ teaspoon basil
¼ cup dry red wine
Salt and pepper
Hot cooked green noodles

1. In a large skillet, or pan, cook onion in fat until soft but not browned; stir occasionally.
2. Add pot roast pieces, beef gravy, mushrooms, basil, and wine.
3. Bring to a boil; reduce heat. Cover tightly and simmer for 15 minutes, stirring occasionally. Taste sauce and correct seasoning, if necessary, with salt and pepper.
4. If sauce is too thin, remove cover during the last 5 minutes of cooking.
5. Serve meat and sauce over hot cooked noodles.

Pot Roast with Zucchini
(4 servings)

Frozen cooked pot roast pieces for 4 servings
2   tablespoons cooking fat
1½ pounds small zucchini, sliced ⅛-inch thick
   (do not peel or parboil)
½   cup chopped onion, fresh or frozen
¼   cup dry sherry wine
2½ cups tomato juice
½   teaspoon basil
1   small bay leaf
Salt and pepper

1. In a Dutch oven, or large skillet, cook zucchini in fat until lightly browned. Add onion and cook until soft but not browned.
2. Add pot roast pieces, sherry, tomato juice, basil, and bay leaf.
3. Bring to a boil; reduce heat. Cover and simmer for 10 minutes, or until zucchini is done, stirring occasionally. Discard bay leaf.
4. Taste sauce and correct seasoning, if necessary, with salt and pepper.
5. If a thicker sauce is desired, remove cover during the last 5 minutes of cooking.

Spaghetti with Pot Roast Sauce
(4 servings)

Frozen cooked pot roast pieces for 4 servings
2   tablespoons cooking fat
½   cup chopped onion, fresh or frozen
2   cans (8 ounces each) tomato sauce
1   can (6 ounces) tomato paste
1½ cups water
¼   cup dry red wine
1   teaspoon basil
½   teaspoon oregano
Salt and pepper
Spaghetti, cooked and drained
Grated Parmesan cheese

1. In a large pan, cook onion in fat until soft, but not browned; stir occasionally.
2. Add pot roast pieces, tomato sauce, tomato paste, water, wine, basil, and oregano.
3. Bring to a boil; reduce heat. Cover and simmer for 20 minutes, stirring occasionally. Taste sauce and correct seasoning, if necessary, with salt and pepper. If sauce is too thick, add a small amount of hot water.
4. Serve meat and sauce over hot cooked spaghetti, and sprinkle with Parmesan cheese.

Super Pot Roast Soup
(4 servings)

Frozen cooked pot roast pieces for 4 servings
2   tablespoons cooking fat
½ cup chopped onion, fresh or frozen
1   can (10¾ ounces) condensed tomato soup, plus 1 can water

1 can (10¾ ounces) condensed minestrone soup, plus
  1 can water
1 can (15 ounces) kidney beans and liquid
Salt and pepper
½ cup elbow macaroni

1. In a Dutch oven, or large pan, cook onion in fat until onion is soft but not browned; stir occasionally.
2. Add pot roast pieces, soups, water, and kidney beans and liquid.
3. Bring to a boil; reduce heat. Cover and simmer for 10 minutes, stirring occasionally. Taste soup and correct seasoning, if necessary, with salt and pepper.
4. Cook macaroni according to manufacturer's directions; drain. Add to mixture and cook until macaroni is heated through.
5. Serve hot in soup bowls.

Sweet and Sour Pot Roast Stew
(4 servings)

Frozen cooked pot roast pieces for 4 servings
2 tablespoons cooking fat
½ cup chopped onion, fresh or frozen
½ cup catsup
1 can (8 ounces) tomato sauce
2 cups water
¼ cup vinegar
¼ cup brown sugar, lightly packed
1 teaspoon prepared mustard
1 tablespoon Worcestershire sauce
1 cup potatoes, cut in 1-inch cubes
1 cup carrots, cut in ¼-inch slices
1 cup celery, thinly sliced
Salt and pepper to taste

1. In a Dutch oven, or large pan, cook onion in fat until soft but not browned; stir occasionally.
2. Add remaining ingredients.
3. Bring to a boil; reduce heat. Cover tightly and simmer for about 15 minutes, or until vegetables are done. Stir occasionally.
4. If a thinner sauce is desired, add a small amount of hot water.

Sweet and Spicy Pot Roast
(4 servings)

Frozen cooked pot roast pieces for 4 servings
4   slices bacon, diced
1   can (10½ ounces) condensed onion soup
1   soup can water
½ cup crushed gingersnaps
⅓ cup brown sugar, lightly packed
⅓ cup red wine vinegar
Salt and pepper
Hot cooked noodles or rice

1. In a large skillet, or pan, cook bacon until almost crisp. Remove and set aside. Pour off fat drippings.
2. Add pot roast pieces, onion soup, water, gingersnaps, brown sugar, vinegar, and bacon pieces.
3. Bring to a boil; reduce heat. Cover and simmer for 10 minutes, stirring occasionally. Taste sauce and correct seasoning, if necessary, with salt and pepper.
4. Serve over cooked noodles or rice.

Supreme Pot Roast Stew
(4 servings)

Frozen cooked pot roast pieces for 4 servings
2   tablespoons cooking fat
½   cup chopped onion, fresh or frozen
1   package beef flavor mushroom mix
2½ cups water
2   tablespoons dry sherry wine
2   medium-size carrots, scraped and cut in ¼-inch slices
2   medium-size potatoes, pared and cut in 1-inch cubes
Salt and pepper

1. In a Dutch oven, or large pan, cook onion in fat until soft but not browned; stir occasionally.
2. Sprinkle mushroom mix over onion and add water; mix well.
3. Add pot roast pieces, wine, and carrots. Bring to a boil; reduce heat. Cover and simmer for 5 minutes, stirring once.
4. Add potatoes and cook for 8 to 10 minutes, or until vegetables are done.
5. Taste sauce and correct seasoning, if necessary, with salt and pepper.

Zesty Pot Roast with Macaroni
(4 servings)

Frozen cooked pot roast pieces for 4 servings
2   tablespoons cooking fat
½ cup chopped onion, fresh or frozen
1   small green pepper, diced
¾ cup chili sauce
1   tablespoon brown sugar
1   tablespoon vinegar
Liquid from green beans plus water to make 1 cup
Salt and pepper
¾ cup elbow macaroni
1   can (1 pound) cream-style corn
1   can (1 pound) cut green beans, drained (save liquid)

1. In a Dutch oven, or large pan, cook onion and green pepper in fat until onion is soft but not browned; stir frequently.
2. Add pot roast pieces, chili sauce, brown sugar, vinegar, and the 1 cup of liquid.
3. Bring to a boil; reduce heat. Cover and simmer for 10 minutes, stirring occasionally. Taste sauce and correct seasoning, if necessary, with salt and pepper.
4. Cook macaroni in boiling salted water until barely tender; drain.
5. Add macaroni, corn, and green beans. Mix thoroughly and simmer for 5 minutes, stirring frequently.

6

More About Quantity Cooking

How to Turn Various Cuts of Inexpensive Beef
into a Variety of Different, Thrifty Meals

In the preceding section the how-to of getting nine different
meals from sixteen pounds of beef blade roast was explained.
Because of its versatility, it's an especially good technique.
I use this method whenever beef chuck blade roast is on
sale at my local market.

Needless to say, though, very often some other cut is
the special of the day. In which case, I buy whatever is on
sale—whether it be stew meat, round steak, short ribs, or
ground beef—and adapt the time- and money-saving techniques of quantity cooking to my purchase. I hope you
will do the same.

On the next few pages, you will find more step-by-step
guides for turning various inexpensive cuts of beef—bought
in quantity at special prices—into a variety of different,
thrifty meals.

How to Get 3 Different, Thrifty Meals
from 4 Beef Chuck Blade Steaks

An average beef chuck blade steak, cut ¾ inch thick,
weighs about 2 pounds. Your total purchase, then, would

be about 8 pounds of beef. Because the beef chuck blade roast contains quite a bit of bone, getting 3 different meals (of four 4-ounce servings of meat each) from 8 pounds of this particular cut is a greater achievement than one might suppose.

When I buy this cut, I serve the tender part, which is the portion containing the backbone, for the immediate meal. The balance—enough for 2 more meals—is prepared and frozen.

I. Divide the Meat

1. Place meat on a cutting board and, with a sharp knife, remove from each steak the section containing the backbone. (The grain of the meat and the direction in which the different muscles run provide a kind of guide.) Cover and refrigerate the steaks.
2. Cut the remaining portions of the steaks into bite-size pieces—1-inch-by-1-inch-by-1-inch cubes are a good size to work with.

II. Freeze Meat Cubes (Refer to Page 137, How to Freeze Bite-Size Pot Roast Pieces in Meal-Size Amounts).

The frozen meat cubes may then be used in any of the 30-minute recipes calling for bite-size pot roast pieces, beginning on page 140.

III. For the Immediate Meal, Use Beef Chuck Blade Steaks in Any of the Following 4 Recipes.

Beef Chuck Blade Steak and Vegetables
(4 servings)

Tender sections, containing the backbone, cut from 4
    beef chuck blade steaks
Unseasoned instant meat tenderizer (optional)
2 tablespoons cooking fat
Salt and pepper
½ cup chopped onion, fresh or frozen
1 package spaghetti sauce mix, plus any additional
    ingredients called for on the label
1 (1 pound) can small whole potatoes, drained
1 (1 pound) can cut green beans, drained

1. Before using tenderizer, remove meat from refrigerator and let stand, in a covered container, for not more than 1 hour.
2. Use tenderizer according to directions on the label. DO NOT ADD SALT.
3. In a Dutch oven, or large pan with a tight-fitting cover, brown the meat in the fat. If meat has *not* been tenderized, season with salt and pepper after browning. Remove meat and pour off fat drippings.
4. In remaining drippings, cook onion until soft but not browned. Stir often.
5. Add spaghetti sauce mix plus any ingredients called for on the label.
6. Return meat to pan. Cover and simmer for 1½ hours, or until done. (Less time is required for tenderized meat.) Or cook in a 325°F. oven for the same amount of time. In either case, turn the meat once about midway through the cooking.
7. Add vegetables during the last 5 minutes of cooking.
8. If desired, thin the sauce by stirring in a small amount of hot water. Correct seasoning with salt and pepper.
9. Serve steaks with sauce and gravy.

Beef Chuck Blade Steak with Gravy
(4 servings)

Tender sections, containing the backbone, cut from 4
    beef chuck blade steaks
Unseasoned instant meat tenderizer (optional)
Salt and pepper
2 tablespoons cooking fat
½ cup chopped onion, fresh or frozen
1 cup water

Gravy:
¼ cup flour
½ cup water

1. Before using tenderizer, remove meat from refrigerator and let stand, in a covered container, for not more than 1 hour.
2. Use tenderizer according to instructions on the label. DO NOT ADD SALT.
3. In a Dutch oven, or large pan with a tight-fitting cover, brown the meat in the fat. If meat has *not* been tenderized, season with salt and pepper after browning. Remove meat and pour off fat drippings.
4. In remaining drippings, cook onion until soft but not browned. Stir often.
5. Add 1 cup water and return meat to pan. Cover and simmer for 1½ hours, or until done. (Less time is required for tenderized meat.) Or cook in a 325°F. oven for the same amount of time. In either case, turn the meat once, about midway through the cooking.
6. When done, remove the meat and keep warm.
7. To make 2 cups gravy, pour pan drippings into a 2-cup measure. Let stand for 1 minute to allow fat to come to the top. Discard all but about 4 tablespoons (or less) fat.

Add enough water to measure 1½ cups liquid. Return to pan.

8. In the same cup, measure ½ cup cold water and blend in flour. Add slowly to liquid in the pan. Bring to a boil, stirring constantly, and cook until thickened (about 3 minutes). Correct seasoning with salt and pepper.

9. Serve steaks accompanied by gravy.

Beef Chuck Blade Steaks with Spaghetti Sauce
(4 servings)

Tender sections, containing the backbone, cut from 4
    beef chuck blade steaks
Unseasoned instant meat tenderizer (optional)
2 tablespoons cooking fat
Salt and pepper
½ cup chopped onion, fresh or frozen
1 package spaghetti sauce mix, plus any additional
    ingredients called for on the label
Spaghetti, cooked and drained
Parmesan cheese

1. Before using tenderizer, remove meat from refrigerator and let stand, in a covered container, for not more than 1 hour.

2. Use tenderizer according to instructions on the label. DO NOT ADD SALT.

3. In a Dutch oven, or large pan with a tight-fitting cover, brown the meat in the fat. If the meat has *not* been tenderized, season with salt and pepper after browning. Remove meat and pour off fat drippings.

4. In remaining drippings, cook onion until soft but not browned. Stir often.

5. Add spaghetti sauce mix plus any ingredients called for on the label.

6. Return meat to pan. Cover and simmer for 1½ hours, or until done. (Less time is required for tenderized meat.) Or cook in a 325°F. oven for the same amount of time. In either case, turn the meat once about midway through the cooking.

7. If desired, thin the sauce by stirring in a small amount of hot water. Correct seasoning with salt and pepper.

8. Spoon the sauce over spaghetti. Sprinkle with cheese. Serve with the steaks.

Beef Chuck Blade Steak in Savory Sauce
(4 servings)

Tender sections, containing the backbone, cut from 4
   beef chuck blade steaks
Unseasoned instant meat tenderizer (optional)
2   tablespoons cooking fat
Salt and pepper
½   cup chopped onion, fresh or frozen
1   medium-size green pepper, cut in ½-inch strips
1½ to 2 cups tomato juice
¼   cup dry sherry wine

1. Before using tenderizer, remove meat from refrigerator and let stand, in a covered container, for not more than 1 hour.

2. Use tenderizer according to instructions on the label. DO NOT ADD SALT.

3. In a Dutch oven, or large pan with a tight-fitting cover, brown the meat in the fat. If the meat has *not* been tenderized, season with salt and pepper after browning. Remove meat and pour off fat drippings.

4. In remaining drippings, cook onion until soft but not browned. Stir often.

5. Add green pepper, tomato juice, and sherry.

6. Return meat to pan. Cover and simmer for 1½ hours, or until done. (Less time is required for tenderized meat.) Or cook in a 325°F. oven for the same amount of time. In either case, turn the meat once about midway through the cooking.
7. If a thicker sauce is desired, cook uncovered for the last 5 minutes. Correct seasoning with salt and pepper.
8. Serve the steaks with the sauce.

How to Get 3 Different, Thrifty Meals from 2 Beef Chuck Arm Pot Roasts

Here is another thrifty plan for cooking in quantity. The end result of this one is: (1) a beef stew, (2) Swiss steak, and (3) a pot roast. Not only is this a time- and money-saver like the other plans, it's a real fuel-conserver, too, since all 3 meals are cooked in the oven at the same time (in different containers, of course).

The average beef chuck arm pot roast is about 2 inches thick and weighs about 3½ pounds. Your total purchase, then, would be about 7 pounds of beef.

When I follow this plan, I serve the pot roast as the immediate meal. I store one of the others in the refrigerator for use within two or three days. The third meal is frozen.

I. DIVIDE THE MEAT
1. With a sharp knife cut off the rounded (boneless) end of each roast and cut into 1-inch cubes. (You should have a total of about 2 pounds of cubes.) These will be used for stew.
2. From the center of each roast cut out the section containing the bone. These will be used for pot roast. Total weight of the two pieces will be approximately 3 pounds. (If you find this is more than you need for one meal,

remember that any leftovers do very nicely for sand-wiches.)
3. Slice each of the remaining two pieces of the roast into 1-inch thicknesses. These four 1-inch thick slices, weighing about 2 pounds in all, will be used for Swiss steak.

II. PREPARE MEAT FOR THE OVEN

1. *Stew:* In a large skillet, brown meat cubes in 2 table-spoons fat. Season with salt and pepper. When browned, remove meat to a shallow oven-proof dish or pan. Add ½ cup water. Make a lid of heavy-duty aluminum foil and seal tightly over the container. Set aside.
2. *Pot Roast:* In the same skillet, brown pot roast meat on all sides. Season with salt and pepper. Remove meat to a shallow oven-proof dish or pan. Add ½ cup water. Make a lid of heavy-duty aluminum foil and seal tightly over the container. Set aside.
3. *Swiss Steak:* Again in the same skillet, brown Swiss steak pieces on both sides. Season with salt and pepper. When browned, remove meat to a shallow oven-proof dish or pan. Pour off fat drippings in the skillet. In the remaining fat, cook ½ cup chopped fresh or frozen onion until soft, but not browned. Stir often. Add ¾ cup water or tomato juice and, if desired, 2 tablespoons sherry wine. Simmer until browned-on bits of meat are blended into the liquid. Pour liquid over the steaks. Make a tight lid of heavy-duty aluminum foil and seal tightly over container.

III. TO COOK, PLACE ALL THREE CONTAINERS IN A PRE-HEATED 325°F OVEN

1. *Stew:* Cook approximately 1¼ to 1½ hours, or until done. Turn meat after about 30 minutes. Add a small amount of hot water if necessary.
2. *Pot Roast:* Cook 1½ to 2 hours, or until done. Turn meat after about 1 hour. Add a small amount of water if neces-

sary. (Vegetables, if used, should be added during the last 35 minutes.)

3. *Swiss Steaks:* Cook 1¼ to 1½ hours, or until done. Turn meat after about 30 minutes. Add a small amount of hot water or tomato juice if necesssary.

Note: If meat for the various dishes weighs more than the approximate weights given, cooking time should be increased accordingly. Test for doneness by piercing with a sharp-tined fork. When forks enters easily, meat is done.

IV. To FREEZE STEW MEAT, REFER TO PAGE 137 (How to Freeze Bite-Size Pot Roast Pieces in Meal-Size Amounts).

V. To FREEZE SWISS STEAK AND GRAVY, REFER TO PAGE 266 (How to Prepare Cooked Food for the Freezer).

VI. USE THE FOLLOWING RECIPE FOR MAKING BEEF STEW WITH FROZEN STEW MEAT:

Frozen cooked beef stew meat
2 tablespoons cooking fat
½ cup chopped onion, fresh or frozen
4 cups water
1 package beef stew seasoning mix
2 medium-size potatoes pared and cut in 1-inch cubes
4 medium-size carrots, scraped and sliced ¼-inch thick
Salt and pepper

1. In a Dutch oven, or large pan with a tight-fitting cover, cook onion in fat until soft but not browned. Stir often.
2. Add water and beef stew seasoning mix.
3. Add frozen beef stew meat, potatoes and carrots. Bring to a boil. Then reduce heat, cover, and simmer for 10 to 12 minutes, or until vegetables are done. Stir occasionally.
4. Correct seasoning with salt and pepper, and serve.

VII. PREPARE FROZEN SWISS STEAKS AND GRAVY

1. Place unwrapped frozen Swiss steaks and gravy in a skillet. (Loosen difficult-to-remove foil by holding under warm tap water for just a few seconds; it is *not* necessary to thaw the meat for any of the following recipes.)
2. Turn heat to low; increase slightly as food begins to thaw. Stir occasionally.
3. Heat to serving temperature. If gravy separates during thawing and reheating, stir constantly until reconstituted to original thickness.
4. If desired, a packaged gravy mix or canned gravy may be used to supplement frozen gravy.

4 Swiss Steak Variations

The frozen cooked Swiss steaks are fine when they are simply taken from the freezer and heated to serving temperature, but I prefer to dress them up a bit and use them in one of the following recipes.

Swiss Steak with Vegetable Soups
(4 servings)

Frozen cooked Swiss steak for 4 servings
2 **tablespoons cooking fat**
1 **large onion, thinly sliced**
1 **can (10¾ ounces) condensed vegetable soup**
1 **can (10¾ ounces) condensed tomato soup**
2 **tablespoons dry sherry wine (optional)**
Salt and pepper

1. In a Dutch oven, or large pan, cook onion in fat until soft but not browned; stir occasionally.
2. Add soups and sherry; mix well. Add Swiss steaks.

3. Bring to a boil; reduce heat. Cover tightly and simmer for 10 minutes. Turn meat and continue simmering for 5 minutes.
4. Taste soup and correct seasoning, if necessary, with salt and pepper.

Swiss Steak in Tomato Sauce
(4 servings)

Frozen cooked Swiss steak for 4 servings
2 tablespoons cooking fat
½ cup chopped onion, fresh or frozen
1 can (10¾ ounces) condensed tomato soup
1 can (4 ounces) sliced mushrooms, drained (save liquid)
½ cup liquid (mushroom juice plus water to make ½ cup)
2 tablespoons dry sherry wine
½ teaspoon basil
¼ teaspoon oregano
Salt and pepper

1. In a large skillet, cook onion in fat until soft but not browned; stir occasionally.
2. Add soup, mushrooms, liquid, sherry, basil, and oregano; mix well.
3. Bring to a boil; reduce heat. Cover tightly and simmer for 10 minutes. Turn meat and continue simmering for 5 minutes.
4. Taste sauce and correct seasoning, if necessary, with salt and pepper.

Note: If more sauce is desired, use two cans of soup.

Swiss Pepper Steak
(4 servings)

Frozen cooked Swiss steak for 4 servings
1 can (10½ ounces) condensed onion soup
½ cup catsup
2 tablespoons dry red or dry sherry wine
1 medium-size green pepper, cut in ½-inch strips
Salt and pepper

1. In a large skillet, or pan, combine soup, catsup, wine, and green pepper strips; mix well. Add Swiss steaks.
2. Bring to a boil; reduce heat. Cover tightly and simmer for 10 minutes. Turn meat and continue simmering for 5 minutes.
3. Taste sauce and correct seasoning, if necessary, with salt and pepper.

Swiss Steak Chili
(4 servings)

Frozen cooked Swiss steak for 4 servings
2 tablespoons cooking fat
½ cup chopped onion, fresh or frozen
1 medium-size green pepper, chopped
1 can (15 ounces) tomato sauce with tomato bits
1 can (8 ounces) tomato sauce
1 tablespoon (or to taste) chili powder
1 can (15 ounces) kidney beans
Salt and pepper

1. In a large skillet, or pan, cook onion in fat until soft but not browned; stir occasionally.
2. Add green pepper, tomato sauce with tomato bits, tomato sauce, and chili powder; mix well. Add Swiss steaks.

3. Bring to a boil; reduce heat. Cover and simmer for 10 minutes, stirring occasionally. Turn meat once during cooking.
4. Add kidney beans and simmer for 5 minutes.
5. If sauce is too thick, add a small amount of hot water. Taste sauce and correct seasoning, if necessary, with salt and pepper.

How to Prepare and Freeze Ground Beef for a Number of Different Meals

I always try to have a good supply of cooked ground beef in the freezer and ready to go. It's a staple and lends itself to a number of appetizing dishes—dishes that come about as close to being "instant meals" as one can get—including many of the recipes calling for frozen cooked pot roast pieces (beginning on page 140). Needless to say, I buy in quantity when the price is right.

(Incidentally, even if your freezer space is very limited, you can save time and money by browning enough ground beef for two meals and freezing one meal-size portion for future use.)

I. TO BROWN GROUND BEEF
1. Shape meat into a large patty, about 1 inch thick. Place in a skillet over medium heat. Brown on each side, then break into 1-inch chunks. Cook until redness disappears, stirring occasionally. Season with salt and pepper.
2. Note: It is better not to try to brown any more than 1½ pounds of ground beef at once in any one pan. (When working with very large quantities of meat, you can speed up the process by browning in more than one pan at once.)

II. To PREPARE FREEZER WRAP

1. Use a 9-inch layer cake pan for each meal-size portion (four 4-ounce servings) of meat to be frozen.
2. Invert pan. Cut enough foil to completely wrap up pan. Mold center of the foil over bottom of the pan.
3. For easy identification, mark contents and date while foil is shaped over pan. Then remove foil, turn pan right side up, and place shaped part of foil inside pan.
4. With a slotted spoon remove browned beef from skillet. Shake off as much of the fat drippings as possible and place beef in foil-lined pan.
5. Arrange meat in one layer. If two layers are necessary, place a length of foil over the first layer before adding the second.
6. Complete the freezer wrap by bringing ends of foil together over top and center of pan. Fold down in 1-inch locked folds, being careful not to draw the foil too tightly. Exclude as much air as possible and fold ends over several times to make a locked seam.

III. To COOL AND FREEZE THE MEAT

1. BACTERIA MULTIPLY RAPIDLY IN GROUND MEAT, SO QUICK-COOLING IS IMPORTANT. DO NOT ALLOW MEAT TO COOL SLOWLY AT ROOM TEMPERATURE. To quick-cool, place foil-wrapped meat (with pan) over a 9-inch layer cake pan filled with ice cubes.
2. When cool to the touch, place meat and pan in freezer.
3. When frozen solid, remove foil-wrapped meat from pan and place in a regular plastic freezer bag. Squeeze out as much air as possible, twist top of bag, and secure with a closure. (Without the freezer bag, even the smallest hole in the foil would expose the meat to air and thus dry it out.)
4. Return meat to the freezer.

7 Almost-Instant Meals Made with Frozen Ground Beef

Following are seven of my favorite recipes calling for frozen ground beef. No need for thawing here. The beef goes directly from freezer to pan (though, of course, I hope you will remove the freezer wrap first).

Remember, too, that frozen ground beef can substitute for frozen pot roast pieces in many of the recipes beginning on page 140.

Spaghetti with Ground Beef Sauce
(4 servings)

Frozen cooked ground beef for 4 servings
1 package spaghetti sauce mix, plus ingredients
   called for in mix
8 ounces or more spaghetti, cooked and drained
Parmesan cheese

1. In a large pan, prepare spaghetti sauce according to manufacturer's directions.
2. Add beef to sauce and simmer for length of time called for in sauce mix.
3. Spoon meat sauce over cooked spaghetti and sprinkle with Parmesan cheese.

Ground Beef with Baked Beans
(4 servings)

Frozen cooked ground beef for 4 servings
2   tablespoons cooking fat
½ cup chopped onion, fresh or frozen
1   can (1 pound, 12 ounces) baked beans
½ cup catsup
1   tablespoon prepared mustard
2   teaspoons (or to taste) chili powder
Salt and pepper

1. In a large skillet, or pan, cook onion in fat until soft but not browned; stir occasionally.
2. Add baked beans, catsup, mustard, chili powder, and ground beef.
3. Bring to a boil; reduce heat. Cover and simmer for 15 minutes, stirring occasionally.
4. Taste sauce and correct seasoning, if necessary, with salt and pepper.
5. If sauce is too thick, add a small amount of water.

Chili Rice with Ground Beef
(4 servings)

Frozen cooked ground beef for 4 servings
2   tablespoons cooking fat
½ cup chopped onion, fresh or frozen
1   medium-size green pepper, chopped
1   package chili mix
1   cup instant rice
1   can (6 ounces) tomato paste
3   cups water
1   can (15 ounces) kidney beans
Salt and pepper

1. In a Dutch oven, or large pan, cook onion and green pepper in fat until onion is soft but not browned; stir occasionally.
2. Add chili mix, ground beef, rice, tomato paste, and water; mix well.
3. Bring to a boil; reduce heat. Cover and simmer for 10 minutes, stirring frequently.
4. Add kidney beans. Taste sauce and correct seasoning, if necessary, with salt and pepper. Continue simmering until beans are heated through.
5. If sauce is too thick, add a small amount of water.

Ground Beef Creole with Noodles
(4 servings)

Frozen cooked ground beef for 4 servings
4 slices bacon, diced
1 cup chopped onion, fresh or frozen
1 medium-size green pepper, chopped
1 cup thinly sliced celery
1 can (15 ounces) tomato sauce with tomato bits
1 can (8 ounces) tomato sauce
½ cup water
1 cup grated Cheddar cheese
1 package (8 ounces) egg noodles
Salt and pepper

1. In a Dutch oven, or large pan, fry bacon. Remove with a slotted spoon and set aside. Remove all but 2 tablespoons of fat.
2. Cook onions, green pepper, and celery until onion is soft but not browned; stir occasionally.
3. Add bacon, tomato sauce with tomato bits, tomato sauce, water, Cheddar cheese, and ground beef.
4. Bring to a boil; reduce heat. Cover and simmer for 15

minutes, stirring occasionally. Taste sauce and correct seasoning, if necessary, with salt and pepper.

5. Meanwhile cook noodles according to package directions; drain.

6. Serve meat sauce over cooked noodles.

Ground Beef and Butter Beans
(4 servings)

Frozen cooked ground beef for 4 servings
2 tablespoons cooking fat
½ cup chopped onion, fresh or frozen
1 medium-size green pepper, chopped
1 can (15 ounces) tomato sauce
2 tablespoons sherry wine
2 tablespoons brown sugar
2 cans (15 ounces each) cooked dry butter beans, drained (save liquid)
Salt and pepper
Hot cooked noodles (optional)

1. In a Dutch oven, or large pan, cook onion and green pepper in fat until onion is soft but not browned; stir occasionally.

2. Add ground beef, tomato sauce, wine, and brown sugar; mix well.

3. Bring to a boil; reduce heat. Cover and simmer for 10 minutes, stirring occasionally.

4. Add butter beans and continue simmering for 5 minutes. Taste sauce and correct seasoning, if necessary, with salt and pepper.

5. If sauce is too thick, add liquid from beans.

6. Serve meat sauce over noodles.

Beef Curry in Tomato Sauce
(4 servings)

Frozen cooked ground beef for 4 servings
2   tablespoons cooking fat
1   tablespoon curry powder
½ cup chopped onion, fresh or frozen
2   cans (10¾ ounces each) condensed tomato soup
1   teaspoon sugar
1   teaspoon vinegar
1   tablespoon Worcestershire sauce
Salt and pepper
Hot cooked rice, egg noodles, or green noodles

1. In a Dutch oven, or large pan, cook onion in fat until onion is soft but not browned; stir occasionally.
2. Blend in curry powder and cook for 1 minute.
3. Add ground beef, tomato soup, sugar, vinegar, and Worcestershire sauce.
4. Bring to a boil; reduce heat. Cover and simmer for 10 minutes, stirring occasionally. Taste sauce and correct seasoning, if necessary, with salt and pepper.
5. If sauce is too thick, add a small amount of water.
6. Serve meat sauce over rice.

Ground Beef Stew with Taco Seasoning Mix
(4 servings)

Frozen cooked ground beef for 4 servings
2 tablespoons cooking fat
½ cup chopped onion, fresh or frozen
1 can (10¾ ounces) condensed tomato soup
3 soup cans water
1 package taco seasoning mix
4 carrots (or more), scraped and cut in ½-inch slices
2 medium-size potatoes, pared and cut in 1-inch cubes
2 or more stalks celery cut in 1-inch pieces
1 can (1 pound) pork and beans in tomato sauce
Salt and pepper

1. In a Dutch oven, or large pan, cook onion in fat until soft but not browned; stir occasionally.
2. Add soup, water, and taco seasoning mix; mix well.
3. Add carrots, potatoes, and celery. Bring to a boil; reduce heat. Cover and simmer for 5 minutes, stirring occasionally.
4. Add ground beef and continue simmering, covered, for 5 minutes.
5. Add pork and beans; simmer for 2 minutes, or until vegetables are done.
6. Taste sauce and correct seasoning, if necessary, with salt and pepper.

How to Prepare and Freeze Meatballs in Quantity

The world abounds in meatball-lovers. If several of them live in your house, you'll find the instructions for making and freezing meat balls in quantity very useful indeed.

I. THE BASIC MEATBALL RECIPE

3   **pounds ground beef**
1½ **teaspoons salt**
¼   **teaspoon black pepper (approximately)**
¾   **cup finely chopped onion**
¾   **cup dry bread crumbs**
3   **eggs**

Note: For the sake of convenience, prepare one-third of the recipe at a time.

1. In a bowl, lightly mix together 1 pound meat, ½ teaspoon salt, dash black pepper, ¼ cup onion, and ¼ cup bread crumbs. Push mixture to one side of bowl.
2. Add 1 egg and beat with a fork. Blend egg and meat mixture.
3. Place mixture on a sheet of wax paper and shape into a flattened rectangle, approximately 10 inches long by 4 inches wide.
4. With a knife, divide the rectangle into 12 equal parts.
5. Roll each part into a ball. Place balls in a bowl and refrigerate.
6. Repeat instructions for two more batches.

II. TO COOK MEATBALLS
1. Lightly grease a rimmed cookie tray (or line tray with greased aluminum foil).
2. Arrange meatballs on tray, allowing space of at least 2 inches between each ball.
3. Bake in a 400°F. oven for 20 minutes.
4. Turn each ball and continue baking until browned (between 5 and 8 minutes).

III. TO FREEZE MEATBALLS
1. Place cooked meatballs on a clean cookie tray. Cover with foil and allow to cool.

2. When cool to the touch, place tray in freezer.
3. When meatballs are frozen, place in a regular plastic freezer bag lined with an ordinary supermarket plastic bag. Squeeze out as much air as possible, twist bag tops, and secure with a closure. (There's no need to label the contents since they're visible through the plastic.)
4. Return meatballs to the freezer.

3 Quick-and-Easy Meatball Meals

Use frozen cooked meatballs in the following recipes. Or, for a nice change of pace, try them in some of the recipes calling for frozen cooked pot roast pieces. In either case, thawing is unnecessary.

Spaghetti with Meatball Sauce
(4 servings)

Frozen cooked meatballs for 4 servings
2   tablespoons cooking fat
½   cup chopped onion, fresh or frozen
1   can (15 ounces) tomato sauce
1   can (6 ounces) tomato paste
1½ cups water
¼   cup dry red wine
1   teaspoon basil
½   teaspoon oregano
Salt and pepper
8   ounces, or more, spaghetti, cooked and drained
Grated Parmesan cheese

1. In a Dutch oven, or large pan, cook onion in fat until soft but not browned; stir occasionally.
2. Add tomato sauce, tomato paste, water, wine, basil, and oregano; mix well. Add meatballs.

3. Bring to a boil; reduce heat. Cover and simmer for 20 minutes, stirring occasionally. Taste sauce and correct seasoning, if necessary, with salt and pepper. If sauce is too thick, add a small amount of water.
4. Serve meatballs and sauce over cooked spaghetti and sprinkle with Parmesan cheese.

Meatball Stew
(4 servings)

Frozen cooked meatballs for 4 servings
2 **tablespoons cooking fat**
1 **medium-size onion, thinly sliced**
2 **cans (10¾ ounces each) condensed tomato soup**
1 **soup can water**
2 **medium-size potatoes, pared and cut in 1-inch cubes**
4 **or more carrots, scraped and cut in ½-inch slices**
Salt and pepper

1. In a Dutch oven, or large pan, cook onion in fat until soft but not browned; stir occasionally.
2. Add tomato soup, and water; mix well. Add meatballs, potatoes, and carrots.
3. Bring to a boil; reduce heat. Cover and simmer for 10 to 12 minutes, or until vegetables are done. Stir occasionally.
4. Taste sauce and correct seasoning, if necessary, with salt and pepper. If sauce is too thick, add a small amount of water.

Meatball Stroganoff with Mushroom Soup
(4 servings)

Frozen cooked meatballs for 4 servings
2   tablespoons cooking fat
½ cup chopped onion, fresh or frozen
1   can (10½ ounces) condensed cream of mushroom soup
¼ cup dry sherry wine
1   can (4 ounces) sliced mushrooms, drained
½ teaspoon caraway seeds(optional)
½ cup, or more, dairy sour cream
Salt and pepper
Cooked buttered noodles

1. In a large skillet, cook onion in fat until soft but not browned; stir occasionally.
2. Add soup, sherry, mushrooms, and caraway seeds; mix well. Add meatballs.
3. Bring to a boil; reduce heat. Cover and simmer for 15 minutes, stirring occasionally.
4. Remove pan from heat and blend in sour cream. Taste sauce and correct seasoning, if necessary, with salt and pepper.
5. Heat, but do not allow sauce to boil or it may curdle. (Note: The flavor of the sauce is not affected should it curdle.)
6. Serve over hot buttered noodles.

How to Prepare and Freeze Individual Meat Loaves

I sometimes use the meatball recipe on page 243 to make individual meat loaves. The ingredients are the same, and so is the procedure for cooking and freezing, except that the meat mixture is shaped into little loaves—each about twice the size of a single meatball. Two of these make an "average" serving.

The loaves may be browned in a skillet or on a tray in the oven. Try them in some of the recipes calling for frozen cooked pot roast pieces, beginning page 140.

Braised Meat Loaf with Creole Sauce
(6 servings)

1½ pounds ground beef
¼ cup minced onion
½ cup dry bread crumbs
1 teaspoon salt
¼ teaspoon black pepper
1 egg
1 can (10¾ ounces) condensed tomato soup
Dry bread crumbs (to coat meat)
3 slices bacon
½ cup chopped onion, fresh or frozen
¼ cup chopped green pepper
¼ cup chopped celery
½ soup can water
Salt and pepper

1. In a large bowl, combine ground beef, minced onion, bread crumbs, and salt and pepper. Push mixture to one side.
2. Break egg into bowl and beat slightly. Add 2 tablespoons tomato soup to egg, and mix.
3. Combine meat and egg mixtures. Shape into two loaves for easier handling. Coat lightly with bread crumbs. This portion of recipe may be done ahead of time. Cover and refrigerate.
4. In a Dutch oven, or large pan, cook bacon until crisp.

Remove and set aside. Brown meat loaves on all sides and remove from pan. Pour off all but 2 tablespoons of drippings.

5. Add onion, green pepper, celery, remaining tomato soup, and water. Crumble bacon and add to sauce.

6. Return meat loaves to pan. Cover tightly and simmer for 45 minutes. Stir occasionally, spooning sauce over meat. Taste sauce and correct seasoning, if necessary, with salt and pepper.

7. If sauce is too thin, remove cover during the last 5 minutes of cooking.

Braised Individual Meat Loaves
(4 to 6 servings)

1½ pounds ground beef

¼ cup minced onion

2 tablespoons chopped parsley

½ cup dry bread crumbs

1 teaspoon salt

⅛ teaspoon black pepper

1 egg

¼ cup catsup

Dry bread crumbs (to coat meat loaves)

2 tablespoons cooking fat

½ cup chopped onion, fresh or frozen

1 can (15 ounces) tomato sauce

1 can water

2 tablespoons dry sherry wine

8 small carrots, scraped and cut in 1-inch pieces

1 large potato, pared and cut in 1-inch cubes

½ pound fresh green beans (remove tips and cut in
　　1-inch pieces) or 1 package (10 ounces) frozen green beans

Salt and pepper

1. In a large bowl, combine ground beef, minced onion, parsley, bread crumbs, and salt and pepper. Push mixture to one side.
2. Break egg into bowl and beat slightly. Add catsup to egg, and mix.
3. Combine meat and egg mixtures. Shape into 4 or 6 loaves, about 1¼-inch thick. Coat loaves lightly with dry bread crumbs. This portion of recipe may be done ahead of time. Cover and refrigerate.
4. In a Dutch oven, or large skillet, brown loaves in fat. Remove from pan and pour off fat drippings.
5. Cook onion in drippings remaining in pan until soft but not browned; stir often. Add tomato sauce, water, and sherry. Return loaves to pan.
6. Bring to a boil; reduce heat. Cover and simmer for 10 minutes.
7. Add vegetables, season with salt and pepper. Simmer 25 to 30 minutes, or until meat and vegetables are done.
8. Taste sauce, correct seasoning, and thicken with flour, if necessary.

Note: If frozen green beans are used, add during the last 15 minutes of cooking.

7

Budget Beef
in the Great Outdoors:

How to Barbecue the Thrift Cuts

Everyone loves a barbecue. It's easy. It's fun. And there's something about cooking and dining alfresco that heightens the taste of even the humblest food. So, though we might prefer to regale our guests with gorgeous fork-tender steaks, we know that even the lowly frankfurter is somehow magically transformed by outdoor cooking, and it can be served with impunity.

I enjoy the steaks *and* the frankfurters. But I've also found a wonderful alternative to both: some of those less tender budget cuts of beef—the ones we've been discussing all through this book—make absolutely marvelous barbecue fare. Blade and arm steaks from the chuck, top round steak, flank steak, and short ribs—all can be done to sizzling, juicy perfection on an outdoor grill, with just a little help from a tenderizer or marinade (or both).

A marinade, remember, tenderizes and adds flavor. Meat to be barbecued should be marinated at least overnight, and preferably for 24 to 48 hours. (The longer the marinating time the more tender the results.) For more about marinades, see page 38.

Some commercial tenderizers add a bit of flavor, though not as much as a marinade. All reduce the necessary cooking time by about one-fourth, so be guided accordingly.

Note: A cut 1½ inches or more in thickness naturally requires more cooking than a thinner cut. If you want to reduce the cooking time of a thick cut, slice it into several smaller pieces. (This also results in more servings with browned surfaces.)

Barbecued Beef with Savory Sauce
(6 to 8 servings)

3- to 4-pound beef chuck blade roast, boneless
Unseasoned meat tenderizer
1¼ cups catsup
2   tablespoons Worcestershire sauce
2   tablespoons wine vinegar
1   tablespoon prepared mustard
2   tablespoons brown sugar
1   package onion soup mix, less 3 tablespoons*
¼   cup flour

1. Remove meat from refrigerator and allow to stand at room temperature not more than one hour.
2. Use tenderizer, following manufacturer's directions. Do not add salt. Allow meat to stand 30 minutes.
3. Meanwhile combine remaining ingredients in a bowl.
4. Brown meat slowly on grill of barbecue unit (or on top of kitchen range).
5. Tear off a 5-foot length of 18-inch heavy duty foil; fold over to double.
6. Spoon half of sauce onto center of foil. Place meat on

* Pour contents of package on a sheet of wax paper and mix thoroughly. Remove 3 tablespoons for Onion Soup Mix Bread (recipe on page 173).

top and spoon remaining sauce on meat. Fold foil over meat and seal securely, using freezer wrap.

7. Cut a double thickness of extra foil to place under meat on grill. Cook slowly 1½ to 2 hours, or until done. Do not turn meat.

Barbecued Beef Arm Roast

(6 to 8 servings)

3- to 4-pound beef chuck blade roast, boneless
Unseasoned meat tenderizer

Marinade:

⅓ **cup salad oil**
2 **tablespoons lemon juice**
½ **cup burgundy, or dry red wine**
¼ **teaspoon garlic powder**
½ **teaspoon basil**
½ **teaspoon oregano**
½ **teaspoon dry mustard**

1. Remove meat from refrigerator and allow to warm to room temperature not more than 1 hour.
2. Tenderize meat, following manufacturer's directions. Do not add salt. Allow meat to stand 30 minutes.
3. Meanwhile combine marinade ingredients in a small bowl and let stand for 30 minutes to blend flavors. Stir several times.
4. Pour half of marinade into a shallow glass baking dish. Place meat on top of marinade and pour remainder of marinade over meat. Cover dish with foil.
5. Marinate meat in refrigerator for 24 hours, turning occasionally.
6. Drain meat; sear both sides, then grill over slow coals about 25 minutes on each side, or to desired doneness, basting with reserve marinade.
7. Slice meat diagonally, across the grain.

Beef Chuck Steak in Beer Marinade
(4 to 5 servings)

1 beef chuck blade steak, cut ³⁄₄ inch thick and weighing about
2¹⁄₂ pounds
Unseasoned meat tenderizer

Marinade:

¹⁄₃ **cup salad oil**
2   **tablespoons honey**
1   **cup beer**
1   **teaspoon oregano**
¹⁄₂ **teaspoon paprika**
1   **teaspoon onion powder**
¹⁄₄ **teaspoon garlic powder**

1. Remove meat from refrigerator and allow to warm to room temperature not more than 1 hour.
2. Tenderize meat, following manufacturer's directions. Do not add salt. Allow meat to stand 30 minutes.
3. Meanwhile combine marinade ingredients in a small bowl and let stand for 30 minutes to blend flavors. Stir several times.
4. Pour half of marinade into a shallow glass baking dish. Place meat on top of marinade and pour remainder of marinade over meat. Cover dish with foil.
5. Marinate meat in refrigerator for 24 hours, turning occasionally.
6. Drain steak and broil at moderate temperature to desired doneness, basting with reserve marinade.

Family Barbecued Steak
(4 to 5 servings)

1 beef chuck blade steak, cut ¾ inch thick and weighing about
  2½ pounds
Unseasoned meat tenderizer

Marinade:

¼ **cup salad oil**

2 **tablespoons honey**

⅓ **cup wine vinegar**

¼ **cup dry sherry wine**

1 **teaspoon onion powder**

¼ **teaspoon garlic powder**

¼ **teaspoon rosemary**

¼ **teaspoon oregano**

¼ **teaspoon dried dill weed**

½ **teaspoon paprika**

1. Remove meat from refrigerator and allow to warm to room temperature not more than 1 hour.
2. Tenderize meat, following manufacturer's directions. Do not add salt. Allow meat to stand 30 minutes.
3. Meanwhile combine marinade ingredients in a small bowl and let stand for 30 minutes to blend flavors. Stir several times.
4. Pour half of marinade into a shallow glass baking dish. Place meat on top of marinade and pour remainder of marinade over meat. Cover dish with foil.
5. Marinate meat in refrigerator for 24 hours, turning occasionally.
6. Drain steak and broil at moderate temperature to desired doneness, basting with reserve marinade.

Barbecued Flank Steak
(4 to 5 servings)

1 beef flank steak (1½ to 1¾ pounds)
Unseasoned meat tenderizer

Marinade:

¼ **cup salad oil**
2   **tablespoons lemon juice**
½ **cup burgundy, or dry red wine**
1   **teaspoon onion powder**
¼ **teaspoon garlic powder**
¼ **teaspoon dry mustard**
6 to 8 **peppercorns**
1   **small bay leaf**

1. Remove meat from refrigerator and allow to warm to room temperature not more than 1 hour.
2. Tenderize meat, following manufacturer's directions. Do not add salt. Allow meat to stand 30 minutes.
3. Meanwhile combine marinade ingredients in a small bowl and let stand for 30 minutes to blend flavors. Stir several times.
4. Pour half of marinade into a shallow glass baking dish. Place meat on top of marinade and pour remainder of marinade over meat. Cover dish with foil.
5. Marinate meat in refrigerator for 24 hours, turning occasionally.
6. Drain steak and broil at moderate temperature to desired doneness, basting with reserve marinade.
7. To serve, carve thin diagonal slices across the grain.

Barbecued Short Ribs, Hawaiian Style
(4 to 5 servings)

4 pounds beef rib short ribs
Unseasoned meat tenderizer

Marinade:

2 tablespoons salad oil
3 tablespoons honey
1 can (20 ounces) sliced pineapple, drained
Pineapple juice (about 3/4 cup)
1 tablespoon brown sugar
1/4 cup soy sauce
1/4 cup dry sherry wine
1 teaspoon powdered ginger
1/4 teaspoon garlic powder

1. Remove meat from refrigerator and allow to warm to room temperature not more than 1 hour.
2. Tenderize meat, following manufacturer's directions. Do not add salt. Allow meat to stand 30 minutes.
3. Meanwhile combine marinade ingredients in a small bowl and let stand for 30 minutes to blend flavors. Stir several times.
4. Pour half of marinade into a shallow glass baking dish. Place meat on top of marinade and pour remainder of marinade over meat. Cover dish with foil.
5. Marinate meat in refrigerator for 24 hours, turning occasionally.
6. Drain ribs and broil at moderate temperature to desired doneness, basting with reserve marinade.
7. Serve ribs with pineapple spices dipped in marinade and lightly broiled.

8

Freezer Facts and Just About Everything Else

How to Freeze Meat, Prepare Freezer Wrap, Prepare Cooked Food, Reheat Frozen Food, and Prepare Sandwiches for Freezing

I really cannot emphasize too much the importance of proper storage techniques, especially where meat is concerned. Meat is perishable, more so than many of us suspect. And if we're going to pay good money for it, we certainly ought to do everything we can to maintain flavor and quality during the time it takes to get it from market to table. Otherwise, even the thriftiest buy is no buy at all.

Here are some important pointers on the care and storage of meat:

REFRIGERATE MEAT IMMEDIATELY UPON RETURNING HOME FROM THE MARKET.

Prepackaged meat (from the supermarket) may be refrigerated in its original packaging.

Meat wrapped in butcher paper should be rewrapped, loosely, in wax paper or aluminum foil before being refrigerated. (Butcher paper absorbs juice and tends to stick to the meat.)

Cured and smoked meats, sausages, frankfurters, etc.,

should also be stored in the refrigerator, unless the label indicates otherwise. Leave them in the original packaging until ready to use.

Canned hams, picnics, and other perishable canned meats should be stored, unopened, in the refrigerator unless otherwise indicated on the label. *Do not freeze canned meats.*

FREEZE ANY MEAT YOU DO NOT PLAN TO SERVE WITHIN TWO OR THREE DAYS OF PURCHASE. The two important exceptions to this rule are ground meat and meat cubes, and variety meats. Both are more perishable than, say, the large chunky cuts.

Ground meat and meat cubes should be served within *two* days of purchase—or, frozen on the day of purchase.

Variety meats should either be cooked or frozen on the day of purchase.

MEAT PURCHASED FROZEN SHOULD GO DIRECTLY INTO THE FREEZER—unless, of course, it is to be defrosted for cooking.

THE ICE-CUBE SECTION OF A REFRIGERATOR IS NOT INTENDED FOR USE AS A FREEZER; it simply is not cold enough for a long-term storage. As a general rule, meat may be safely frozen and kept in the ice-cube compartment for no more than one week.

Only a freezer or the freezer section of a refrigerator (as opposed to the ice-cube compartment) is capable of maintaining temperatures of 0°F. or below, required for long-term storage of a week or more.

How to Freeze Meat

It's most important to freeze meat while it's fresh and in top condition; quality and flavor will be no better when it is removed from the freezer than when it was put in. Assuming freshness and good quality to begin with, most meat can be satisfactorily frozen if properly wrapped, frozen quickly, and kept at 0°F. or below.

Prepackaged meat may be frozen, in the original packaging, with an overwrap of freezer paper (sealed and marked with contents and date) for a period of from two to three weeks. But to maintain good flavor and quality, any meat that is to be stored for longer than three weeks should be removed from the retail packaging and properly rewrapped for freezing.

1. SELECT THE FREEZER WRAP

A good freezer wrap, tightly sealed, locks air out of the package and keeps moisture in. There are a number of excellent wraps on the market, and I think it's preferable to choose from among them than to try to devise one of your own.

Pliable wraps, such as aluminum freezer foils, transparent moisture-vapor-proof wraps, and certain types of plastic bags, are good for wrapping bulky, irregularly shaped cuts. Laminated freezer paper and various-sized plastic bags are suitable for some meat.

2. PREPARE THE MEAT

To conserve space within the freezer, trim off any excess fat and remove bones (unless to do so would give the meat a hacked-up appearance at serving time).

Do not use salt or seasoning. Though salt is commonly thought of as a preservative, it has the opposite effect in freezer storage: salted meat has a shorter freezer life than unsalted. As for other seasonings, since freezer storage tends to intensify their flavor, it's better to add them later, during cooking or thawing.

3. WRAP IN MEAL-SIZE AMOUNTS

Don't make the mistake of lumping two pounds of loose ground beef together in one package, for example, when one pound is what you ordinarily use for a meal. Whenever possible, estimate the amount you and your family get through at any one time, and wrap accordingly.

It's a good idea to place a double thickness of freezer wrap between chops, patties, or individual pieces of meat—they'll be that much easier to separate when it's time to cook or thaw them.

4. WRAP TIGHTLY AND PRESS OUT AS MUCH AIR AS POSSIBLE.

When air is able to penetrate the wrap, moisture is drawn from the food, and the result is what is commonly called "freezer burn"—visible dry patches on the surface.

The "freezer wrap," illustrated opposite, is the preferred method of wrapping for the freezer.

5. MARK THE CONTENTS AND DATE

I prefer using a felt-tip pen for this. The name of the cut and the date on which it was frozen are essential. You might want to indicate the weight, or the approximate number of servings, too.

I find it a big help to keep a kind of inventory of what's inside the freezer; it's a simple matter of noting on a sheet of paper the date and contents of each package as it goes into the freezer. (Small magnets are used to hold the paper to the outside of the freezer door.)

6. FREEZE IMMEDIATELY AT 0°F., OR LOWER, IF POSSIBLE

When packages first go into the freezer, arrange them so that there is at least a small amount of space between them. This facilitates quick initial freezing.

In order to maintain an unfluctuating low temperature, try to avoid introducing very large amounts of meat—or anything else—at one time.

TIME LIMITS

Too-long freezer storage does affect flavor. And though one could store large cuts of beef for up to a year at 0°F., I can't imagine why anyone would want to do so (unless, of course, it was a matter of working through a whole side of beef).

How to Prepare the Freezer Wrap
(commonly called the drug-store wrap)

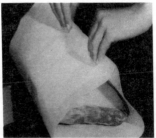

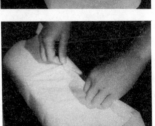

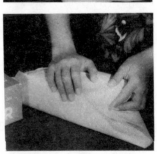

1. Use enough paper so that the edges, held together above the food, can be folded down (1 inch per fold) at least three times.

2. Place food in the center of the paper. (Separate individual servings—such as steaks, chops, or patties—with sheets of freezer paper so they will come apart easily.)

3. Bring the two edges together above the food and fold down in 1 inch locked folds until the paper is drawn tight against the food.

4. Press to force out air.

5. Hold remaining edges close to the food and fold into triangles.

6. Bring the triangles under the package, away from the top fold. Seal with freezer tape and mark each package to show contents, number of servings, and date of freezing.

Note: When aluminum foil is used as a freezer wrap, the procedure is basically the same as for above. Steps #5 and 6 are omitted, however, and instead the ends are simply folded over and over to form a locked seam, then pressed tightly up against the food.

It is not necessary to use freezer tape with aluminum foil.

263

The recommended maximum storage period for ground beef is 4 months, though I think it makes sense to try to use it up within 3 months. Recommended maximum storage for other fresh beef is between 6 and 12 months, though again I would try to use it up faster—say, within 6 months.

Freezing of cured meats, such as ham and bacon, is usually discouraged. However, bacon can be frozen and stored for up to 1 month, and whole hams for up to 2 months.

Frankfurters should be frozen for no more than 1 month.

Cold cuts should not be frozen, as freezing has an adverse affect on their flavor and texture.

REFREEZING DEFROSTED MEAT IS NOT RECOMMENDED

If *partially* thawed meat still contains ice crystals, it may be safely refrozen. (Do rewrap if the package has been opened.) Remember, though, that refreezing does result in some drip loss.

When completely thawed, meat should be cooked within 24 to 36 hours.

How to Cook Frozen Meat

Depending on how it is to be used, frozen meat may be thawed either prior to or during cooking.

TO THAW BEFORE COOKING

It is best to thaw meat in the main section of your refrigerator, still in the original freezer wrap. Approximate refrigerator thawing times are as follows:

LARGE ROASTS	4 to 7 hours per pound
SMALL ROASTS	3 to 5 hours per pound
1-INCH STEAKS	12 to 14 hours

TO COOK MEAT IN THE FROZEN STATE

ROASTING: Allow one-third to one-half more cooking time. In other words, if 3 hours' roasting time is required for unfrozen meat, test for doneness after 4 hours.

Use the same method for roasting frozen cuts as for fresh or thawed meat: Place meat on a rack in a 300°F. or 325°F. oven. Do not cover pan. Do not add water. And do not baste during cooking. When the meat has been in the oven for approximately half the estimated cooking time, insert a meat thermometer. (Do not try to force the thermometer into the meat—it may not yet be completely thawed.)

BROILING: Place meat to be broiled at least 4 inches below the source of heat so that it will be cooked to the desired degree of doneness without becoming too brown on the outside.

Thin frozen steaks require very little more broiling time than thawed or fresh.

Any meat to be coated with egg and crumbs should be partially defrosted so that the coating will adhere to the meat.

PANBROILING: Use a hot skillet to which a scant tablespoon of cooking fat has been added. (With a *hot* skillet the meat has a chance to brown before it thaws.) When the meat is browned, reduce heat and continue cooking. Turn the meat occasionally to prevent overbrowning.

BRAISING: If meat is to be floured before browning, thaw slightly. Then dredge with flour. When flouring is not desired, thawing is unnecessary. In either case, cooking time will be approximately the same as for fresh or thawed meat.

How to Store Cooked Food

Whether it's to be stored in the refrigerator or prepared for the freezer, special care should be taken with cooked food.

Because bacteria thrive in temperatures between 40°F. and 120°F., freshly cooked food, especially broth, soup, sauces, and gravies, spoil rapidly when allowed to cool slowly at room temperature (which, in a warm kitchen, is probably anywhere from 70°F. on up).

The possibility of spoilage is reduced if cooked food is cooled as quickly as possible. The best way to quick-cool is to place the container of food on top of a large container filled with ice cubes and a small amount of cold water.

The cooling process starts at the outer edges, while the center retains heat longest. If there is a large quantity of food to be cooled, it is advisable to divide it into several small portions and place each over ice. Occasional stirring further speeds the cooling process.

Food may be refrigerated when lukewarm to the touch. For *How to Prepare Cooked Food for the Freezer*, see below.

IMPORTANT: Before serving refrigerated or frozen broth, soup, sauce, or gravy, cook at a hard, rolling boil for 3 or 4 minutes.

How to Prepare Cooked Food for the Freezer

Cooking and freezing ahead—whether it be meat or soup or vegetables or anything else—can be the means to significant savings of time and money. But even so, it's hardly worth the bother if the end product isn't just as appetizing and appealing as it would be fresh from the store. Unfortunately, many times home-cooked frozen foods do lose something in the process because freezing is done in such a way that by the time food finally gets to the table it is soggy with overcooking.

Let me explain: When food is reheated from the frozen state, thawing starts from the outer edges and gradually works toward the center. Often, the center is still cold (if not frozen solid) by the time the outer edges are thawed. By the time the center has reached serving temperature, the outer edges are *overcooked*.

For various reasons, defrosting *before* heating is not the answer to this particular problem. To begin with, thawing in the refrigerator takes quite a long time—and one of the reasons for cooking and freezing ahead in the first place is to *save* time. On the other hand, allowing food to defrost at room temperature is not advisable because of the danger of rapidly multiplying bacteria.

But, if food is frozen in such a way that the time needed for reheating is minimal—say, 30 minutes or less—there will be little, if any, overcooking.

FOR THIS REASON, IT IS RECOMMENDED THAT THE THICKNESS, OR DEPTH, WITHIN THE CONTAINER OF ANY FOOD TO BE FROZEN BE NOT MORE THAN 2 INCHES. Often, this will mean freezing in two medium-size or small containers instead of one large one. I hope you will keep this in mind when freezing any cooked food—other than liquids, such as soups.

The following is a step-by-step guide for preparing just-cooked food for the freezer:

1. PREPARE THE FREEZER WRAP. I find it very convenient to freeze an entree, or whatever, in aluminum foil shaped to fit the pan or casserole in which it will be reheated for serving.

To do this, make a foil liner by cutting enough 18-inch heavy-duty aluminum foil to completely wrap up the container you plan to use for reheating. Allow enough additional foil to make a folded seal over the food.

Invert the container and mold the center of the foil over it.

2. MARK CONTENTS AND DATE. Do this while the foil is still shaped over the inverted container.

3. LINE THE CONTAINER. Remove foil from the inverted container; turn the container right side up; place molded foil *inside* the container.

4. ADD FOOD TO BE FROZEN, then cover immediately with a tight-fitting lid or foil shaped to fit. (Note: Frozen cooked food keeps better when covered with a gravy or sauce, which, in effect, seals out the air.)

5. QUICK-COOL WITH ICE CUBES. Because of the danger of rapidly multiplying bacteria, do not allow food to cool at room temperature. Instead, place the covered container of food over a large container (a 9-inch cake pan does very nicely) filled with ice cubes. Occasional stirring hastens the cooling process.

When cool to the touch, place covered container of food in the freezer or freezer section of the refrigerator.

6. REMOVE FROZEN FOIL-WRAPPED FOOD FROM CONTAINER. If this is difficult, turn the container upside down under warm tap water for just a few seconds; the food should then slip out easily. (Be sure to hold onto the food with one hand to keep it from falling out into the sink!)

7. COMPLETE THE FREEZER WRAP by bringing the two long ends of the foil together over the top and center of the food and folding down in 1-inch locked folds. Exclude as much air as possible, fold the ends over several times to make a locked seam, and press tightly to the food.

8. PROTECT FOIL-WRAPPED FOOD WITH A PLASTIC FREEZER BAG. This is important because the foil may be ripped as food is shifted around within the freezer—and even the smallest hole in the foil would expose the food to air and thus dry it out.

Squeeze air out of the bag, twist the top, and secure with a closure.

9. RETURN FROZEN FOOD TO FREEZER.

How to Freeze Cooked Leftover Vegetables

What do *you* do when confronted with a half-cup of leftover peas or carrots or cut corn or any cooked vegetable for that matter? Chances are you do what a lot of others do: stow them away in the refrigerator fully intending to use them the next day. Or the next. And chances are the vegetables end up in the garbage.

But why not freeze them instead? It's easy to do, and there are many, many uses for them. I often add them to stews and soups and to some of the pot roast recipes in this book. (I allow ½ cup or more per serving; they go into the pot, still frozen, during the last few minutes of cooking.)

To freeze leftover cooked vegetables:

1. PLACE COOLED COOKED VEGETABLES IN A PIE PLATE, or other flat container. Arrange so that there is a small amount of space between each piece.

2. COVER WITH ALUMINUM FOIL AND PLACE IN FREEZER.

3. WHEN FROZEN, TRANSFER THE VEGETABLES TO A LARGE, WIDE-MOUTH JAR (choose one with a tight-fitting lid). The jar is kept in the freezer, of course, and you may add more frozen vegetables whenever you like.

How to Reheat Frozen Cooked Food

1. DO NOT THAW FROZEN COOKED FOOD. It should go directly from freezer to skillet or saucepan to serving dish.

2. REMOVE THE FREEZER WRAP. If a foil wrap is difficult to remove, loosen it by holding the package upside down under warm tap water for a few seconds.

3. PLACE IN A SKILLET OR SAUCEPAN OVER LOW HEAT. As the food begins to thaw, heat may be slightly increased.

4. HEAT TO SERVING TEMPERATURE, STIRRING OCCASIONALLY.

Note: Constant stirring will restore the original consistency of gravies or sauces that separate during thawing and reheating.

How to Prepare Sandwiches for Freezing

Packing lunches is a chore hardly anyone enjoys, and I suspect it's not so much because of the work involved as it is the rather odd hours at which it ordinarily needs to be done: either late in the evening when we'd rather be relaxing, or—worse—during the early-morning rush.

One can rid oneself of at least some of the burden of everyday lunch making by freezing whole batches of sandwiches in advance. Wrapped in a double thickness of wax paper, sandwiches can be stored in the freezer for about a week; wrapped in aluminum foil or plastic wrap, they keep for up to three weeks.

In preparing sandwiches for the freezer, choose a time of day when you can work for an hour or so without interruption.

Decide how many sandwiches you're going to make (I usually do a week's worth at once), then lay out as many slices of bread as you'll need. If you're working with bread from an irregularly shaped loaf (like some rye, French, and Italian bread), pair slices according to size. Unless some particularly finicky member of the family insists, don't remove the crusts; they help hold the sandwich together.

Spread softened butter or margarine (or peanut butter or cream cheese) on each slice, covering it thinly but evenly all the way to the edges. The spread helps keep the bread moist and acts as a kind of barrier preventing salad dressing, mustard, barbecue sauce, etc., from soaking through when the sandwich is thawed. (Never use melted butter or margarine; it will make the bread soggy.)

If you like, the butter or margarine may be seasoned with just a *little* bit of chili sauce, mustard, horseradish, etc.

If you're using meat for the filling, several thin slices are preferable to a single thick slice. It tastes better and it's easier to eat.

Leftovers, of course, are naturals for sandwiches. Was beef pot roast on the dinner menu? Then cool the meat and use it for sandwiches. Do the same with roast pork, ham, corned beef, meat loaf, etc. And meatballs, thinly sliced, with a drizzle of sauce, make marvelous sandwiches, especially on crusty slices of French or Italian bread.

Whatever goes between the two slices of bread (and it should be a protein food, such as meat, chicken, tuna fish, cheese, or egg), do insure freshness by wrapping with care. One's primary concern in wrapping sandwiches, as in wrapping any food for the freezer, is to make an air-free, airtight package.

TO WRAP SANDWICHES IN WAX PAPER: Place sandwich in the center of a double thickness of wax paper. Bring the long edges together and fold over at least twice, or until the paper fits snugly. Turn the sandwich over, press out as much air as possible, then bring the remaining ends together and seal with a strip of freezer tape. Mark contents with a felt-tip pen.

TO WRAP SANDWICHES IN ALUMINUM FOIL: Regular foil (as opposed to heavy-duty or freezer foil) is fine for sandwiches. Place sandwich squarely in the center of the foil. Bring the long edges together and fold over at least twice, or until the foil fits snugly. Press out as much air as possible, fold remaining ends to make a locked seam, and press tightly to the sandwich. Freezer tape is unnecessary. Mark contents with a felt-tip pen.

TO WRAP SANDWICHES IN PLASTIC WRAP: Place sandwich in the center of the wrap. Mark contents on a slip of paper and place on top of the sandwich. Bring one long end of the wrap up over the sandwich and overlap with the other end. Press out as much air as possible, then bring remaining ends under the sandwich, pressing gently to make them adhere. Freezer tape is unnecessary.

TO FREEZE: Make sure sandwiches are not in direct contact with freezer shelf or wall. Otherwise, ice crystals will form, causing the bread to become soggy when thawed.

A good idea is to arrange sandwiches in a shoe box with

lid. (The lid provides further protection from air.) Another possibility is to freeze the sandwich in its own paper lunch bag. (When I do this, I sometimes include a napkin and a frozen dessert.)

Frozen sandwiches should go directly from freezer to lunch box. They'll thaw within the box. (Thawing takes approximately 3 to 3½ hours, so by the time lunchtime rolls around, they're ready to eat.) It is important, though, that the sandwiches be eaten as soon as possible after thawing—especially during the hot summer months when there is danger of rapid spoilage.

You'll find, incidentally, that putting a frozen sandwich in a lunchbox is like equipping it with its own little built-in refrigerator; it will help keep frozen desserts cool and fresh fruits and vegetables deliciously crisp. (A foil liner inside the lunch box will keep the contents cooler even longer.)

Keep in mind that lunch should be a *meal*—and that the contents of a lunch box should supply about one-third of the day's nutritional requirements. So, in addition to a sandwich, do include a fruit, a vegetable (try carrot and celery sticks wrapped in a lettuce leaf), milk, and a dessert, plus, perhaps, an extra little snack surprise (pepperoni sticks and beef jerky are favorites at our house).

A BIT ABOUT BREADS

I like to use a variety of breads for sandwiches: whole wheat, rye, pumpernickel, oatmeal, raisin, cinnamon, French, Italian, and quick breads, in addition to enriched white. Hamburger buns and frankfurter rolls are nice for a change. So are hard rolls—slice these lengthwise and scoop out most of the doughy insides (save this to make crumbs for meat loaf, meatballs, etc.).

Most bread stays fresh for two or three days if the original wrapper is intact. When opened, it will remain fresh for several more days if stored in a dry, well-ventilated bread box or drawer, and for up to a week in the refrigerator. (It might be a good idea, especially if your family is quite small, to store most of a loaf in a plastic bag in the refrigerator and the remainder—for immediate use—in its original wrapper in the bread box or drawer.)

And did you know that it is easier to spread firm butter or margarine on bread that has been refrigerated for an hour or so?

FREEZER STORAGE TIPS FOR BREAD

Bread may be stored in its original wrapper in the freezer for about a week (possibly two).

For long-term storage, place the loaf, still in its original wrapper, in a plastic bag, exclude as much air as possible, twist the bag top, and secure with a closure.

Frozen bread may be thawed, made into sandwiches, and returned to the freezer, provided it has not been left at room temperature for more than a few hours.

Brief Descriptions

Capsule of Main Ingredients Needed

To save you from hunting, maybe fruitlessly, through every word of the more than 200 recipes offered in this book, here is an easy way to decide on the type of meal you want to serve and the main ingredients you'll require for it. The recipes are arranged chronologically here and grouped under the relevant chapter in which they occur. This may be your short cut to sanity on one of those days when *everything* happens at once!

Recipes from Chapter 3— 37 Hearty Meals Made with the Chunky Cuts

1. *Savory Pot Roast*
   Chopped onion, condensed bouillon soup, catsup.
2. *Zesty Pot Roast*
   Chopped onion, condensed tomato soup, vinegar, canned applesauce.
3. *Beef Pot Roast with Mushroom Soup–Wine Gravy*
   Chopped onion, condensed cream of mushroom soup, burgundy wine, chopped parsley, garlic powder.
4. *Pot Roast with Tomatoes and Corn*
   Thinly sliced onion, canned tomatoes, paprika, kernel corn.

5. *Pot Roast, Italian Style*

   Chopped onion, chopped carrots, chopped celery, tomato paste, tomato sauce, red wine, beef bouillon cubes, basil, oregano. Serve with spaghetti and grated Parmesan cheese.

6. *Pot Roast in Barbecue Sauce*

   Ingredients for the barbecue sauce include catsup, chopped onion, Worcestershire sauce, vinegar, prepared mustard, and brown sugar.

7. *Hawaiian Pot Roast*

   Soy sauce, pineapple tidbits and juice, ginger, thinly sliced onion, cut celery, canned mushroom slices; gravy thickened with cornstarch.

8. *Pot Roast with Dill Gravy*

   Onions and dill seed flavor the basic cooking liquid, with gravy made by thickening meat stock with flour and blending in dairy sour cream.

9. *Bavarian Pot Roast*

   Ginger, apple juice, tomato sauce, cinnamon, vinegar, bay leaf.

10. *Pot Roast, Oriental Style*

    Chopped onion, green pepper, soy sauce, sherry wine, fresh or ground ginger, canned sliced mushrooms; gravy thickened with cornstarch. Serve over hot rice.

11. *Pot Roast Teriyaki*

    Curry powder, honey, soy sauce, sherry wine, ginger; gravy thickened with corn starch. Serve over hot rice.

12. *Pot Roast, Mexican Style*

    Thinly sliced onion, paprika, tomato sauce, catsup, brown sugar, chili powder, vinegar, Worcestershire sauce, canned baby lima beans or kernel corn.

13. *Sloppy Joe Pot Roast*

    Tomato sauce, Sloppy Joe seasoning mix, potatoes, carrots, zucchini.

14. *Pot Roast with Onion Soup Mix and Vegetables*

    Onion soup mix, carrots, celery.

15. *Pot Roast with Beef Stew Seasoning Mix*
    Thinly sliced onion, tomato sauce, sherry wine, beef stew seasoning mix.
16. *Individual Pot Roasts with Bouillon Noodles*
    Thinly sliced onion, tomato juice, Worcestershire sauce; noodles cooked in diluted canned beef bouillon.
17. *Pot Roast with Tomato Red Wine Sauce*
    Chopped onion, tomato sauce, red wine, bay leaf, garlic powder.
18. *Beef Pot Roast, Danish Style*
    Meat marinated in a mixture of chopped onion, water, red wine vinegar, ginger, whole cloves, bay leaf. Strained marinade with bouillon cubes becomes the liquid in which meat is cooked. Gravy is thickened with a mixture of flour and brown sugar. One-half cup of dairy sour cream is added to the gravy.
19. *Pot Roast Stroganoff*
    Chopped onion, beef bouillon cube, catsup, sherry wine, Worcestershire sauce, caraway seeds, canned sliced mushrooms. Gravy is thickened and dairy sour cream added. Served over hot noodles.
20. *Hungarian Pot Roast with Noodles*
    Chopped onion, tomato juice, paprika, dairy sour cream. Served over hot noodles.
21. *Pot Roast with Enchilada Sauce Mix*
    Thinly sliced onion, chopped green pepper, tomato sauce, enchilada sauce mix.
22. *Beef Pot Roast, French Style*
    Chopped onion, tomato sauce, red wine, garlic powder, bay leaf, bouquet garni or mixed herbs.
23. *Fruited Pot Roast*
    Chopped onion, finely chopped carrots and celery, garlic powder, red wine, mixed dried fruit.
24. *Pot Roast in Savory Cheese Sauce*
    Sliced onion, condensed Cheddar cheese soup, tomato sauce, canned sliced mushrooms, oregano, basil.

25. *Barbecued Chili Pot Roast*

   Chopped onion, tomato sauce, green pepper, paprika, brown sugar, chili powder, prepared mustard, vinegar, Worcestershire sauce.

26. *Chili Bean Pot Roast*

   Chopped onion, tomato sauce, chili powder, red kidney beans.

27. *Pot Roast in Savory Wine Gravy*

   Onion soup mix, potatoes, carrots, red wine, thyme, bay leaf.

28. *Pot Roast with Horseradish Sauce*

   Chopped onion, tomato juice, prepared horseradish, sherry wine.

29. *Pot Roast, Spanish Style*

   Mix salt, pepper, marjoram, cinnamon, ground cloves, minced parsley, garlic powder in olive oil; spread on meat and let stand for 1 hour. After browning meat, the liquid consists of onion, green pepper, tomato sauce with tomato bits, red wine, and orange juice. Sauce is thickened with cornstarch-water mixture.

30. *Supreme Pot Roast*

   Chopped onion, condensed golden mushroom soup, sherry wine, carrots, potatoes.

31. *Oven Pot Roast, Bag Style*

   Browning of meat not necessary. Meat and ingredients placed in a special plastic bag, with tomato sauce, chopped onion, green pepper, and taco seasoning mix, and bake in a 350°F. oven for 2 hours.

32. *My Favorite Pot Roast*

   Condensed tomato soup, chili sauce, sherry wine, onion soup mix, potatoes, carrots.

33. *Pot Roast with Beef Mushroom Mix*

   Chopped onion, condensed tomato soup, beef flavor mushroom mix, sherry wine, garlic powder, oregano.

34. *Pot Roast in Wine Marinade Sauce*

   Red wine marinade includes an herb bouquet (bay

leaves, peppercorns, cloves, thyme), wine vinegar, oil, garlic powder, and thinly sliced onion and carrots. After marinating, meat is cooked in a sauce of the marinade, bacon, chopped fresh tomatoes, beef bouillon cubes.

35. *Spicy Pot Roast*

Base of tomato juice seasoned with garlic powder, ground cloves, mace, allspice, lemon juice, and bay leaves.

36. *Pot Roast, Flemish Style*

One cup beer, red wine vinegar, dark brown sugar, thinly sliced onion, minced garlic, thyme, bay leaf, beef bouillon cubes, potatoes, carrots.

37. *Pot Roast with Spicy Wine Sauce*

Dijon-style mustard, together with garlic powder, catsup, red wine, Worcestershire sauce—all add up to a spicy taste in the sauce; served over hot noodles.

Recipes from Chapter 4—
19 Tasty Recipes Calling for Thrift Steaks and Other Nonchunky Cuts

1. *Braised Short Ribs and Gravy*

A good standby recipe when short ribs are a special buy at the market. Be sure to try sherry wine in the gravy.

2. *Short Ribs with Garbanzos*

An all-in-one-dish—meat and vegetables. Chopped onion, green pepper, celery, condensed tomato soup, Worcestershire sauce, prepared mustard, paprika and garbanzos. Double the recipe: serve one portion for immediate meal and freeze the other. Don't freeze the garbanzos, though—add them when reheating the frozen meal.

3. *Short Ribs with Stewed Tomatoes*

    Chopped onion, green pepper, canned stewed toma-
    toes, and chili powder. Served over hot fluffy rice, or
    noodles.

4. *Barbecued Short Ribs*

    A tasty barbecue sauce—and so handy to have a
    frozen meal like this, especially after a round of golf
    or weeding the garden.

5. *Swiss Steak with Brown Gravy*

    A basic recipe for quantity cooking of beef round
    steak when it is a market special. Double or triple
    the recipe and serve your family a variety of 30-minute
    meals using this cut of meat: Swiss Steak with Veg-
    etable Soups, Swiss Steak in Tomato Sauce, Swiss
    Pepper Steak, Swiss Steak Chili (recipes on pages
    232 to 235).

6. *Barbecued Beef Round Steak*

    Having frozen meals on hand adds to a homemaker's
    repertoire; constant variety of meals and her family
    will not have occassion to say, "What, again!" A
    quick-and-easy-to-make-barbecue sauce.

7. *Round Steak in Chili Wine Sauce*

    A very tasty sauce made so by the use of red wine;
    add green pepper, tomato sauce with tomato bits, and
    the right amount of chili powder to suit your taste.

8. *Round Steak in Creole Sauce*

    Sauce ingredients: condensed tomato soup, Wor-
    cestershire sauce, garlic powder, chopped green
    peppers, thinly sliced celery.

9. *Braised Individual Round Steaks*

    Place carrot and pepper strips in the center of a piece
    of round steak; roll and fasten with wooden picks,
    skewers, or tie with string.

10. *Brisket of Beef, Pot Roast Style*

    Fresh brisket of beef takes on a different cooking
    method—braising, rather than cooking in liquid. Pap-

rika adds flavor to the sauce; carrots and potatoes round out this dish.

11. *Brisket of Beef Stew*

A delicious, unusual, tasty stew is the result of using this cut of meat. Ingredients include chopped onion, beef stew seasoning mix, potatoes, carrots, and peas.

12. *Corned Beef Dinner*

A good standby dinner with a bonus for leftovers—make sandwiches for the lunchbox and freeze. (See instructions on *How to Prepare Sandwiches for Freezing*, page 270.)

13. *Marinated Flank Steak*

This marinade will be a big hit, whether broiling indoors or outdoors.

14. *Braised Stuffed Flank Steak*

Lots of flavor in this dish: poultry seasoning in the stuffing; tomato sauce with tomato bits, green pepper, celery, and sliced mushrooms in the sauce.

15. *Flank Steak in Wine Sauce*

Thinly sliced onion, tomato sauce, red wine, garlic powder, parsley, oregano, basil, sliced mushrooms. Served over cooked noodles.

16. *Flank Steak with Savory Sauce*

An unusual taste—meat cooked in French dressing (not the creamy type), then topped with bleu cheese. Gravy is delicious and a very different flavor. Worth the try.

17. *Marinated Beef Stew*

A good recipe to keep in mind when a bottle of burgundy or a dry red wine has been opened and 1 cup of its content left over from a dinner party. The marinade calls for thinly sliced onion, thyme, garlic powder, chopped parsley, and bay leaf.

18. *Easy Pot Roast Casserole*

No browning of meat—an all-in-one casserole. Ingredients include sliced onion, condensed consommé, red wine, marjoram, thyme, garlic powder, carrots, potatoes. Takes a slow oven and a long time.

19. *Beef Shanks in Tomato Sauce*

Serve this inexpensive cut one night and steak the next, but do dress up the beef shanks with sherry wine in the tomato-juice sauce, and add a touch of basil; potatoes go well with the sauce.

Recipes from Chapter 5—
102 Quick-and-Easy Recipes Using
Frozen Cooked Pot Roast Pieces

1. *Barbecue Pot Roast and French Fries*

Add frozen French fries to barbecue sauce—one less pot to wash. The sauce permeates the meat and potatoes, and shoestring potatoes cook faster.

2. *Budget Pot Roast Bean Soup*

A happy balance of protein and vegetables— chopped onion and celery, pork and beans, canned stewed tomatoes, beef bouillon cubes, Worcestershire sauce.

3. *Creole Pot Roast*

Chopped onion, green pepper, and celery, plus condensed tomato-rice soup make this an easy dish to prepare. Leftover vegetables can be used to extend the quantity.

4. *Deviled Pot Roast*

Recipe calls for 1 tablespoon dry mustard, tomato sauce, tomato juice, sherry wine, brown sugar, Worcestershire sauce, thinly sliced carrots. Served over green noodles.

5. *Hearty Pot Roast Vegetable Soup*

Dry onion soup mix (½ package), canned stewed tomatoes, and tomato sauce make up the basic part of this recipe. Cook frozen mixed vegetables in the liquid—no extra pan to wash. Or use canned vegetables; cooked rice or macaroni; leftover vegetables.

6. *Italian Pot Roast Stew*

   Tomato juice, tomato paste, sliced mushrooms, carrots, garbanzo beans, with a flavoring of basil and oregano.

7. *Pleasing Pot Roast Stew*

   Carrots, potatoes, zucchini, whole-kernel corn; in a tomato-juice sauce flavored with basil, paprika.

8. *Pot Roast with Baked Beans*

   Canned baked beans in tomato sauce, chili powder, catsup, and prepared mustard.

9. *Pot Roast with Barbecue Beans*

   Canned beans in barbecue sauce makes this a quick dish to prepare.

10. *Pot Roast in Barbecue Wine Sauce*

    Red wine in the barbecue sauce gives it a "different" flavor. The bay leaf enhances the flavor, but in a subtle way.

11. *Pot Roast Bean Paprikash*

    Make up a sauce of tomato paste, water, and beef bouillon cubes. Add 4 teaspoons paprika, kidney beans; flavor with bay leaf and garlic powder—then add sour cream. Serve over noodles.

12. *Pot Roast with Butter Beans in Tomato Sauce*

    A combination of flavors and texture—green pepper, sherry wine, condensed tomato soup, and canned butter beans (large limas).

13. *Pot Roast with Burgundy Sauce*

    Condensed golden mushroom soup and red wine. Served over buttered noodles.

14. *Pot Roast with Butter Beans*

    The sauce is flavored with prepared mustard, lemon juice, brown sugar, and tomato paste. Water is base for the liquid.

15. *Pot Roast Cacciatore*

    Sherry wine, basil, oregano, and bay leaf flavors the tomato sauce; sliced mushrooms are included in the recipe. Served with spaghettini.

16. *Pot Roast and Cabbage*

    Chopped onion, tomato juice, and sherry wine; add cooked chopped cabbage for a tasty combination.

17. *Pot Roast Cacciatore Stew*

    Hunter-style stew with canned stewed tomatoes, carrots; flavored with chili powder, oregano, and parsley. Add cooked seashell macaroni and grated Parmesan cheese.

18. *Pot Roast Casserole with Poppy Seed Biscuits*

    A casserole ready to serve in 30 minutes. Condensed tomato soup, sherry wine, canned green beans. Butter ready-to-bake refrigerator biscuits and sprinkle with poppy seeds; place on mixture. Bake 10 to 12 minutes in a 450°F. oven.

19. *Pot Roast Chili*

    Chili in a half hour. Break up chunks of canned tomatoes with a potato masher, or whirl in a blender for a few seconds.

20. *Pot Roast with Chili Limas*

    Thinly sliced carrots and celery, and baby lima beans (canned or frozen), cooked in a tomato-juice sauce flavored with chili powder and oregano.

21. *Pot Roast Chili with Mushroom Soup Sauce*

    A dramatic switch, using condensed cream of mushroom soup, especially when blended with a can of tomato sauce with tomato bits. The tomato bits in the sauce give it enough body to offset a smooth sauce. Chopped onion, celery, red kidney beans, and chili powder round out the ingredients.

22. *Pot Roast Chili with Red Wine–Herb Sauce*

    Chili powder, oregano, basil, red wine, and a subtle touch of garlic powder added to the canned tomatoes brings forth a most delightful flavor to the pot roast pieces and kidney beans.

23. *Pot Roast Chili Rice*

    Instant rice is cooked in a sauce made up of chopped onion and green pepper, tomato paste, and water; seasoned with garlic powder and chili powder.

24. *Pot Roast and Chinese Chop Suey Vegetables*

    Two cans of condensed golden mushroom soup, canned Chinese chop suey vegetables, flavored with soy sauce and served over hot rice, brings on a delightful reaction.

25. *Pot Roast Chop Suey*

    Canned chop suey vegetables, soy sauce, ginger, molasses, bouillon soup; thickened with cornstarch.

26. *Pot Roast Chuck Wagon Chowder*

    Chopped green pepper and celery, stewed tomatoes, canned chili beans. Additional chili powder optional.

27. *Pot Roast Circus Mulligan*

    Chopped onion, celery, and green pepper, plus cream-style corn all in tomato sauce.

28. *Pot Roast Company Fare*

    Combine condensed cream of celery soup with salad dressing for the sauce; add thin strips of green pepper and sliced mushrooms. Served over noodles.

29. *Pot Roast and Corn Chips*

    Canned tomato sauce, tomato paste, chopped onion, celery, and green pepper, chili powder. Served over corn chips and sprinkled with Cheddar cheese.

30. *Pot Roast with Corn Niblets and Corn Chips*

    Chopped onion, green pepper, condensed tomato soup, corn niblets; flavored with chili powder and served over corn chips.

31. *Pot Roast Country-Style Stew*

    Combining a can of tomato soup with a can of bean-with-bacon soup and adding a can of mixed vegetables (or leftover cooked vegetables) makes this a hearty stew in less than 30 minutes.

32. *Pot Roast Creamy Herbed Stew*
   Condensed cream of celery soup thinned with milk and blended with marjoram will delight many hungry husbands. Add fresh carrots sliced ¼ inch thick, potatoes cut in ½-inch cubes, and frozen peas. A beef bouillon cube brings out the flavor.

33. *Pot Roast Curry Sauce and Macaroni*
   Elbow macaroni mixed in a curry-flavored Cheddar cheese cream sauce.

34. *Pot Roast Curry with Fruit*
   Pineapple tidbits, apples, raisins, banana, beef bouillon, and curry powder. Surprising taste, approved by my husband.

35. *Pot Roast in Curry-Mushroom Sauce*
   Condensed cream of mushroom soup, sherry wine, sliced mushrooms, curry powder, and sour cream make up the sauce. Served over rice or fine noodles.

36. *Pot Roast in Curry-Sour Cream Sauce*
   Sauce consists of beef bouillon cubes dissolved in hot water, sherry wine, and Worcestershire sauce, and is thickened with a mixture of curry powder and flour. Recipe calls for 1 teaspoon of fresh grated ginger or ½ teaspoon ground ginger. Refer to instructions on *How to Freeze Fresh Ginger*, which follows this recipe.

37. *Pot Roast Goulash Supreme*
   Chopped onion, green pepper, and celery, sherry wine, condensed tomato and mushroom soups, frozen cut corn; flavored with garlic powder and paprika. Add thin spaghetti cut in 1-inch pieces.

38. *Pot Roast Goulash with Poppy Seed Noodles*
   Chopped onion, 1 tablespoon paprika, tomato sauce, canned stewed tomatoes; seasoned with garlic pow-

der, oregano, basil, thyme, marjoram, and served over buttered poppy seed noodles.

39. *Pot Roast with Garbanzo Bean Curry Sauce*
    Tomato soup sauce, curry powder, and garbanzo beans.

40. *Pot Roast with Green Pepper Sauce*
    Green peppers cut in ½-inch strips, tomato sauce, flavored with prepared mustard and Worcestershire sauce.

41. *Pot Roast Indienne*
    Thinly sliced carrots and celery, beef bouillon, and curry make this an appetizing dish.

42. *Pot Roast with Onion Soup Mix Sauce, Italiano Style*
    The sauce calls for onion soup mix and Italian herbs. Part of the onion soup mix is used as a spread for hot Italian bread (recipe follows). Serve meat and sauce over cooked spaghetti.

43. *Pot Roast with Canned Italienne Zucchini*
    Flavored canned zucchini in a tomato sauce with sherry wine.

44. *Pot Roast Jamboree*
    Chopped onion and green pepper, tomato sauce, canned whole-kernel corn, sliced ripe olives, flavored with oregano, garlic powder, and allspice. Add grated Cheddar cheese. Served over hot cooked noodles; or noodles may be mixed in with sauce.

45. *Pot Roast Jumble*
    Blending one can of condensed minestrone soup, one can of pork and beans, and an 8-ounce can of tomato sauce, and flavored with chopped celery, celery leaves, and basil, makes the task of preparing a quick dinner (after a day's work or shopping) a joy.

46. *Pot Roast with Kidney Beans and Red Wine*
    Chopped onion cooked in fat, 2 cans kidney beans and liquid, and ⅔ cup red wine—a real quickie, and so tasty.

47. *Pot Roast Kidney Bean Stew*

    Red kidney beans give this stew a different twist. Sliced celery and carrots in a diluted tomato sauce, flavored with bay leaf and a touch of thyme.

48. *Pot Roast with Lima Beans in Mustard Sauce*

    Frozen baby lima beans in a mustard sauce with brown sugar and sherry wine. Water is base for the liquid.

49. *Pot Roast Lima Bean Stew*

    Canned large limas (butter beans), carrots, and celery in tomato juice with a touch of bay leaf.

50. *Pot Roast Macaroni and Bean Dinner*

    Chopped onion and green pepper, condensed tomato soup, kidney beans; add catsup for flavor and cooked elbow macaroni for a complete dish. Lots of nourishment and protein.

51. *Pot Roast Minestrone Soup*

    Frozen mixed vegetables, celery and leaves, cabbage, tomato sauce, kidney beans, elbow macaroni, canned potatoes—all in one pot. Truly a hearty meal!

52. *Pot Roast in Mushroom Gravy*

    Canned mushroom gravy, sherry wine, thinly sliced carrots, cut green beans; served over cooked noodles.

53. *Pot Roast with Mushrooms and Herb Gravy*

    Canned sliced mushrooms, tomato sauce, catsup, sherry, oregano, applesauce, cut green beans.

54. *Pot Roast with Mushroom Soup Sauce and Green Peppers*

    Chopped onion, condensed cream of mushroom soup, sherry wine, sliced mushrooms, and thinly sliced green pepper. Serve over small seashell macaroni.

55. *Pot Roast with Noodles in Catsup Sauce*

    Chopped onion and celery; one bottle (14 ounces) catsup, flavored with Worcestershire sauce and garlic powder. Serve over hot noodles.

56. *Pot Roast Noodle Chili*

Canned stewed tomatoes, chili powder, tomato paste, and kidney beans; thin noodles added at end.

57. *Pot Roast Noodle Quickie*

Bring 4 cups tomato juice to boiling point; blend in sherry wine and 1 package onion soup mix. Reduce heat; add pot roast pieces. Simmer for about 10 minutes. Add cooked thin noodles; and simmer for about 3 minutes more. To serve, sprinkle with shredded Cheddar cheese.

58. *Pot Roast Noodle Soup*

Recipe calls for 2 packages beef noodle soup mix and sherry wine for flavor. Use canned, frozen, or leftover vegetables.

59. *Pot Roast Omar Khayyam*

Chopped onion, tomato juice, and sherry wine for the sauce; frozen peas or cut green beans cooked in the sauce. Canned or leftover vegetables may also be used.

60. *Pot Roast with Onion-Tomato Sauce*

The flavor derived from basil in this sauce of tomato soup, sherry wine, thinly sliced onion and sour cream, plus the colorful green noodles, make this dish a delight to be repeated often.

61. *Pot Roast Orientale*

A sweet-and-sour sauce with pineapple tidbits, mushrooms, soy sauce, thinly sliced onion, green pepper strips, and toasted sesame seeds. In a small saucepan, cook sesame seeds over medium heat until toasted, about 5 minutes—do not use oil, butter, or any fat to toast seeds.

62. *Pot Roast and Peas in Tomato Sauce*

The flavor of curry powder, paprika, and garlic powder in tomato sauce is a combination sure to make a hit. Add canned peas and liquid for a quick meal.

63. *Pot Roast in Pepper Tomato Sauce with Cheddar Noodles*

     Chopped onion, thin strips of green pepper, bouillon, canned tomatoes; flavored with soy sauce. Served over noodles mixed with Cheddar cheese.

64. *Pot Roast Pepper Steak, Chinese Style*

     Thinly sliced green pepper, sliced onion, fresh tomato, sherry wine, canned condensed consommé, soy sauce, fresh or ground ginger—thickened with cornstarch.

65. *Pot Roast Pork and Beans Chili*

     This combination is bound to be a favorite in many households. The ingredients are condensed tomato soup, chopped green pepper, chili powder, and canned pork and beans.

66. *Pot Roast Ratatouille*

     A derivative of the popular French vegetable dish. Eggplant, green pepper, zucchini, fresh or canned tomatoes. Garlic and basil for flavor.

67. *Pot Roast with Red Wine and Vegetables*

     The flavor of red wine in beef consommé is pleasant, and three vegetables—thinly sliced green pepper, celery, and carrots—makes this a hearty repast.

68. *Pot Roast with Ripe Olives in Tomato Sauce*

     A little on the exotic side; onion, sherry wine, beef bouillon, tomato paste, chili powder, and ripe olives. Serve over noodles.

69. *Pot Roast and Sausage in Green Pepper Sauce*

     Pot roast pieces and Italian sausage in a sauce of tomato juice, green peppers, sherry wine, bouillon cubes, garlic powder. Add frozen French fries during the last 5 minutes of cooking, or serve over rice or spaghettini.

70. *Pot Roast Shepherd's Pie*

     Make this 30-minute casserole with canned gravy or gravy mix, canned or frozen vegetables, or several leftover vegetables; with a top-crust layer of mashed potatoes or refrigerator biscuits. Sherry wine enhances the flavor.

71. *Pot Roast Sloppy Joe Stew*

   The excellent flavor of the Sloppy Joe seasoning mix blends very well with canned tomato sauce. Add frozen peas and carrots and cooked elbow macaroni to make a complete meal in one dish. This recipe is especially adaptable to leftover cooked vegetables.

72. *Pot Roast Smothered with Onions*

   Two large onions, thinly sliced, simmered in hot fat, flavored with basil and oregano, cooked in consommé; add sliced mushrooms. Thicken sauce with cornstarch and add ½ cup dairy sour cream. Prepare for requests on this dish.

73. *Pot Roast with Sour Cream–Tomato Sauce*

   Chopped onion, sherry wine, tomato sauce, prepared mustard, and sour cream comprise the sauce ingredients. Frozen peas or cut green beans are cooked in the sauce.

74. *Pot Roast Stew*

   Beef stew seasoning mix puts a delectable flavor in this dish and thickens the sauce to the right consistency. Vegetables: carrots and potatoes.

75. *Pot Roast Beer Stroganoff*

   An unusual, delicious sauce using beer as the liquid. Other ingredients are thinly sliced onion, paprika, canned sliced mushrooms, Worcestershire sauce, and sour cream. Served over hot noodles.

76. *Pot Roast Stroganoff with Brown Gravy Mix*

   One of the variations of this popular dish.

77. *Pot Roast Stroganoff with Canned Gravy*

   Quick and easy with canned beef gravy on the shelf. Flavored with sherry wine and caraway seeds.

78. *Pot Roast Stroganoff with Mushroom Soup*

   Another variation in the sauce of this popular dish. The flavor of sherry wine enhances it. Add mushroom slices and a few caraway seeds.

79. *Pot Roast Stroganoff with Onion Soup Mix*
    Instead of fresh onions, onion soup mix is used (½ package) with tomato paste, sherry wine, water, canned sliced mushrooms, and sour cream.

80. *Pot Roast with Stroganoff Sauce Mix*
    Easy to prepare; excellent flavor.

81. *Pot Roast Stroganoff with Tomato Juice Sauce*
    A slightly different twist and a delightful flavor, because this recipe calls for tomato juice as the liquid. Sherry wine and sour cream, of course.

82. *Pot Roast Stroganoff with Vegetables*
    A good coverup for an accumulation of leftover vegetables. This recipe calls for Stroganoff sauce mix. Canned or frozen mixed vegetables lend themselves equally well.

83. *Pot Roast with Green Beans and Corn*
    Frozen vegetables are cooked in tomato sauce with chopped onion and green pepper; flavored with sherry wine and a hint of basil and oregano.

84. *Pot Roast Supper Chili*
    Canned tomato soup is the sauce with green pepper, raw rice, Cheddar cheese, corn niblets, and chili powder for flavoring.

85. *Pot Roast with Sweet and Sour Barbecue Sauce*
    Tomato sauce, pineapple tidbits, prepared mustard, brown sugar, chopped green pepper, and vinegar.

86. *Pot Roast with Sweet and Sour Sauce, Chinese Style*
    Strips of green pepper, pineapple tidbits, sherry wine, catsup, lemon juice, vinegar, fresh tomato, soy sauce; cornstarch to thicken the sauce.

87. *Pot Roast with Taco Seasoning Mix*
    Bless the various seasoning mixes; this one will be a favorite. Start with onion and green pepper cooked in fat, tomato sauce, water, taco seasoning mix. Served over rice or noodles.

88. *Pot Roast with Tomatoes and Beef Stew Seasoning Mix*
    The combination of flavors—stew seasoning mix,

stewed tomatoes, and frozen mixed vegetables—
can't be beat.

89. *Pot Roast in Tomato-Curry Sauce*
Chopped onion, diced apple, curry powder, and
tomato juice—flavors that blend well together.

90. *Pot Roast with Tomato Sauce and Mushrooms*
Tomato sauce, consommé, sliced mushrooms, basil,
oregano, bay leaf, red wine. Served over spaghetti
with Parmesan cheese. Recipe calls for two tablespoons tomato paste, but it's no problem to freeze
the balance of opened can of tomato paste in tablespoon amounts (recipe follows).

91. *Pot Roast with Vegetables, Chinese Style*
Thinly sliced onion, celery, frozen, French-cut green
beans, canned bean sprouts and sliced mushrooms,
thickened with soy sauce and cornstarch. Served
over hot rice.

92. *Pot Roast with Vegetables*
Chopped onion and green pepper, cubed potatoes,
and frozen cut green beans in a sauce of canned
tomatoes, flavored with basil.

93. *Pot Roast and Vegetables in Curry Sauce*
A hearty sauce with curry flavor; carrots and peas are
the vegetables. Add small seashell macaroni.

94. *Pot Roast Vegetable Soup, Italian Style*
Loaded with vegetables—celery, cabbage, carrots,
canned tomatoes, and flavored with bay leaf and
oregano.

95. *Pot Roast in Wine Sauce*
Start with the basic ingredients of onion cooked in
fat, add canned beef gravy, sliced mushrooms, basil,
and red wine. Served over green noodles.

96. *Pot Roast with Zucchini*
Fresh zucchini with the flavor of sherry wine, basil,
and bay leaf, in a tomato-juice sauce.

97. *Spaghetti with Pot Roast Sauce*
Canned tomato sauce, tomato paste, basil, oregano,

and red wine makes this sauce truly Italian—in spite of the fact that it takes only 30 minutes to prepare.

98. *Super Pot Roast Soup*

The flavor derived from combining condensed minestrone soup and tomato soup, plus kidney beans and cooked elbow macaroni, make this a super soup.

99. *Sweet and Sour Pot Roast Stew*

A surprising blend of flavors in this concoction, and it's one of our favorites. Chopped onion, catsup, tomato sauce, water, vinegar, brown sugar, prepared mustard, Worcestershire sauce, cubed potatoes, and sliced carrots and celery. ·

100. *Sweet and Spicy Pot Roast*

Condensed onion soup, brown sugar, red wine vinegar, and diced bacon. Sauce thickened with crushed gingersnaps.

101. *Supreme Pot Roast Stew*

Beef flavor mushroom mix is the secret ingredient in this delicious stew with carrots and potatoes. Sherry wine also enhances the flavor.

102. *Zesty Pot Roast with Macaroni*

Chopped onion, green pepper, chili sauce, brown sugar, vinegar, canned cream-style corn, and canned green beans. Add cooked elbow macaroni.

Index

Recipes are arranged by name as well as under the specific beef cut called for.

An asterisk (*) preceding an entry means that recipe calls for frozen, cooked pot roast pieces.